Contents

D0475053

Children in Difficulty
Second Edition

Written by two practising clinicians, this book is a guide for those who work with children. In clear, simple language it focuses upon some of the most common, yet incapacitating, difficulties which are frequently encountered by young children and adolescents. After introducing and discussing different forms of therapy and treatment used in clinical work with children, the book provides a series of chapters, each dealing with a specific difficulty. Drawing upon recent research findings, and employing detailed case illustrations, it seeks to help the reader to understand the nature of each problem and offers a guide as to how the child in difficulty can best be helped.

This new edition has been fully updated to include new material on conditions such as dyspraxia and ADHD. The authors also make full references to advances in the field of special education since the first edition was published, and provide the reader with a variety of sources for further reading and information.

This accessible and practical book will be of particular value to those working in education, social work, health and childcare settings and anyone else who needs to be able to recognise and help children in difficulty.

Julian Elliott is Professor of Education at the University of Durham. **Maurice Place** is Visiting Professor at the University of Northumbria.

Children in Difficulty

A guide to understanding and helping
Second edition

Julian Elliott and Maurice Place

RoutledgeFalmer
Taylor & Francis Group

LONDON AND NEW YORK

First published 1998 by Routledge
Second edition published 2004 by RoutledgeFalmer
11 New Fetter Lane, London EC4P 4EE

Simultaneously published in the USA and Canada
by RoutledgeFalmer
29 West 35th Street, New York, NY 10001

RoutledgeFalmer is an imprint of the Taylor and Francis Group

Typeset in 11/12pt Garamond 3 by
Graphicraft Limited, Hong Kong
Printed and bound in Great Britain by
MPG Books Ltd, Bodmin

British Library Cataloguing in Publication Data
A catalogue record for this book is available from the
British Library

Library of Congress Cataloging in Publication Data
Elliott, Julian, 1955–
  Children in difficulty : a guide to understanding and helping /
Julian Elliott and Maurice Place. – 2nd ed.
      p. cm.
  Includes bibliographical references and index.
  ISBN 0-415-32543-9 (Hardback : alk. paper) –
ISBN 0-415-32544-7 (Paperback : alk. paper)
    1. Child psychotherapy.   2. Child psychopathology.
    3. Adolescent psychotherapy.   4. Adolescent psychopathology.
    1. Place, Maurice. II. Title.

  RJ504 .E43 2004
  618.92'8914–dc22
                                                            2003024358
ISBN 0-415-32543-9 (hbk)
ISBN 0-415-32544-7 (pbk)

Figures

Chapter 1

Introduction

There are few issues which can raise stronger feelings in the average person than those which relate to children. Be it outrage at their challenging behaviour, or distress at injury or neglect, adults quickly become moved by issues which involve children. Even more fascinating is the way that each person knows how the situation or behaviour should be handled – and usually this means that the delinquent needs more punishment, or the hurt child needs more care. While such emotional responses are very understandable, they are not always the correct way to intervene in a situation to ensure that matters will be improved. But how should you intervene in delicate situations and be confident that you are helping?

Helping takes a number of forms from being a sympathetic listener to the employment of highly specialised and complex approaches. What is presented in this book is not only what an individual might do, but what is undertaken by others working in the caring professions. Readers, therefore, need to judge whether they have the expertise to undertake some of the techniques described and must carefully consider the point at which it is necessary to refer to others.

The general rules of child management can be easily stated with the four 'C's:

- care and warmth;
- consistency and predictability;
- control and maintaining appropriate boundaries;
- commitment.

For any chance of success all four elements must be present in significant measure, but specific circumstances may require emphasis upon one strand for a period – a sick child tends to need more care, a wayward child more control. However, although life's events may require these changes of emphasis it is important to remember that even at such times all the elements need to be tangibly present, and the balance between the four needs to be present in reasonable degree if problems are to be managed or prevented.

Louise was fifteen years of age and was having difficulties in school. When challenged by the teachers over trivial matters she would become angry and storm from the classroom. Her parents said that she had behaved like this at home ever since being a toddler. The parents said that when these episodes occurred at home they either gave in to her wishes or tried to calm her down by offering treats or rewards. The parents adopted this placating style when Louise was eighteen months of age, because it was then that she was diagnosed as having a major hormonal problem, and the doctors said it would be dangerous for her if she became upset. Over the years the parents had continued to believe that Louise's life would be in danger if she became too upset and so made every effort to avoid such situations ever arising.

Situations such as this are not common, but seeing children whose behaviour is troublesome because they have not been managed with a balanced regime is. Too much control, which is not tempered by a caring warmth, creates angry, and at times violent, children. Too little control, and the young person will live to the limit of that control, quickly exceeding it and usually only being pulled up by the limits which society imposes in the form of laws. Perhaps lack of parental commitment exerts the most detrimental effects for it removes the child's sense of being claimed, and for some youngsters, for example children who are being fostered, this may already be a very fragile emotion.

When confronted with a challenging situation, how is the best course of action determined, and perhaps even more crucially, how is that action carried out? In the following chapters there are descriptions of how to deal with the more common challenges that arise within everyday life. To be able to intervene effectively it is important to have a structured way of understanding the information that is gathered by locating it in the context of the child's development, current functioning and the wider issues of family and environment.

Determining the origin of the difficulties

There are many influences which work upon a child and help to determine how he or she will behave, and these can be summarised as:

- genetic;
- physical;
- attachment difficulties;
- dynamic influences;
- parenting issues;

- traumatic and significant life events;
- societal themes.

The genetic make-up which the child has inherited from the parents is increasingly seen as a significant influence on many diverse aspects of a child's growth, development and ultimate functioning. The belief that problems within the parents can be passed on to their children has been persuasive since biblical times. The advent of scientific study, and the work of George Mendel, the Augustinian monk, gave a clear understanding of the principles of heredity, and prompted research in many areas to try to determine the part genetics plays in the origin of many disorders and syndromes. For example, Heston (1966) looked at the children of schizophrenic patients and found that they were more likely to develop the disease than the general population. Such studies, together with studies of twins, have gradually supported a view that genetic influences often make a contribution to the emotional and behavioural difficulties which children show (Skuse 2000).

A related theme to genetic influences is that of physical make-up, and particularly the complex chemical structures which control all of our bodily systems, and alter emotions and behaviour. The detail and complexity of such elements make them beyond the scope of this text, but by way of illustration we can look at one particular body chemical: serotonin (or 5-HT). Work over the years has highlighted that certain disorders (particularly depression, anxiety and eating disorders) are more frequently seen in females, whereas others (such as alcoholism, aggressiveness and suicide) are seen more frequently in males. In animals as well as humans the female shows a tendency to an increased synthesis and turnover of serotonin, and evidence is now accumulating that this may be the chemical which moderates the emotional responses to adverse experiences throughout the animal kingdom (Steiner *et al.* 1997). Any dysfunction in serotonin's action and emotional problems are therefore likely to arise. This leads to the speculation that this brain chemical may have a significant role in the origin or maintenance of these disorders, so opening a new avenue of potential treatment for them.

In addition to these intrinsic physical factors there are also extrinsic elements to consider. Physical illnesses or disorders can exert direct effects upon emotional well-being. For instance, it is well known that children with epilepsy experience a significantly greater level of emotional disturbance than children without this condition (Meltzer *et al.* 2000), and similar increases are also noted in conditions such as asthma (Mrazek *et al.* 1998), and almost half the children who have had head injuries show emotional and behavioural difficulties (Max *et al.* 1998).

An area that is now being recognised to be of great influence upon a person's long-term functioning is his or her capacity to form meaningful attachments. Attachment is defined as a 'lasting psychological connectedness between human beings' (Bowlby 1969). It fosters a sense of security by maintaining proximity – giving a firm base from which to learn about wider environment. It gives a sense of 'felt' security and provides the internal representation upon which to model all future relationships. Having a sense of secure attachment means that the child can recognise emotions, show empathy and behave morally. It also makes a significant contribution towards helping the child develop feelings of self-worth and develop a positive view about life.

Of all bonds that contribute to the sense of attachment, the mother–infant bond is perhaps the most crucial, but the development of attachment is not a passive process. From the age of about three months the infant becomes increasingly aware of subtle communication and so as the parent responds to the child's needs, the child detects warmth and affection from the parent and begins to develop trust in its carer, an essential foundation upon which all subsequent development hinges. Such positive attachment also provides relative protection from the negative effects of adverse events, and this further strengthens the bond between caregiver and child. In the average child, the foundation created by this sense of attachment is then built upon through a sequence of developmental steps, with each step extending and developing aspects of the child's functioning and personality. It is important to recognise that this attachment process is not only an emotional change, but can actually make physical changes to the brain, changing its very architecture (Place 2003).

The next strand to be considered when addressing why a problem is happening is the present family atmosphere and the influences that exist within it. We are social animals and feel most comfortable when part of a group which wants us to be there. We respond to subtle changes in atmosphere, and will often do things we would not have chosen to do because the group we are with makes it seem right. This is even more true for children who have still to acquire the sense of personal determination which allows adults to resist these influences and expectations. It is not surprising, therefore, that a young person's behaviour can be powerfully influenced by the relationships within the family and the way that these relationships are expressed. For example, if a child feels a close alliance with a particular member of the family, or becomes caught in conflict between parents, then he or she may try to deal with the confusion of feelings by reacting in a challenging or distressed way. In practice many problems that present are in fact signposts to troubles within the family, and if these troubles are not recognised and addressed then resolution of the problems is far less likely. When these dynamic elements predominantly involve the parents then that most fundamental of influences, the nature and quality of parenting, can be changed. These changes will range from the subtle, but powerful, dynamic changes seen if, for instance, a parent begins working away from home and so is less available to the family, to the impact upon a child of being physically abused.

It is a feature of life that periodically we experience significant changes and unexpected events within our lives. Children have less-well-developed mechanisms of coping to respond to these events and so depend quite heavily on the adults around them for support and help. Thus the history of the child's life often contains important clues and themes which have clearly had a strong influence in shaping the child's present pattern of behaviour. The death of a parent, serious illness in brothers or sisters, being the victim of abuse or neglectful parenting – such themes are very powerful in prompting behavioural and emotional reactions which can quickly become part of a child's routine responses. Sometimes the history is more a family myth than actual events – but if powerful enough it may establish patterns of behaviour.

John was seven years of age and lived with his mother in a quiet part of town. He was seen in the neighbourhood as a helpful and pleasant boy, and school had only praise for his work there. John's mother presented to the adult mental health services because she was miserable. She explained that since her husband had left she had found it hard to manage John's behaviour. John's father had been the main disciplinarian because she had never been able to control John's outbursts. She explained that as a teenager she had been expected to look after her older brother, who had also been called John. He had often been violent towards her and seemed to take particular delight in tormenting her. On the night of her son's birth her brother John had been killed while committing a robbery, and she was convinced that her son had taken on this malevolent spirit. The family's wish to have her child named after her dead brother compounded this belief.

The important theme here is not the veracity of John's mother's belief but merely the strength with which she believed it. Growing up with a parent who expects you to be difficult and violent towards her is very likely to encourage such behaviour to surface.

As we shall see later, a child's development occurs in stages and the established elements of development that result from each stage are incorporated into the next one. In this way, early life experiences are used to develop competencies, and a child who has successfully met all the challenges of a particular developmental stage is well equipped to take on the next stage (Sroufe and Rutter 1984). If there have been difficulties or upheavals, however, these can create vulnerabilities which are also carried forward, with the result that the child arrives at the later stages of development with less than the optimal resources to respond to new challenges. This is known as Werner's Orthogenetic Principle (Werner 1948) and illustrates one mechanism by which problems at a particular age can still be exerting influence many years later.

Finally, there is the influence of the peer group and the subculture in which the young person is living. The need to conform to the wishes and plans of significant people is a feature of all humans' make-up, but at different phases of life the significant people tend to change. For example, in infancy the parents are central, but in adolescence the peer group becomes more influential. If conformity to the peer group demands involvement in dangerous or troublesome activity then the teenager is clearly at risk if the need to participate is felt strongly. Much of the delinquent behaviour seen in society is committed by teenagers who are part of a group pursuing excitement or physical gain. Similarly, if a peer group is criticising or teasing a young person, these negative statements can be powerful in making the adolescent feel badly about himself or herself.

Peer group influence is but one specific example of the impact which subculture can have upon the behaviour or emotional state of a child. A further example is given by the work of Rutter, who in his detailed study of the influence of schools (Rutter *et al.* 1979) highlighted the relationship between a school's ethos and children's behaviour, as well as the levels of vandalism and graffiti, irrespective of the type of area from which the pupils of the school were drawn.

Understanding the areas which can influence functioning allows the information that is gathered to be used to clarify the influences which underlie the difficulties. It also points to certain areas of enquiry which it is wise to pursue if a full understanding of the problem is to be achieved.

Developmental themes

As well as these elements of influence it is important to remember that children are also developing organisms. This means that each child has to proceed through various stages of development in a variety of ways. Each of these helps to equip him or her for future life as an adult. There have been many suggestions as to how to conceptualise these processes, focusing on many different aspects of development, but in the context of this text the psychological/social sequence described by Erikson (1959) is perhaps the most helpful (Figure 1.1). This developmental process illustrates the elements that are most influential in a child's life at each stage of development, and although others will still exert some influence, this process highlights the features which are exerting most influence at each age level. For example, in the Industry phase it is teachers and peers who exert the most influence. All parents will have experienced this when trying to help a child with homework, and the child becomes distressed because 'it is not the way my teacher said to do it'. The possibility that there may be other methods is not

Trust v. Mistrust Birth to 1 year	Infants must learn to trust others. There must be minimal uncertainty, and with each demand satisfied the infant grows in trust. Maternal care fosters the child's sense of self-identity. Insufficient warmth and care and the infant views the world as a dangerous place and can become mistrustful of adults. The mother-figure is the primary agent.
Autonomy v. Shame and Doubt 1 to 3 years	The child's self-will emerges usually focused upon demanding to be able to control and order events. These strivings need to be matched by the parents, determination to maintain a clear sense of boundaries but combined with explicit care and security to safeguard the child's developing sense of self-esteem. Parental figures are paramount.
Initiative v. Guilt 3 to 6 years	Children at this age attempt to act grown up and project having some self-control. They seek to broaden their world and strive to achieve physical independence from their parents. They begin to notice sex and role differences, and explore them through play. The members of the family are key agents.
Industry v. Inferiority 6 to 12 years	Relates to parents and other adults on an equal basis. The child compares self to peers. Teachers and peers have the greatest influence.
Identity v. Confusion Adolescence	The teenager is seeking a path through the maze of life options to establish his or her own unique identity. Striving for emotional independence from parents. Key influences are peers, significant adults and society (but not parents).

Figure 1.1 Erikson's developmental process

something the child can recognise easily at this age, but, more importantly, the way teachers demonstrated the task must be right because of their importance in the young person's world.

These stages should not be seen as gateways. The completion of the tasks in each stage is not a prerequisite to moving on to the next stage, but they do equip the child to cope with the next stage better and in a more robust fashion. This means that problems during any stage do not prevent the child developing, but make it more difficult for him or her since crucial knowledge and skills may be lacking. For example, a child who has not fully developed social skills during the Industry phase will find negotiating the process of dating in adolescence especially difficult. Of course the earlier that the difficulties occur the more profound the disruption might be, and many developmental theorists have linked major illness processes, such as psychopathic personality disorder, to difficulties in the first months of life. The young person may traverse the remaining stages well, and this may correct much of the initial disturbance, but the disruption of those early stages presents the young person with a far steeper hill to climb.

A key factor, therefore, in trying to predict how a traumatic event might be dealt with is to consider the child's age. After eighteen months of age infants begin to understand that they are independent entities separate from their parents. Self-regulation becomes increasingly important, but to achieve this the child has also to learn frustration tolerance. Marked tantrums are common as this is developed, but if the relationship with parents has been solid and secure up to this point then these 'explosions' are facilitated by an internal picture that the child has of the parents being available and sensitive to emotional needs. This helps the infant to feel free to express negative feelings directly, confident that the parents will be supportive through times of distress. It is interesting to note that the quality of this attachment between an infant and parents can be in great measure predicted from the mother's description of her baby while she is pregnant (Benoit *et al.* 1997). This suggests that in the early stages of this evolving attachment it is the contribution of the parents which is the most influential.

In young children the usual medium for coming to understand such emotions and the events occurring around them is through the world of play. By about two years of age toddlers' sense of self provides sufficient differentiation for them to begin to recreate experiences in play. It is interesting to note that children who have been abused at this young age find it difficult to develop all the skills of this stage, and so they engage in less symbolic play, find it difficult to play with peers, and are generally more aggressive (Alessandri 1991).

Although children can recognise that events have occurred through the mechanical processes of repetition that play offers, their sense of the world is not sufficiently developed for them to set the events in any context. This means that at this age a child can't anticipate events or consequences very easily, because the context that would act as a warning is missing.

By four years of age the child can repress one view in preference to another and so there is the beginning of a recognition that there can be alternative origins for problems other than the child's action. Now the recognition of other sources of influence begins to become apparent, and the play takes on a richer content as the roles of others in making things happen are gradually explored. By six years of age this ability is fully developed and the child is able to relate the cause of events to origins which the child recognises he or she can't influence. Children also begin to evaluate their competence by comparing themselves to others (Dweck and Elliott 1983), and with this comes the start of seeing peer approval as important, an influence which reaches its peak in adolescence. The areas of this influence tend, however, to be different in boys and girls, for while boys seek approval for their actions, it is a girl's view of herself that is most strongly influenced by the views of others (Cole *et al.* 1997).

The significance of this developing awareness is that if traumatic events should occur early in a child's life it is likely that he or she will believe him- or herself responsible. The help offered to children has therefore not only to take account of what the child may have experienced but at what age it has occurred so that the correct emphasis can be given to the therapeutic help.

A structured assessment

When confronted with any type of problem, the first impulse may be one of bewilderment. Where to start? It is nearly always best in such situations to recognise that there is no danger in silence. A quiet and reflective style will probably start the information flowing, and if all that is happening is weeping and distress then silent support is equally comforting. Although there is a need to know in order to be able to understand, the first response should be one of availability and support. From this basis the immediate issues can usually be clarified, and together these two themes give an excellent platform from which to begin to obtain the detail upon which decisions can be based.

The way forward

Armed with the detail of the situation it is then possible to formulate the next steps. There may be a clear recognition that more specialised help is needed, and the task then becomes to help the child, and the family, to see how important this may be.

In most cases, however, the information is used to inform the process of assistance being offered by the concerned adult. For most situations, being clear and decisive can prove very beneficial. The young person feels less confused because an adult is bringing clarity, and if they are agreeable to help, then they feel less frightened and alone. Not all young people want to be helped, and sadly there are a few who are set on a self-destructive path from which they will not be deviated. Knowing one's personal and professional limitations, while not underestimating innate skills, is the starting point for deciding what a particular individual's role should be. If the problem is one detailed in the following pages, then the themes described will help to clarify how best to proceed.

Sources of further help

www.brightfutures.org/publications/index.html
www.rcpsych.ac.uk/info/help/adol/index.htm
www.aacap.org/publications/factsfam/index.htm
www.nimh.nih.gov/publicat/index.cfm

Initial themes

1 Clarify the issues – who is concerned, and why? If there are discrepancies, this may be significant.
2 Details of the current problem – duration, intensity, circumstances and consequences.
3 The attitudes of the key people – the youngsters themselves, parents, teachers, etc.

Developmental history

Is there anything in the child's history which might be influencing the behaviour?

School functioning

The key areas here are academic performance – is the youngster struggling in lessons?

• relationships with teachers;
• relationships with other children – don't forget the powerful impact of being bullied.

Peer relationships

Are there any friends? What are they like, how much of an influence do they wield?

Hobbies and interests

Are there elements of variation in the child's life or is he or she overly focused on a single issue or area, or perhaps even on no areas at all?

Traumatic events

Have significant things happened in the life of the family or directly to the youngster which seem linked to the present issues?

Family relationships

Although these can be asked about, the most effective way of evaluating family relationships is to observe them in action – who speaks most?

• the tone of exchanges
• who holds the authority (it might be a child!)

The child's behaviour

How does the child behave – restless/settled, calm/sad, etc.? All such observations help to clarify the type of difficulties that may exist.

Figure 1.2 The structured assessment

References

Alessandri, S.M. (1991). Play and social behaviours in maltreated pre-schoolers. *Developmental Psychopathology* 3, 191–206.

Benoit, D., Parker, K.C.H. and Zeanah, C.H. (1997). Mothers' representations of their infants assessed pre-natally. Stability and association with infant attachment classifications. *Journal of Child Psychology and Psychiatry* 38, 307–13.

Bowlby, J. (1969). *Attachment and Loss*. London: Basic Books.

Cole, D.A., Martin, J.M. and Powers, B. (1997). A competency-based model of child depression: a longitudinal study of peer, parent, teacher, and self-evaluations. *Journal of Child Psychology and Psychiatry* 38(5), 505–14.

Dweck, C. and Elliott, E. (1983). Achievement motivation. In P. Mussen (ed.) *Handbook of Child Psychology, Volume IV: Socialization, Personality and Social Development*. New York: Wiley.

Erikson, E. (1959). *Identity and the Life Cycle*. New York: International University Press.

Heston, L.L. (1966). Psychiatric disorders in foster home reared children of schizophrenic mothers. *British Journal of Psychiatry* 112, 819–25.

Max, J.E., Koele, S.L., Smith, W.L. (1998). Psychiatric disorders in children and adolescents after severe traumatic brain injury: a controlled study. *Journal of American Academy Child Adolescent Psychiatry* 37, 832–40.

Meltzer, H., Gatward, R., Goodman, R., Ford, F. (2000). *Mental Health of Children and Adolescents in Great Britain*. London: Stationery Office.

Mrazek, D.A., Schuman, W. and Klinnert, M. (1998). Early asthma onset: risk of emotional and behavioural difficulties. *Journal of Child Psychology and Psychiatry* 39, 247–54.

Place, M. (2003). Attachment and identity – its significance in decisions about contact and placement. *Family Law* 33, 260–4.

Rutter, M., Maughan, B., Mortimore, P., Ouston, J. and Smith, A. (1979). *Fifteen Thousand Hours: Secondary Schools and their Effects on Children*. London: Open Books.

Skuse, D. (2000). Behavioural neuroscience and child psychopathology: insights from model systems. *Journal of Child Psychology and Psychiatry* 41, 3–32.

Sroufe, L.A. and Rutter, M. (1984). The domain of developmental psychopathology. *Child Development* 55, 17–29.

Steiner, M., LePage, P. and Dunn, E.J. (1997). Serotonin and gender specific psychiatric disorders. *International Journal of Psychiatric Clinical Practice* 1, 3–13.

Werner, H. (1948). *Comparative Psychology of Mental Development*. New York: International University Press.

Chapter 2

The basics of being helpful

Introduction

Perhaps the most important distinction between the child and the adult client is that children with difficulties rarely seek help themselves. Rather, they are typically referred for help by concerned others, usually the child's family or teachers. It should not be assumed that because the child is deeply unhappy about his or her circumstances and strongly desires change to take place that professional intervention will be welcomed or accepted. Many forms of therapy, particularly the psychotherapies, are based upon an assumption that the client is a willing participant who actively wishes to change. The reality is that many children who are brought to therapists come unwillingly and respond only because of the power imbalances which they perceive. Furthermore, successful work with children is likely to involve direct support and intervention from others, such as parents, teachers, social workers and peers.

This chapter cannot provide an exhaustive account of the many differing forms of therapy. Where this is required the reader is advised to examine the specialised texts referred to in each section.

The talking therapies

Talking with others, outlining the difficulties we are experiencing and receiving advice on how to remedy a difficult situation, is a natural, effective and everyday way of tackling problems. The old adage 'a problem shared is a problem halved' reflects the fact that merely by unburdening ourselves to others our difficulties may often appear less arduous, our sense of confusion and powerlessness less overwhelming. In a world where communication is often brief or misunderstood, where there often appears to be insufficient time for one another, the availability of another who, in a non-judgemental fashion, will try to understand your problems, concerns and frustrations, who will provide a sounding board for your own, often confused understandings and who may suggest ways forward is often rare.

Despite the efficacy of problem-solving discussion between a child and a concerned adult in everyday situations, the types of problem outlined in this book are unlikely to be resolved solely by such means. Unlike the common scene in television sitcoms where the question 'Can we talk about this?' can usually be relied upon to result in greater understanding and awareness of the complexity of interpersonal relationships, the problems of the highly anxious, phobic, aggressive or defiant child are unlikely to be resolved in such a fashion.

A term increasingly used to describe supportive forms of talking is counselling. The use of this as a description of the process of discussing problems has now become so widespread as to render the term virtually meaningless; parents counsel their children, teachers their students, police counsel potential lawbreakers, finance brokers their clients. With regard to children, counselling is frequently used to describe the process of listening to problems, advising on action and explaining the constraints within which the child should operate. Indeed, counselling is misguidedly used as a euphemism for controlling behaviour – the headteacher who asked one of the present authors to 'severely counsel' a wayward five-year-old was by no means exceptional. As is shown in Chapter 8, counselling is often misunderstood and misused.

Such a criticism, however, does not imply that counselling, undertaken appropriately and skilfully, is of little therapeutic value. Indeed, the basic elements of counselling and psychotherapy have shown a tendency to converge over the years, with much cross-fertilisation of approach and technique resulting. Counselling uses a variety of techniques to help people, but often involves assistance to help them express emotion over painful events (Lindemann 1944), communicate their feelings more accurately and develop problem-solving behaviour, and employs empathy and displays of concern to increase self-esteem (Rogers 1951, 1961). In contrast to the psychotherapies, there is, perhaps, less reliance on a theory of development to which themes are referenced, and this makes it very suitable, for instance, as a way of helping people come to terms with traumatic events that are still troubling them (see Chapter 7). In recent years there has also been a rapid growth of pre-emptive counselling: offering assistance to people in the immediate aftermath of an incident. This approach assumes that early intervention, and the rapid ventilation of feelings in a controlled way will prevent problems later. Although this has some theoretical attraction, the results of such processes suggest that this is not totally successful (Bisson *et al.* 1997).

Counselling has perhaps also seen a great expansion because, unlike the psychotherapies, training is easily available. Many academic settings offer basic counselling certificates and diplomas, and there is a well-structured development path up to post-degree level. A danger, however, is that it is often easy for individuals to claim counselling expertise on the basis of very limited training.

While there may be much overlap between the everyday process of listening to and supporting another, and the operation of the many forms of talking therapy (Garfield and Bergin, 1994, identified 400 in their review), the latter is marked by the presence of a theoretical base which underpins practice. While theoretical perspectives vary greatly, talking therapies have several elements in common; these were first pointed out by Frank (1974). At the heart of this commonality is the establishment of a therapeutic relationship. The sense of regard and concern shown by the therapist for the client is a foundation point from which other elements can emerge. A second key theme common to all psychotherapies is facilitating the emergence of emotional arousal. The linking of emotions with recalled events or memories provides the basic material from which therapy proceeds because being able to tolerate such emotions and then recognising their associations is a key element of working through the areas of difficulty.

At the heart of each psychotherapy, however, is the aim of giving the person insight into his or her problems, and their origins, on the assumption that from such self-knowledge he or she will begin to change and the difficulties will be eased. This is perhaps seen at its clearest when dealing with someone who has experienced a traumatic early life and now has difficulties that the therapist believes are occurring as a consequence of those experiences. By helping the person see these links their growing understanding modifies their sense of inevitability and helps them to find new ways of behaving.

The therapist works from a specific theoretical base and the responses reflect the theory of development being used. For example, Freud (1976) used psychosexual development, and the way that basic drives (id) and the higher morality of conscience (superego) interacted with each other to influence behaviour. Such theories offer the child a context in which to view the traumas, and so build a framework from which to analyse beliefs, feelings and reactions. This gives a sense of structure to the emerging understanding. These theoretical frameworks also have common elements: for example, the offering of a predictable space and time dedicated to exploring the themes. Within each session information is gathered which helps the therapist to refine the understanding of the specific difficulties, and these hypotheses are tested by subsequent information. Therapists will then use their specific understanding and the theoretical base to reflect upon the origins of specific behaviours, feelings or beliefs. Most of these therapies also depend upon using the emotion generated within sessions to inform the process. So, for instance, a passage in which the client becomes upset may be specifically noted – because people sometimes experience emotions but have no name for them or, more commonly, may display emotions without realising they are doing so. 'I notice you become angry whenever you mention your father' could be the starting point for a young person to realise such a link. In some hands these interpretations can be quite confrontational (Ashurst 1991).

Another theme which is common to many of the psychotherapies is the way that a therapist uses emotions that arise within him- or herself to highlight the unspoken emotions and feelings of the client. This is described as transference and can arise in many situations. For example, when a mother's death is spoken of by a child, it is possible that the therapist also feels a personal sense of sadness. The commenting on such feelings is seen in some therapeutic styles (particularly psychoanalysis) as a key element of the process. It is important to recognise that within such therapies silence is equally important as a form of emotional communication (Lane *et al.* 2002).

One of the best-known talking therapies is psychoanalysis (Freud 1976), which was the first psychotherapy and whose basic tenets are still at the core of many therapeutic approaches. Its requirement of three to four sessions a week for two years or more means it is not the routine approach in many centres. At the heart of psychoanalytical theory are the assumptions that:

- no item of mental life or pattern of behaviour is accidental, rather it is the outcome of previous experiences;
- thoughts, feelings and other aspects of mental activity and behaviour are trying to achieve something; that is, they are goal-directed;
- unconscious determinants mould and affect the way we perceive and react. These are thoughts of a primitive nature and are shaped by impulses and feelings within the individual of which he or she is unaware;
- early childhood experiences are overwhelmingly important and pre-eminent over more recent experiences.

Other theorists have also seen therapeutic approaches developed from their theories, the most important of which for work with children is that of Melanie Klein (Segal 1964).

Most psychotherapy offered today is less frequent and far less lengthy than that offered by Freud and his followers. Known as short-term dynamic (Davanloo 1980) or brief dynamic psychotherapy (Malan 1963), this work uses similar principles to the longer-term analyses, but there is a greater emphasis upon specific issues, and indeed most brief dynamic therapies depend upon finding a focus from which themes can be explored. Although in such approaches it is still seen as important to make the client aware of unconscious fantasies, the most fundamental therapeutic lever is seen as helping the client to rework relationship patterns that have been damaging. This is achieved through the relationship they develop with the therapist, a process that has been described as the 'corrective emotional experience' (Alexander and French 1946). Because of this emphasis, transference is perhaps of even greater importance in these types of approach, as is the need to establish a good therapeutic relationship quickly.

The appropriateness of the brief psychotherapy approach is illustrated by the finding that the success of psychotherapy in general often depends upon the quality of the relationship that is established between client and therapist (Orlinsky and Howard 1986). This type of brief psychotherapy is indicated if there is also a motivation to change, and the person has a circumscribed problem, with an absence of severe mental disorder (Malan 1976).

The effectiveness of psychotherapy has been examined in over 250 studies. On average, the results from these indicate that about 79 per cent of children will show some benefit from psychotherapy (Weisz *et al.* 1987), although on average children show only a small improvement in their functioning (Weisz and Jensen 2001). Work with adults suggests that no one type of psychotherapy is more effective than another (Andrews 1993), although techniques which focus upon observable behaviour may be particularly valuable for work with children (Kazdin 1990).

Play therapy

Play is the medium by which a child gains an understanding of the world. When confronted by difficult or poorly understood situations the child's natural reaction is to incorporate this into play, and by regular repetition there emerges an explanation and understanding which the child can adopt. The accuracy of this explanation is, however, dependent on many factors, not least of which is the child's limited understanding of the world and its complexities. It is not surprising then that play should be seen as the obvious medium by which to work therapeutically with a young child. The therapeutic approaches are broadly similar to the talking therapies, but the emphasis is shifted to using play as the medium of communication. It can operate on several levels. The play can be used as a method of communicating inner-world feelings and so becomes the exact equivalent of the psychotherapy used in adults. Such work is again rooted in a theoretical model of child development, the most well known being those described by Anna Freud (1966) and Melanie Klein (Segal 1964).

The client-centred non-directive approach described by Rogers (1951, 1961) also has its equivalent in play therapy. The leading exponent of this type of approach is Axeline (1947), whose description of play therapy is the foundation for the many play therapists who are not practising within a formal psychoanalytical structure. She described eight rules for such practice:

1   quickly develop a warm, and friendly relationship;
2   accept the children as they present themselves, not as they should be;
3   the relationships should be permissive, allowing the children to express their feelings freely;
4   recognise and reflect feelings so that the child gains insight;
5   the responsibility for making changes is the child's;
6   the child's wishes give direction;

7   sessions are at the child's pace;
8   the only limitations are those of safety and responsibility within the therapeutic relationship.

Allan was referred at ten years of age because of the aggressive and hostile behaviour he was showing both at home and school. Allan had been adopted by his present family when he was five years of age, his life with his birth family having been one characterised by violence and neglect from being a baby. Allan had no explanation for his behaviour other than to say that he became angry when people 'bugged' him.

A regular sequence of play sessions was established which quickly became dominated by themes of tragedy (people being killed or seriously injured; rescue attempts being sabotaged). Gradually the therapist became a participant in the play and verbalised that it seemed that there was no way to help the characters of the games. Some three months into the sessions an additional theme began to emerge from the play. When the models and toys had been injured or hurt they would seek revenge, and would let nothing stand in the way of it being achieved.

Later, these elements faded somewhat and there were several sessions which focused upon being small and helpless in large, complex and confusing worlds. The therapist reflecting on how small and vulnerable that must feel increased the tempo of the play and its chaotic quality. Almost immediately after commencing the sessions Allan's aggressive behaviour at school faded, but became more evident at home. Seven months after commencing therapy Allan's behaviour at home began to moderate, but when therapy stopped after a year he was still seen by the family as more difficult than his siblings.

This description illustrates how play can be used by a child to portray his or her inner world. It also shows how recognising the link between apparently distinct play activities is often the key to understanding this portrayal. This example also illustrates a key factor that must be considered when deciding if therapy is appropriate. Effective therapy reduces the defences which the child is using to cope with the world, and this can be a very frightening experience. As a result, in the early stages of therapy there is often a deterioration rather than an improvement. Similarly, if the child is not in an environment in which he or she feels safe and secure the ability to take risks in therapy evaporates and little meaningful work is achieved. With the potential for so much emotional impact to occur within the sessions, and the possibility that the child does not feel secure enough to share, it is crucial that the pace of any work done within the sessions is set by the child.

As well as being a medium through which psychotherapy is pursued, play therapy can also be used more directly. As the child works through a difficulty or a painful experience, the play is usually transparent enough for an acute observer to see the underlying themes. This can be used as a basis for exploring such issues in more detail, and can also be used to offer alternative views and explanations. As with all psychotherapies, the sharing of emotions becomes an important element of healing, although within a play context it is easy to transfer such feelings on to other elements of the activity – for example, 'the doll is naughty and must be smacked'.

Brief (solution-focused) therapy

As is discussed below, it is a fundamental tenet in the management of all animal behaviour that more is achieved by reward than by punishment. It is, however, only very recently that this fundamental has seen its expression in a dynamic (i.e. interpersonal) therapy. Brief solution-focused therapy is an approach which can be seen as using this position as a starting point under-pinned by the assumption that successful work depends upon knowing where the client wants to get to. From this flow the principles that understanding the problem is not necessary, and indeed focusing on the problem more than is needed for the client to feel heard is probably counterproductive. The philosophy here is that successful work depends upon taking the positive path, which means determining what the client is trying to achieve, working out the quickest way of achieving this goal, and detailing what he or she is already doing that might start him or her on this path (de Shazer 1991). This philosophy has become summarised in three rules:

1   If it ain't broke, don't fix it.
2   Once you know what works, do more of it.
3   If it don't work, then do something else.

Work usually, therefore, begins by identifying 'exceptions to the rule' of the problem, in other words identifying what is already working, even if this is only in very small pockets. The drive towards emphasising the positive means that even small acknowledgements that things are moving in a positive direction can be the start of a cascade of change which gathers momentum, carrying the client towards his or her desired goals.

There are several aspects to this type of approach which harness these basic themes. For example, a question like 'If a miracle has occurred and the problem is solved what will be the first thing you notice?' (usually described as 'the miracle question') may begin the process of clarifying the desired goals, and identifying the first steps that need to be taken to achieve them. These are then built upon by asking what the first small step they need to take might be to progress towards their goal. As with any therapy, the client will frequently doubt the progress, and usually does so by highlighting times when things have not gone as expected. However, these exceptions can also feed the therapeutic process, because subsequent questions can continue to emphasise the positive – 'Tell me about times it doesn't happen' or, if the statement is that it never stops, then the question might be, 'When does it happen least?' It is also important to realise that any pattern of improvement will consist of both forward and backward steps. When such situations occur the therapist can help the client to identify what resources, skills and techniques have been used to prevent slipping too far backwards, and through this recognition, additional strengths are acknowledged.

The content of a therapeutic session is flexible, the goal for each often being established by simple questions such as, 'How will you know at the end of the session that it was useful to come today?' The general aim of every session, however, is always to follow the basic behavioural principle of emphasising the positive and identifying with the client those exceptions when the problem was stopped or did not occur. Techniques such as rating the occurrence and intensity of good spells can be used to demonstrate progress, but can also be valuable in identifying the next step towards the full solution. The framing of the questions around such elements adds to the overall emphasis upon the positive. For example, examining the most recent scores on the rating scale could prompt the question, 'What will be happening when you are just one point higher on the scale?', a question which contains an implicit assumption that the next point will be achieved. Overall solution-focused therapy is proving to be effective and brief (Lethem 2002), with outcome evaluations showing that, for instance, 60 per cent of cases report improvement (Macdonald 1997), and on average this is achieved by a three-session intervention (Berg and de Jong 1996).

Group therapy

Dynamic group therapy is useful to broadly the same type of person as the individual approach. It adds the extra dimensions of sharing difficulties with others and tends to reduce the sense of isolation, and thoughts that 'I'm the only one'. However, it does require the group members to be able to tolerate the frustrations which arise in sharing relationships, although for some this can have a therapeutic benefit in its own right. In addition to this toleration, the group process usually seeks to encourage group members to give feedback to others, which includes expressing their own feelings about what someone says or does (Yalom 1995). Furthermore, the interaction among group members gives each person an opportunity to try out new ways of behaving along with providing members with an opportunity to learn more about the way they interact with others. They may sometimes re-create the difficulties that brought them to group therapy in the first place, and one of the main goals of group therapy is always gently to confront the person with an unconscious difficulty so it can be resolved.

These themes tend to result in groups being run for children, or parents, who have a shared experience or difficulty. In child abuse, for instance, this type of intervention is commonly used because the sense of personal isolation is reduced. In addition, if the group is working well there can be a tremendous sense of support which allows participants to share far more than they might have done in other circumstances.

Family therapy

Children grow up not in isolation but with myriad influences playing upon them. These influences shape, alter and colour the child's evolving feelings and beliefs so that each adult becomes a unique individual, made up of the way that these developmental experiences interact with the person's genetic make-up and current life events. Recognising the importance of these influences opens a major branch of potential intervention, for if these influences can be changed in a helpful way, a lasting impact upon the adult that is to come may be achieved. In the 1960s many centres began to explore the potential for bringing about such change, and the main focus of this work was the family, for, as Erikson has pointed out (see Chapter 1), it is the family which exerts the most powerful influence in the formative years.

Some therapy styles seek to detail the family's belief system, and acknowledging with them its content can help the family to explore new ways of relating (Byng-Hall 1995). This may involve working with the family in the construction of their family tree (known as a genogram), not only to record linkage, but more especially to recognise family traits and similarities (Lieberman 1979).

Today the most common style of family therapy is that based upon systems theory (Burnham 1986). The approach is less rooted in family history, concentrating instead upon day-to-day interactions and the impact one person's behaviour has on the other members of the family. By way of illustration, consider the child who is fearful of attending school. By considering the child in isolation the conclusion might be that an illness is present, a phobia of school. However, if a wider perspective is taken, it may be discovered that the child has a particularly close relationship with his mother, that he is not fearful of attending school but that his real difficulty is leaving his mother at home alone. His fear, perhaps, might stem from concerns about her health, particularly as she has been prescribed medication similar to that taken by his uncle, who died suddenly some six months ago.

Clearly this story may be greatly expanded, but hopefully it shows how links can arise between apparently disparate elements to cause a problem. The significance of this is that, if these links are not identified and dealt with, the problem will not be resolved. Here, for instance, a programme aimed at helping the child overcome a fear of school would fail even though it is the apparent problem. Family therapy tries to clarify what influences are operating to maintain a problem, and then attempts to change them. This can sometimes be achieved merely by making the influences explicit, but usually also involves the setting of tasks.

Within this main thrust there emerge two broad schools. Structural therapy recognises that certain family patterns and make-ups are more helpful than others and seeks to set tasks and goals that move families towards these patterns. For instance, a child may be acting as a parent, with the new step-parent marginalised and prevented from taking any role within the family. The stepfather's complaint that the child will not go to sleep except in the parental bed has to be seen in this context. Helping the parents develop an equal relationship, to which the children are subordinate, and recognising that there is a boundary around the adults which children have to respect become key in resolving such problems (Mann *et al.* 1990). It is, of course, not always possible to help families achieve such change, but any movement along the path may be deemed to be helpful.

Alternatively, the family pattern of functioning can be used to identify the issues which are specifically maintaining the problem. In this type of approach it is assumed that the symptoms that are presented are in fact an unsatisfactory solution to the family's difficulties, and that by making the present symptoms even less successful at reducing the underlying difficulties a new pattern of family functioning will emerge. The therapeutic strategies used may be the same as a structural approach would identify but in general they tend to be more circumscribed and hence the tasks also tend to be more focused. For instance, asking the stepfather to take charge of bedtime routines in the above example may bring about a structural change, but its primary purpose is to evict the child from the parental bed. A variation on such strategic work can be the use of paradox (Cade 1984), where families who seem to fail to act on professional advice are approached with that very expectation in mind. The underlying principles for the interventions remain the same, but the tasks take on a more challenging quality.

One of the approaches which can be used in a paradoxical approach is that of reframing. Here the symptom is accepted and a different, positive explanation for its occurrence is offered. By offering this positive explanation its value in suppressing the more deep-rooted family problems is reduced, and so it becomes redundant. An example of such an approach might be to identify a child's soiling as a helpful thermometer of the parents' relationship.

In recent years the ethics around paradoxical work have been questioned, but the core elements probably still have a place in the strategic therapist's armoury (Shoham-Solomon and Jancourt 1985).

The effectiveness of family therapy

Research into family therapy has shown that such work, no matter what its style, can bring about major changes in a child's environment and presenting problems (Cottrell and Boston 2002).

Investigations continue to attempt to identify what parts of the family work are the most powerful influences of change. These process studies show how reducing coalitions between a parent and child, and so establishing appropriate parental authority, helps to reduce problem behaviour (Mann *et al.* 1990), as does moving the parent's focus from organisational issues (such as bedtimes) to wider, more emotional themes (Heatherington and Friedlander 1990).

Brief solution-focused family therapy

As was described above, recently there has been a rapid increase in interest in using this type of therapy, and this enthusiasm has also been evident within family therapy work. This is not surprising since the therapy was largely developed from a systemic perspective (de Shazer *et al.* 1986), the techniques are easily transferred into the family context, and the approach is proving to be equally effective when used with families (Gingerich and Eisengart 2000). As its name implies, the task of the therapist within sessions is continually to guide the conversation in the session towards solution talk. To do this the therapist fits in with the family process while highlighting exceptions to the rule that 'the problem is always there', the potential solutions they have already found, and the individual, or family, strengths which they themselves identify.

Sarah was twelve years of age when she was brought by her mother and grandmother because of their concern about the difficult behaviour she was displaying. Problems had begun after her grandfather's death a year ago. Since that time she had been stealing, lying and avoiding school at every opportunity. Both mother and grandmother clearly found Sarah's behaviour very annoying, and although they had identified the onset as coinciding with Sarah's grandfather's death, they found it difficult to understand why she was behaving like this.

The 'miracle question' was used to clarify that Sarah wanted to feel as she had before her grandfather's death, and that the adults wished she would behave as she did then. With this goal in mind, questions were asked which focused upon what they would notice about themselves after they had reached this goal, and by using scaling questions they clarified for themselves how close they were to achieving it. The first session showed they had already moved three points from the low ebb they had been at immediately after Sarah's grandfather died, recognising how this had been achieved and identifying strengths and resources which the family possessed and which they could use to move further forward.

Over the next three sessions each small positive change was highlighted and emphasised. When talk about problems began, exceptions were sought and so the focus was persistently kept upon encouraging solution talk. The homework at the end of each session was to record when each family member saw signs that her goal was being achieved. As this task highlighted the genuine affection which they had for each other, the irritation of the adults towards Sarah dissipated and the problem behaviour stopped. The last session was dominated by descriptions of how much they were now enjoying their time together, and how helpful Sarah had become once more.

Behavioural approaches and therapies

In contrast with the talking therapies, behavioural therapies place less emphasis upon helping the client to achieve insight into why he or she is exhibiting problem behaviour. Rather than dwelling upon the past or considering hypothetical underlying causes of problems, behaviourists are primarily concerned with observable, measurable behaviour in the here and now. In most cases the goal of therapy is to assist the client to change specific problem behaviour in ways which are predetermined.

Behavioural techniques have their origins in experimental studies of animal learning where it was found that behaviour could be systematically changed (conditioned) by modifying its consequences (reinforcement). Behavioural therapies are based upon the principle that all behaviour (adaptive and maladaptive) is learned and can thus be unlearned or replaced by alternative behaviours. Therapy consists of altering the client's environment in such a way that desirable behaviour replaces that which was giving rise to problems.

Behaviour therapies draw upon two major types of learning: classical and operant conditioning. Classical conditioning refers to the process by which a naturally occurring, largely involuntary, behaviour becomes linked with a neutral object or event (a stimulus) in such a way that the two become associated. As a result, the presence of the stimulus results in the behaviour's occurrence. This principle resulted from the famous studies of Ivan Pavlov at the beginning of the twentieth century, which showed how sounding a tuning fork when presenting food to dogs led to an association between the sound and the feeding process. As a result, the dogs would salivate (their typical response when anticipating food) when hearing the tuning fork, even if no meat were presented. Thus the dogs had, through classical conditioning, been taught to salivate at the sound of the tuning fork – a naturally occurring response had been linked to a new stimulus.

The findings from animal studies were subsequently applied to human situations. In a highly influential study, Watson and Rayner (1920) demonstrated the effectiveness of classical conditioning with an eleven-month-old child, Albert. When initially presented with a white rat, Albert showed no fear; when, subsequently, the rat's presentation was accompanied by a sudden, very loud noise, Albert became highly anxious and fearful. After several presentations of the rat and the noise together, the child became intensely fearful of the rat alone. In essence a previously neutral object, the rat, had become the source of a conditioned fear response.

A further study at about this time (Jones 1924) concerned another child, Peter, who was inordinately fearful of rabbits and furry objects. Treatment involved gradual and systematic exposure to a rabbit while he was engaged in pleasurable eating activity. Positive, rather than negative, associations with furry animals were made and Peter's phobia disappeared.

Drawing upon these early studies of classical conditioning, many sophisticated techniques for treating problem behaviours have been developed. Perhaps the simplest example is the bell and pad treatment for nocturnal enuresis (bedwetting). When the sleeping child begins to urinate, a bell awakens the child and further urination is inhibited. This process is repeated nightly and, over time, the child associates the sensations from the bladder as it fills with the exercise of sphincter control. Eventually, the bladder's contents are contained all night without waking.

As Albert's case might suggest, classical conditioning underpins many treatments for phobias and other forms of emotional disorder. Techniques such as systematic desensitisation and emotive imagery (see Chapter 3), for example, through the process of association, involve the gradual substitution of a pleasant, relaxed state for the unpleasant anxiety or fearfulness previously experienced.

Operant conditioning, based upon the pioneering work of B.F. Skinner, is a rather different behavioural technique which emphasises the importance of consequences in maintaining and shaping an individual's behaviour. Where a behaviour is followed by a positive consequence, it is more likely to recur (i.e. it can be said to have been reinforced). Where behaviour is not reinforced, it is less likely to be repeated.

Reinforcement is a key conceptual tool for analysing why people behave as they do and is of particular value for understanding and treating problem behaviour. Frequently, one finds that undesirable behaviour is reinforced in ways that are not always obvious.

Samantha, aged four, was a member of a class of children who were listening to the teacher read from a giant-sized book full of colourful illustrations. She was bored, restless and kept fidgeting. This was beginning to disturb the other children. As a means of deflecting her behaviour, Samantha's teacher asked her to come to the front of the class and help her hold up the book for the other children to see.

While the reactions of the teacher are likely to have resolved the immediate problem caused by Samantha's disruptiveness, a behavioural analysis would suggest that, in the long term, her reaction may have made things worse. The child's undesirable behaviour was rewarded by attention and the allocation of a 'high-status job'. If such situations were repeated, Samantha is likely to associate 'being a nuisance' with desirable outcomes and, as a consequence, the undesirable behaviour would be 'reinforced', that is, it would become stronger and be exhibited more frequently (see Chapter 7 for further case studies).

In contrast, there are many situations where desirable behaviours are not reinforced as frequently or as strongly as they should be. For some adults, because children are expected to behave appropriately, they are rarely rewarded by thanks, praise or more tangible rewards when exhibiting desired behaviour. Over time, the child finds that 'good' behaviour goes unrewarded while 'bad' behaviour often gains adult attention and can alleviate boredom.

It is exceedingly rare for any human behaviour to be reinforced each time it is exhibited and the term 'intermittent reinforcement' describes situations where behaviour is reinforced in an unpredictable fashion. In such situations one can never be certain when rewards will follow behaviour. When reinforcement is stopped completely, the individual will tend to persist in the undesired behaviour for a much greater period of time than in other situations where behaviour had consistently been reinforced. The principle of intermittent reinforcement helps to explain the immense hold which fruit machines exert over people, for the customer always hopes that reinforcement will take place next time!

Alan, aged nine, was allowed one chocolate biscuit a day by his mother, although continually pestered for more. His mother would usually refuse his requests for a second biscuit and, invariably, this would result in scenes where the boy would become highly demanding, either by pleading and coaxing or by becoming verbally aggressive.

On some occasions, his mother's resolve was strong and, however poor Alan's behaviour, her determination to 'stick to her guns' meant that he could not get his own way. On other days, however, her son's temper tantrums and pleading often became too much for her and on such occasions she would give in 'for a quiet life'.

Positive reinforcement (e.g. praise, pocket money) follows the occurrence of a desired response (e.g. making one's bed). Such behaviour should occur more frequently in future. A process where positive reinforcement is used to change behaviour over a number of gradual stages is known as shaping (Chapters 3, 7, 8).

Negative reinforcement an undesirable situation (e.g. being kept in at playtime) is removed upon the occurrence of a desired response (e.g. classwork is completed). Such behaviour should occur more frequently in future (Chapters 7, 8).

Punishment an unpleasant situation (e.g. detention) follows the occurrence of an undesired response (e.g. failure to complete classwork). Such behaviour should occur less frequently in future (Chapters 7, 8).

Extinction undesirable behaviour is not reinforced and, as a result, gradually disappears (e.g. the child exhibiting a tantrum is completely ignored until he or she exhibits acceptable behaviour) (Chapter 7).

Token economy symbolic rewards (e.g. points, stars, tokens) are given in response to desirable behaviour. These can subsequently be exchanged for material items, such as money and sweets, or privileges, such as staying up to watch TV. In some programmes undesirable behaviour may result in a 'fine' where rewards are removed (sometimes known as 'response cost') (Chapters 7, 8).

Contingency contracting an explicit agreement is drawn up between two or more parties which sets out desired and undesired behaviours and the rewards and sanctions which will be made contingent upon these (Chapters 3, 7, 8).

Time-out when specific, undesirable behaviours occur, the child is removed from all sources of positive reinforcement (e.g. the child is required to sit alone in the hall for a fixed period of time) (Chapter 7).

Systematic desensitisation through relaxation training and a gradual exposure to a feared situation (via the imagination or in reality), a fearful or anxious state is gradually substituted by one of relaxation and calmness (Chapter 3).

Emotive imagery closely allied to systematic desensitisation, this involves developing an association between the feared object and a heroic figure with whom the child identifies. This association permits the child to confront and reduce the feared situation (Chapter 3).

Flooding/implosive therapy rather than introducing, through gradual exposure, that which is most feared (as in systematic desensitisation), the child is asked to imagine, or actually experience, this from the outset. Sometimes the feared object or situation is deliberately exaggerated to maximise its initial impact. The situation does not permit escape from the feared object or event and gradually the high level of anxiety lessens. The child comes to realise that the fear is unrealistic and that it can be controlled (Chapter 3).

Modelling the child is asked to observe and imitate behaviour modelled by another (e.g. family member, therapist). Successful performance is subsequently reinforced. Modelling may be used in respect of phobias (e.g. holding a spider in one's hand) or conduct disorders (e.g. tidying up one's toys at bedtime) (Chapter 3).

Figure 2.1 Major forms of behavioural therapy (chapters where these are outlined, or form part of case illustrations, are listed in brackets)

The above case study represents a classic illustration of intermittent reinforcement. Because Alan can never be certain whether prolonging his undesirable behaviour will eventually result in the achievement of his desires, he is likely to persevere with demanding behaviour even when it is not being reinforced. The expectation that his goal will eventually be met is often so strong that parental resolve to resist is unlikely to modify the child's behaviour in the short term. Given such a scenario, it is hardly surprising that parents who decide to 'stand up to their child' often come to believe that their new stance is not working and are tempted to give up. Where this happens, the pattern of intermittent reinforcement is continued and future attempts to take charge are likely to be met by even greater resistance.

In work with challenging children, the selection and effective use of reinforcement to shape behaviour is often more difficult than it might first appear. Children vary greatly in what is reinforcing for them; for example, some may respond to stars and stickers, others may see these as childish and prefer more tangible rewards. While many parents perceive yelling and scolding to be a form of punishment, for some children, receiving parental attention, in whatever form, is highly reinforcing.

It is also often difficult to control reinforcement. The range of possible reinforcers is limited and these may be insufficient to counter the perceived rewards which are associated with the problem behaviour. The child may find peer admiration when disrupting a class, the excitement and emotional rush from stealing a car, the satisfaction obtained from baiting a family member to be far more attractive outcomes than any rewards which parents or teachers might be able to offer.

There are many behavioural techniques which are employed as parts of treatment programmes. Some of the most common forms of therapy are listed in Figure 2.1.

Behaviour therapies have been shown to be among the most effective types of child therapy (Kazdin 1990). They are the cornerstones of treatment for phobias and anxieties and are highly valuable in work with conduct-disordered, challenging children and adolescents. They are accessible to clinicians operating in a wide range of disciplines and under appropriate supervision programmes can be operated by parents, teachers and many other relevant parties.

> Unlike the use of medicines, behaviour therapy has no side-effects; unlike the talking therapies, it does not demand high-level verbal ability; and unlike the group and environmental therapies it does not require the involvement of a range of other people or the regulation of wider environmental factors. Its non-diagnostic and non-stigmatising language helps prevent the formation of negative and excusatory self-concepts, particularly among adolescents with deep disorders and who search for ploys which neutralise therapeutic intervention.
>
> (Hoghughi 1988: 98)

It has become increasingly recognised that narrow behavioural conceptions are often insufficient for understanding and treating complex behaviour disorders. For this reason, behaviour therapists now more readily take into consideration broader issues relating to the functioning and belief systems of the child and the family together with the impact of the wider social context (Messer *et al.* 1993).

Cognitive therapy

Cognitive therapy uses techniques from several sources to pursue its aim of helping people change the way they think about their problems, and their general functioning. As described in the context of treating depression (see Chapter 10), the basic principle on which cognitive therapy is based is that moods and feelings are directly influenced by thoughts and ways of thinking – known as cognitions. These cognitions include the inner dialogue we use to understand events, and the template by which we always judge certain events. So, for example, a summons to the boss's office may always prompt the spontaneous thought 'What have I done wrong?' even though there is nothing to suggest that this is the reason for the request. Using such 'spontaneous' explanations is not usually a cause of problems, but if they become routinely negative and make the person permanently anxious, angry or depressed, they become a source of major difficulty. Cognitive therapy seeks to change such explanations, and so produce a more accurate, and hopefully healthier, view of the world for the individual to live by.

The first major description of this type of therapy was given by Beck (1963, 1964) who studied its use with people who had severe depression. Since that time the therapy has undergone major development, and is now seen as a cornerstone of treatment for several conditions, for example, depression (Williams 1992) and eating disorders (Ricca *et al.* 2000). This value is especially true in children for whom, for instance, drug treatment in depression is not very useful and so cognitive therapy tends to be the first line of response (Curry 2001).

Drug treatments

Drug treatments can only be prescribed by doctors, and so for many situations where problems are being considered by other professionals, the role of drugs is not considered. In adults drug treatments have been a significant part of the way that doctors try to help people with major psychiatric problems. It is not surprising, therefore, that similar endeavours have been seen when trying to assist with emotional and behavioural difficulties that arise in childhood. The efforts have, however, been more muted because of concern about the long-term effects of giving any drug to a child. In addition there is the ethical dilemma that, since problems in childhood can be strongly influenced by many factors, is it right to subdue the symptom and not tackle the cause? This dilemma can be illustrated by the child who demonstrates aggressive behaviour primarily as a result of his or her parents' own marital violence. Should such a child be treated with drugs to minimise what is, in effect, a natural response to such behaviour in his or her caregivers? Interestingly, the response to this question has tended to be different depending on which side of the Atlantic you live. In the UK the giving of drugs to children who do not have physical or demonstrable major psychiatric illness has, until quite recently, been rare. By contrast, American clinicians have been much more likely to explore drug regimes (Campbell and Cueva 1995). The growing number of studies which show that medication can have a positive impact upon young people's lives by, for instance, reducing their aggression (Findling *et al.* 2000) is prompting a shift in prescribing in the UK. Major psychiatric illnesses, such as schizophrenia (Spencer and Campbell 1994) and obsessional compulsive disorder (De Veaugh-Geiss *et al.* 1992), do show a positive response to medication similar to that seen in adults. For some problems, however, e.g. depression, the improvement achieved by medication appears less than in adults, but despite this, may still be the most effective way of reducing the young person's distress in the short term (Michael and Crowley 2002). However, caution is always needed, because most of the medicines used in children and young people have only been officially approved (e.g. licensed by the Drugs Licensing Authority in the UK) for use with adults, and some may show unwanted effects when given to younger people.

Milieu therapy and intensive approaches

Residential units

It has been a traditional response when confronted with someone who has severe emotional or behavioural problems to look to place them in a residential setting which can not only offer continuous assistance and treatment to the individual, but removes them from the community where their problems may be prompting concern or distress. In psychiatry this residential setting has been a hospital, in education a residential school, and in the social services arena may range from a residential family group home to a secure-accommodation provision.

Such settings can offer an intensive intervention, and may permit specific treatment approaches (such as token economy schemes) to be implemented which would be impractical in more limited provisions. Over recent years, however, the role of residential settings has been severely questioned, and their use has tended to dwindle. Removal of children from their families and the community is always a detrimental step and must be weighed against the potential advantages.

The programmes offered in residential settings have to take account of the developmental stage which the child has reached. Regimes that would be suitable for young children would clearly be inappropriate for adolescents, and offering a suitable range of responses in what are usually quite small units is one of the major challenges which residential settings face. As with any effective intervention its content must be tailored to the needs of the individual but usually there are elements of work with the child individually as well as group activities. One of the most powerful elements that is at work in any treatment setting is the milieu. Because so much time is spent in residential settings, the power which this exerts in such environments is particularly important.

Milieu is difficult to define, and yet we all experience it several times a day. As human beings we are sensitive to the mood in a room, or the 'atmosphere' that exists in some meetings. Children are especially sensitive to ambience, and can be strongly influenced by it. Any therapeutic environment, therefore, is not only influencing the child by the stated treatment programme but by way the unit 'feels'. 'First impressions' and 'prevailing atmosphere' are indicators of the milieu which the unit is offering. This is partly to do with the physical environment, but is mostly made up of a blend of warmth and personal regard combined with clear expectations about behaviour and general conduct. A staff view that 'we care about you too much to let you do this' is an excellent foundation for a positive milieu, and once accepted as genuine can be far more powerful in bringing about change than a formal treatment strategy.

In recent times there has been a considerable shift in the focus and use of such resources. The provision of hospital places for children has considerably reduced, while the demand for facilities continues to expand. The decision to seek specialised residential schooling is rarely made to meet a specific educational need, but rather to respond to social and behavioural difficulties. Indeed responding to children and young people whose behaviour is beyond the control of their families, and is disturbing to their community and society in general represents the greatest challenge for the caring professions today. An effective regime for residential settings to deploy to respond to such needs is slowly emerging, but units with such programmes are still few.

Day units

As mentioned above, one of the difficulties with residential treatment is the way that it separates the child from family and community. In recent years there has been a great upsurge in the provision of day treatment programmes (called partial hospitalisation in the United States) as a way of providing an intensity of care with the minimum of disruption to the day-to-day functioning of the child. As well as offering a greater intensity of involvement than can be achieved by outpatient appointments, such programmes allow the child to remain within the family, and this in turn produces issues and information that can be used to inform and progress family change. In addition, with careful planning it is possible to provide very focused treatment packages which are age-specific, and use the continued attendance at school and so on as a positive lever for change (Place *et al.* 1990). By remaining within their community children may also develop support networks through friends, school, and so on. These become particularly important when the day programme comes to an end.

Confronting and challenging inappropriate behaviour is a key element of the programmes offered by a variety of residential settings and day units. Many use the interpretative style described by Redl (1959) and which he called 'the life-space interview'. This seeks to use such situations not only to help children recognise patterns and repetitions in their behaviour, but to assist them in developing new responses which are more appropriate.

The diversity of day unit programmes and the differing goals which they aspire to make it difficult to offer a general view on the effectiveness of such programmes. In units which deal with psychological difficulties about three-quarters of the children continue to have improved functioning two years after discharge (Place *et al.* 1990). These improvements are often not only in the presenting problem but also in the child's self-esteem and hopefulness about the future (Grizenko *et al.* 1993). Long-term follow-up studies show that for both residential and day treatment programmes two-thirds of the children have sustained their improvement after ten years (Erker *et al.* 1993).

Multisystemic therapy

A single type of response that effectively reduces marked antisocial behaviour is proving difficult to find. This has prompted efforts to combine elements of various approaches, and perhaps the most effective of these is the multisystemic therapy developed by Scott Henggeler and his colleagues (1998). The approach is intensive, with each clinician having five or six families, and being available to them throughout every day. Family, behavioural and individual approaches are combined with school, peer and social-network elements, with the exact make-up being determined by the needs of the specific family and young person. There is a high level of supervision for each clinician, and monitoring of progress is routine. It has been used in several countries to intervene with a variety of mainly delinquency-type problems, and the outcomes are quite promising (Henggeler 2002).

Treatment foster care

When remaining with the family is not possible alternative family placement is the usual response. Recently there has been a growing interest in whether children could be helped to overcome their difficulties by placing them in a substitute family whose purpose is to offer a therapeutic regime. For some children whose family of origin is limited in its parenting resources, moving to a family which offers good-quality care may be sufficient to bring about positive change. However, for more damaged children these substitute families have to offer a deliberately therapeutic regime. These placements tend to operate a strict behavioural regime with each of the day's tasks being allocated points for completion. For instance getting up on time, washing and being on time for breakfast would each be rewarded with points that can be traded for activities, CDs, etc.

Interest in using treatment foster care has been increasing since its introduction in the USA (Clark *et al.* 1994), and the results are encouraging enough for programmes to be established around the UK. However, whether children who have received such treatment will maintain the improvement in their functioning in the long term is still to be determined (Reddy and Pfeiffer 1997).

Voluntary agencies

In any locality there is a variety of voluntary and charitable agencies that may be helpful in dealing with difficulties. For instance:

- Relate is a voluntary agency that will help couples to explore, and hopefully resolve, relationship difficulties. Although the agency's workers are volunteers, as with other voluntary agencies, they are trained to ensure they can offer the appropriate skills necessary to help couples address their problems.
- Cruise is a voluntary service which helps both adults and children cope with bereavement.
- Victim Support gives practical advice and support to anyone who has been the victim of crime.
- Rape Crisis offers help and support to people who have been the victims of rape, though they usually only offer services to teenagers and adults.

In addition to such focused agencies the children's charities for example, the NSPCC, Barnardos, National Children's Homes (NCH) are increasingly developing specialised sources of help for specific situations – such as the victims of sexual abuse, or supporting children from very damaging homes who have been adopted. Such services tend to be patchy, although local social services departments can offer advice on their availability.

References

Alexander, F. and French, T. (1946). *Psychoanalytic Therapy. Principles and Application.* New York: Ronald Press.

Andrews, G. (1993). The essential psychotherapies. *British Journal of Psychiatry* 162, 447–51.

Ashurst, P. (1991). Brief psychotherapy. In J. Holmes (ed.) *Textbook of Psychotherapy in Psychiatric Practice*. Edinburgh: Churchill Livingstone.

Axeline, V. (1947). *Play Therapy*. Boston: Houghton-Mifflin.

Beck, A.T. (1963). Thinking and depression. I. Idiosyncratic content and cognitive distortions. *Archives of General Psychiatry* 9, 324–33.

Beck, A.T. (1964). Thinking and depression. II. Theory and therapy. *Archives of General Psychiatry* 10, 561–71.

Berg, I.K. and de Jong, P. (1996). Solution-building conversations: co-constructing a sense of competence with clients. *Families in Society* 2, 376–91.

Bisson, J.I., Jenkins, P.L., Alexander, J. and Bannister, C. (1997). Randomised controlled trial of psychological debriefing for victims of acute burn trauma. *British Journal of Psychiatry* 171, 78–81.

Burnham, J.B. (1986). *Family Therapy*. London: Routledge.

Byng-Hall, J. (1995). *Re-writing Family Scripts*. New York: Guilford Press.

Cade, B. (1984). Paradoxical techniques in therapy. *Journal of Child Psychology and Psychiatry* 25, 509–16.

Campbell, M. and Cueva, J.E. (1995). Psychopharmacology in child and adolescent psychiatry: a review of the past seven years. II. *Journal of the American Academy of Child and Adolescent Psychiatry* 34, 1262–72.

Clark, H.B., Prange, M.E., Lee, B.L. and Adlai, L.B. (1994). Improving adjustment outcomes for foster children with emotional and behavioral disorders: early findings from a controlled study on individualized services. *Journal of Emotional and Behavioral Disorders* 2, 207–18.

Cottrell, D. and Boston, P. (2002). The effectiveness of systemic family therapy for children and adolescents. *Journal of Child Psychology Psychiatry* 43, 573–86.

Curry, J.F. (2001). Specific psychotherapies for childhood and adolescent depression. *Biological Psychiatry* 49, 1091–1100.

Davanloo, H. (1980). *Short-term Dynamic Psychotherapy*. New York: Aronson.

de Shazer, S. (1991). *Putting Difference to Work*. New York: W.W. Norton.

de Shazer, S., Berg, I.K., Lipchik, E. and Nunnally, E. (1986). Brief therapy: focused solution development. *Family Process* 25, 207–22.

De Veaugh-Geiss, J., Moroz, G. and Biederman, J. (1992). Clomipramine hydrochloride in childhood and adolescent obsessional-compulsive disorder: a multicenter trial. *Journal of the American Academy of Child and Adolescent Psychiatry* 31, 45–9.

Erker, G.J., Searight, H.R., Amanat, E. and White, P.D. (1993). Residential versus day treatment for children: a long term follow-up study. *Child Psychiatry and Human Development* 24, 31–9.

Findling, R.L., McNamara, N.K., Branicky, L.A., Schluchter, M.D., Lemon, E. and Blumer, J.L. (2000). A double-blind pilot study of risperidone in the treatment of conduct disorder. *Journal of American Academy of Child Adolescent Psychiatry* 39, 509–16.

Frank, J.D. (1974). Therapeutic components of psychotherapy. A 25 year progress report of research. *Journal of Nervous and Mental Disease* 159, 325–42.

Freud, A. (1966). *The Writings of Anna Freud. Vol. 2. The Ego and Mechanisms of Defense*. New York: International University Press.

Freud, S. (1976). *Introductory Lectures on Psychoanalysis*. Harmondsworth: Penguin.

Garfield, S. and Bergin, A. (1994). Introduction and historical overview. In A. Bergin and S. Garfield (eds) *Handbook of Psychotherapy and Behaviour Change*. Chichester: Wiley.

Gingerich, W.J. and Eisengart, S. (2000). Solution-focused brief therapy: a review of the outcome research. *Family Process* 39, 477–98.

Grizenko, N., Papineau, D. and Sayegh, L. (1993). Effectiveness of a multimodal day treatment program for children with disruptive behavior problems. *Journal of the American Academy of Child and Adolescent Psychiatry* 32, 127–34.

Heatherington, L. and Friedlander, M.L. (1990). Complementarity and symmetry in family therapy communication. *Journal of Counselling Psychology* 37, 261–8.

Henggeler, S.W., Clingempeel, W., Brondino, M.J., Pickrel, S.G. (2002). Four-year follow-up of multisystemic therapy with substance-abusing and substance-dependent juvenile offenders. *Journal of American Academy of Child Adolescent Psychiatry* 41, 868–74.

Henggeler, S.W., Schoenwald, S.K., Borduin, C.M., Rowland, M.D., Cunningham, P.B. (1998). *Multisystemic Treatment of Antisocial Behavior in Children and Adolescents*. New York: Guilford.

Hoghughi, M. (1988). *Treating Problem Children*. London: Sage.

Jones, M.C. (1924). The elimination of children's fears. *Journal of Experimental Psychology* 7, 382–90.

Kazdin, A.E. (1990). Psychotherapy for children. *Annual Review of Psychology* 41, 21–54.

Lane, R.C., Koetting M.G., Bishop, J. (2002). Silence as communication in psychodynamic psychotherapy. *Clinical Psychology Review* 22, 1091–1104.

Lethem, J. (2002). Brief Solution Focused Therapy. *Child and Adolescent Mental Health* 7, 189–92.

Lieberman, S. (1979). *Transgenerational Family Therapy*. Guildford: Biddles Ltd.

Lindemann, E. (1944). Symptomatology and management of acute grief. *American Journal of Psychiatry* 101, 101–48.

Macdonald, A.J. (1997). Brief therapy in adult psychiatry – further outcomes. *Journal of Family Therapy* 19, 213–22.

Malan, D.H. (1963). *A Study of Brief Psychotherapy*. London: Social Science Paperbacks.

Malan, D.H. (1976). *The Frontiers of Brief Psychotherapy*. London: Hutchinson.

Mann, B.J., Borduin, C.M., Henggeler, S.W. and Blaske, D.M. (1990). An investigation of systematic conceptualizations of parent–child coalitions and symptom change. *Journal of Consulting and Clinical Psychology* 58, 336–44.

Messer, S.C., Morris, T.L. and Gross, A.M. (1993). Clinical behavior therapy with children. In A.S. Bellack and M. Hersen (eds) *Behavior Therapy in the Psychiatric Setting*. New York: Plenum Press.

Michael, K.D. and Crowley, S.L. (2002). How effective are treatments for child and adolescent depression? A meta-analytic review. *Clinical Psychology Review* 22, 247–69.

Orlinsky, D. and Howard, K. (1986). Process and outcome in psychotherapy. In S. Garfield and A. Bergin (eds) *Handbook of Psychotherapy and Behavioural Change*. Chichester: Wiley.

Place, M., Rajah, S. and Crake, T. (1990). Combining day patient treatment with family work in a child psychiatry clinic. *European Archives of Psychiatry and Neurological Sciences* 239, 373–8.

Reddy, L.A. and Pfeiffer, S.I. (1997). Effectiveness of treatment foster care with children and adolescents: a review of outcome studies. *Journal of the American Academy of Child and Adolescent Psychiatry* 36, 581–8.

Redl, F. (1959). A strategy and technique of the life-space interview. *American Journal of Orthopsychiatry* 29, 1–15.

Ricca, V., Mannucci, E., Zucchi, T., Rotella, C.M., Faravelli, C. (2000). Cognitive-behavioural therapy for bulimia nervosa and binge eating disorder. A review. *Psychotherapy and Psychosomatics* 69, 287–95.

Rogers, C.R. (1951). *Client-centred Therapy*. London: Constable.

Rogers, C.R. (1961). *On Becoming a Person*. London: Constable.

Segal, H. (1964). *Introduction to the Work of Melanie Klein*. London: Heinemann.

Shoham-Solomon, V. and Jancourt, A. (1985). Differential effectiveness of paradoxical interventions for more versus less stress-prone individuals. *Journal of Counselling Psychology* 32, 499–513.

Spencer, E.K. and Campbell, M. (1994). Children with schizophrenia: diagnosis, phenomenology, and pharmacotherapy. *Schizophrenic Bulletin* 20, 713–25.

Watson, J.B. and Rayner, R. (1920). Conditioned emotional reactions. *Journal of Experimental Psychology* 3, 1–14.

Weisz, J.R. and Jensen, A.L. (2001). Child and adolescent psychotherapy in research and practice contexts: review of the evidence and suggestions for improving the field. *European Child and Adolescent Psychiatry*, 10 Suppl 1: 112–18.

Weisz, J.R., Weiss, B., Alicke, M.D. and Klotz, M.L. (1987). Effectiveness of psychotherapy with children and adolescents: a meta-analysis for clinicians. *Journal of Consulting and Clinical Psychology* 55, 542–9.

Williams, J.M.G. (1992). *The Psychological Treatment of Depression*. 2nd edn. London: Routledge.

Yalom, I.D. (1995). *The Theory and Practice of Group Psychotherapy*, New York: Basic Books.

Chapter 3

School refusal

Introduction

Children may not wish to attend school for many reasons, ranging from boredom in class, to fear of classmates, to a reluctance to leave their parents. The list of reasons is long and applies to most children at some time during the 15,000 hours that they typically spend in school.

Most children are likely to miss occasional days from school at some stage during their childhood because of what may often appear to an onlooker to be trivial fears or anxieties. Perhaps a lesson has been misunderstood and a teacher's anger is feared, or a best friend has teamed up with someone else. Usually such difficulties are resolved or quickly forgotten and school attendance soon resumes. Some children maintain a strong dislike of school throughout their childhood but accept the requirement to attend regularly. A much smaller proportion cease to attend school for a prolonged period of time; these are the individuals who usually come into contact with helping agencies.

Truants or school refusers?

A major distinction is often drawn between truants and school phobics (the latter are now more commonly termed school refusers). Although truants also choose not to attend school they are usually perceived as experiencing no major psychological difficulty in attending; rather they prefer not to. In contrast, school refusers may wish to attend but often find that they cannot. To some extent, then, one distinction between truancy and school refusal centres upon volition. Truancy is widely perceived as one variant of acting-out behaviour, often associated with delinquency and disruptiveness, whereas school refusal is typically perceived as a form of neurosis characterised by anxiety and fearfulness. This widely held distinction is complicated because some writers (e.g. Kearney 1995) include all those who refuse to attend school, both truants and school phobics, under the broader, all-encompassing heading of school refusal. This chapter, however, will maintain the generally accepted distinction between truants and school refusers.

In distinguishing school refusal from truancy, Berg *et al.* (1969) noted that unlike truants, refusers tend to share the following features:

- severe difficulty in attending school, often amounting to prolonged absence;
- severe emotional upset, which may involve such symptoms as excessive fearfulness, temper tantrums, misery or complaints of feeling ill without obvious organic cause when faced with the prospect of going to school;
- during school hours, the child remains at home with the knowledge of the parents;
- absence of significant antisocial disorders such as juvenile delinquency, disruptiveness and sexual activity.

In contrast, truants are more likely to attend school on a sporadic basis. They are typically not excessively anxious or fearful about attending school, nor do they usually complain about physical discomfort. Truants are more likely to conceal the absence from their parents, often by wandering the streets during the day, and are more likely to engage in antisocial acts. In a comparative study of truants and school refusers (Galloway 1983) parental reports indicated that truants were more influenced by peers and had a greater history of lying, stealing and wandering from the home out of school hours. In contrast, school refusers were reported as having more concerns about academic matters, were more anxious about parental well-being and were reluctant to leave the home. There were, however, no significant differences in peer relationships, the frequency of eating and sleeping difficulties or the proportion of cases of enuresis.

It should be recognised, however, that truants and school refusers do not always fall into clear-cut groups and a relatively small proportion of absentees show features of both truancy and school refusal. In one study of one hundred chronic absentees, for example, Bools *et al.* (1990) found that approximately 10 per cent of the sample demonstrated both emotional and antisocial conduct disorders.

Prevalence

Estimates of the prevalence of school refusal vary considerably, primarily because of the differing criteria that have been used to define the term. Where estimates of school refusal, not including truancy, are employed (consistent with the use of the term in this chapter) figures in the USA and UK generally range from 0.4 per cent to 2 per cent of the population.

Types of school refuser

Hersov (1977: 458–9) outlines a common picture of school refusal immediately recognisable to those with experience of such difficulties:

The problem often starts with vague complaints about school or reluctance to attend progressing to total refusal to go to school or to remain in school in the face of persuasion, entreaty, recrimination and punishment by parents and pressures from teachers, family doctors and education welfare officers. The behaviour may be accompanied by overt signs of anxiety or even panic when the time comes to go to school and most children cannot even leave home to set out for school. Many who do return home halfway there and some children, once at school, rush home in a state of anxiety. Many children insist that they want to go to school and are prepared to do so but cannot manage it when the time comes.

In addition to the psychological distress noted above, such children often complain of physical illness such as headaches, stomach aches, dizziness or vomiting for which there are no organic causes. In many cases these physical symptoms disappear once the child is allowed to remain at home. The high levels of anxiety may also be compounded by depression leading to tearfulness, sleeping difficulties, irritability and low self-esteem.

Although such a picture is common, it is important to recognise that there is no single form of school refusal. Major areas of controversy centre on, first, the extent to which school refusal should be seen as a consequence of fear of being in school rather than of separating from parents and home, and, second, whether there is a difference between those children whose non-attendance is sudden, as opposed to developing over a long period. In both issues the influences of age and gender are seen as important mediating factors.

Although Broadwin (1932) is credited as being the first writer to describe a form of persistent school absence marked by fearfulness and prolonged refusal to attend, Johnson et al. (1941) coined the term 'school phobia' to describe this phenomenon. According to these early theorists, the school-refusing child had an excessively strong love attachment to the parent and fantasised about returning to the nourishing and protective maternal situation enjoyed in infancy. The mothers of such children were perceived as having similarly unfulfilled emotional needs and, as a result, became overprotective of their child and overdemanding of attention. It was thought that anger, resentment and hostility experienced by both mother and child in the resolution of the quest for independence/dependence resulted in anxiety about separation directly resulting in school refusal. This view became highly popular in the 1950s and 1960s to the extent that some writers (e.g. Johnson 1957) saw school phobia being replaced by separation anxiety as the key diagnostic criterion.

Separation anxiety is now seen by many practitioners as an inadequate explanation for all cases of school refusal. The theory does not explain why the peak age for school refusal is between the ages of eleven and thirteen (Last et al. 1987) rather than in the early years of schooling as the theory would suggest. Furthermore, many school-phobic children appear to have little difficulty in separating from their parents for other social/recreational activities. Given these weaknesses in the theory, many contemporary writers tend to place equal emphasis upon the school itself as the source of anxiety (Pilkington and Piersel 1991).

In identifying differing types of school phobia, a distinction is often drawn between acute and chronic school refusal, a factor that may be important in the devising of appropriate interventions. Berg *et al.* (1969) suggested that where absence had been preceded by at least three years' trouble-free attendance, irrespective of current duration, the school refusal should be considered as acute. Other cases should be considered as chronic. Studies comparing children falling into these two categories have repeatedly demonstrated that chronic refusal is associated with a greater dependency, neurosis, a higher incidence of parental mental illness, less sociability and lower self-esteem. In contrast, acute refusal is associated with higher levels of depression.

Given the greater incidence of problems experienced by chronic cases and findings indicating that such children are often unlikely to be provided assistance by support services for several months, it is hardly surprising that the prognosis for chronic refusal is poorer than for acute cases (Berg 1970). Indeed, it is arguable that chronic cases are merely acute cases that have been allowed to persist over time.

Studies have been inconsistent and variable in determining both age and sex differences (Trueman 1984), although there is some evidence to suggest that separation anxiety is more a feature of younger female children while fear of school tends to be more prevalent in older male children (Last *et al.* 1987). There is some evidence, however (e.g. Smith 1970), that cases are high at the time of school entry and peak between the ages of eleven and thirteen (at a time when most children transfer from primary to secondary schooling). In general, studies suggest that older school refusers suffer from more severe disorders and have a poorer prognosis (Atkinson *et al.* 1985). Intellectual functioning in school refusers, contrary to earlier thinking, tends to mirror that of non-school refusers of comparable ages (Trueman 1984).

It is now widely accepted that school refusal is not a unitary syndrome but, rather, multicausal and heterogeneous. As such, rather than focusing upon simple school phobia/separation anxiety or acute/chronic onset distinctions, it may be more helpful for practitioners to examine the needs of the child that are met by non-school attendance (Kearney and Silverman 1990; Evans 2000). Understanding what the child gains by not attending school should help the practitioner derive the most effective forms of intervention. Kearney and Silverman's clinical and research work has led them to the conclusion that, for each individual, school refusal is maintained by one or more of four major categories (see Figure 3.1). Preferred modes of intervention for each of these categories can be outlined (see Chapter 2) and their effectiveness measured over time.

Category I	Avoidance of specific fearfulness or general overanxiousness related to the school setting. This includes cases where one or more particular features of school (a corridor, toilets, test situations, a particular teacher) are feared.
Category 2	Escape from aversive social situations. This focuses on situations where problems centre upon unsatisfying relationships with others (peers and/or teachers). Often this incorporates an evaluative element.
Category 3	Attention-getting or separation-anxious behaviour. This may be manifested by tantrums and/or somatic complaints where the child's intention is primarily to stay at home with a parent or important other.
Category 4	Rewarding experiences provided out of school. Children who fall into this category may wish to remain at home because this provides opportunities for engaging in preferred activities such as watching the television or associating with friends.

Figure 3.1 Kearney and Silverman's functional categories for school refusal

Assessment

The heterogeneous nature of school refusal is such that a detailed assessment of the child is necessary in order to derive the most appropriate intervention. It is important that consideration is given to the child's affective, cognitive and behavioural functioning both generally and in relation to the specific context of the refusal. Most practitioners favour the employment of a range of procedures, including child interviews (in both one-to-one and whole-family settings), the employment of self-report questionnaires, ratings of the child by significant others (e.g. parents and teachers), self-monitoring by the child (e.g. the use of a diary to record feelings and behaviours), direct behavioural observation of the child in the home and school setting and an assessment of family dynamics.

At the initial stages information about the child's general functioning at home and at school is sought. The precise nature of the refusal is explored in greater detail in order to ascertain the extent of the child's difficulty. Subsequently, consideration of specific aspects of the child's environment that induce fearfulness, together with examination of the responses of others to this, are examined. At this early stage, the practitioner may discover that school refusal is a secondary symptom of another, more pervasive difficulty. This may be a genuine physical illness, severe depression, agoraphobia, a complex learning difficulty, or more generally defiant or challenging behaviour.

Many practitioners advocate the use of self-report instruments that gauge children's perceptions of their feelings and emotions. Widely used measures include the Children's Manifest Anxiety Scale – Revised (Reynolds and Paget 1983), the Fear Survey Schedule for Children – Revised (Ollendick

1983), the Children's Depression Inventory (Kovacs and Beck 1977; see Chapter 10) and the Social Anxiety Scale for Children – Revised (La Greca and Stone 1993).

Such scales typically ask children to respond to a variety of situations printed on a questionnaire. The Fear Survey Schedule for Children – Revised, for example, lists eighty situations that are potentially fearful (e.g. spiders, being in a fight, failing a test, having to go to hospital). For each, the child is asked to indicate whether he or she experiences no fear, some fear or a lot of fear. As a number of the situations relate to school contexts, this measure provides a useful means of differentiating between those whose difficulties relate specifically to one or more aspects of school life and those who experience a wider form of separation anxiety (Ollendick and Mayer 1984).

The only self-report measure that specifically addresses school-refusal behaviour is the School Refusal Assessment Scale (Kearney and Silverman 1993) which attempts to ascertain what needs are served by the child's school-refusal behaviour. This scale, available in child, teacher and parent versions, originally contained sixteen items, whereby four questions each measure the relative influence of one of the four maintaining conditions (see Figure 3.1). More recently, Kearney (2002a) has produced revised student and parent versions, each now containing twenty-four (six per function) questions. Ideally, the scale should be used in conjunction with direct observation of the child at home, in particular at the beginning of the school day (Kearney 2001).

An important issue to assess in understanding what maintains any phobic behaviour is whether it is negatively or positively reinforced, that is whether the 'reward' is escaping from something unpleasant (negative reinforcement) or achieving a pleasing experience (positive reinforcement). In relation to school refusal, such an analysis involves considering whether avoidance of school is maintained because:

1   it results in the reduction or elimination of unpleasant experiences, such as no longer being teased by schoolmates (negative reinforcement); or
2   avoidance of school results in an increase in the experience of desirable outcomes, such as playing at home on one's computer (positive reinforcement).

Clearly, the intervention programme will differ greatly according to the nature of the factors that maintain the behaviour. An illustrative example is provided below.

Richard, a fourteen-year-old, was an only child living at home with his mother and her partner. Two years earlier his natural parents had separated, and shortly after his mother's new boyfriend moved in on a permanent basis. Richard spoke widely of his liking for his mother's new partner, though he readily admitted that he would like to see his parents reunited.

Richard was referred to an educational psychologist on the grounds of his prolonged absence from school. His parents informed the psychologist that in order to persuade the boy to return to school they had bought him a motorcycle for use in the woods near his home. Richard, however, subsequently reneged on his promise to return to school and was now stating that he would only return to school if he were bought a more powerful machine. His mother informed the psychologist that she was prepared to accede to this request if it led to a return to school but she wasn't optimistic that this would be the case.

Detailed examination of Richard's situation resulted in the following observations:

1　There was little evidence of fearfulness and/or anxiety when Richard was in school (prior to the onset of the refusal and during a brief, ultimately unsuccessful, staged return trial programme).

2　Richard's day at home was undemanding and generally pleasurable. He got up late, watched the television or played with his computer. His mother and her partner were at work all day so he spent his time at home alone. Most evenings he met his schoolmates in the woods and rode his motorcycle. Occasional attempts to restrict his use of the motorcycle had been introduced but these appeared to make no impact upon his unwillingness to attend school. His mother had therefore ceased to use this threat as a means of persuasion.

3　Richard enjoyed good relations with most people with whom he came into contact. Apart from friction concerning his non-attendance at school, there was little conflict or hostility in the home. Richard appeared to have accepted his mother's partner and enjoyed going out with him to fish or to play sports. There was no indication of any specific difficulties at school (e.g. academic problems, bullying or harassment). His behaviour in class was good and his teachers were mystified by his unwillingness to attend.

4　From the outset, Richard was eager to establish a positive relationship with those professionals who were attempting to help him. His presentation of himself as relaxed and sociable was backed up by a rather jocular manner that appeared somewhat inappropriate.

5　Richard could not articulate any reasons for not attending school other than to state that he 'couldn't face it'. When pressed, he would clam up and become silent. If another topic was raised he would immediately become communicative once more. When asked about his bargaining over the replacement motorcycle he replied that he wanted it so badly that he would force himself to attend school.

6   Richard's mother was meeting regularly with her husband in order
    to persuade him to exert influence over their son. Father was com-
    ing to the house on a regular basis but family discussions usually
    ended with Dad losing his temper with Richard.

The investigation of Richard's case indicated that his school refusal was
maintained primarily by the fourth of Kearney and Silverman's (1993)
categories, that is, his school refusal behaviour was being positively
reinforced by his out-of-school experiences. His enjoyable daytimes,
together with the power he was exerting over the adults in his life,
appeared to combine in the maintenance of his school refusal. This
power not only resulted in his bargaining for material things but gave him
control over his parents, frequently bringing them together, possibly in
the hope that they might ultimately be reunited. School refusal may be
a powerful weapon for a child who feels generally powerless to control a
break-up of the family.

There was no indication that the other three functional categories had
any bearing on this case. The implications for intervention were clear:
change the reinforcement schedules operating at home by relating access
to enjoyable activities at home and in the evenings to school attendance
and establishing a more appropriate daily routine (e.g. bedtimes, getting
up in the morning); and engage the family in therapeutic work geared
to the resolution of the family-based problems and tensions that were
leading to the school refusal.

Intervention approaches

The many different conceptions and manifestations of school refusal, each
with differing underlying causes and symptoms, have led to fierce debate
about the most appropriate interventions and it has proven impossible
to derive any one strategy that has proven effective or appropriate for all
school refusers. What is clear is that if either support agencies or the school
fail to work collaboratively, and fail to understand the contribution that
other professionals will be making, the chances of a successful return are
greatly reduced. The following sections deal initially with types of clinical
intervention and then go on to consider the central role which the school
plays.

In treating school refusal, a distinction is often made between psychodynamic approaches, which are concerned with disturbances of thought, feeling
and behaviour, and which are typically addressed by means of some form
of individual, group or family therapy, and behaviour therapy approaches
based upon the premise that disordered behaviour is learned and can thus
be unlearned through the use of a variety of 'behavioural' techniques. With

regard to school refusal, behavioural approaches usually involve a graduated weakening of the relationship of school attendance with associated negative emotions, and ensuring that rewards and sanctions in the child's life become contingent upon desired behaviour (i.e. school attendance).

A number of techniques are used to address school refusal. These are based upon applications of talking therapy, behavioural techniques and medication (see Chapter 2). The most widely advocated techniques are:

- systematic desensitisation through relaxation
- emotive imagery
- shaping and contingency management
- modelling
- social skills training
- cognitive therapy
- family therapy
- medication.

Each of these will be briefly described below, although for a more detailed account of research studies, see Elliott (1999).

Systematic desensitisation

Systematic desensitisation usually consists of a three-stage procedure (the reader is referred to Kratochwill and Morris (1991) for a more detailed account):

1 Teaching the client to become progressively relaxed. King et al. (1995) outline a helpful format of relaxation training that involves progressive muscle relaxation. The programme involves systematically tensing and relaxing muscle groups (e.g. arms and shoulders, legs and feet) with, for younger children, the assistance of associated mental imagery. It is suggested that no more than three muscle groups should be introduced in each fifteen- to twenty-minute session.

2 Constructing a hierarchy of anxiety-evoking situations. The child and practitioner agree upon a target fear (such as attending school). The child is presented with a number of blank cards and is asked to write down briefly about each situation (e.g. undressing for PE) where that fear is evoked. The child is asked to outline situations where there are differing degrees of fearfulness or other forms of emotional discomfort. Cards are then ranked in order of fearfulness. Additional cards are completed as necessary in follow-up sessions until there is a hierarchy ranging from zero-level fearfulness to that which evokes the most extreme emotions.

3   Replacing anxiety by relaxation for each of these situations. Once the child has become skilled at practising relaxation techniques he or she is asked to imagine each of the situations on the cards, commencing in ascending order. Usually, three or four situations are considered in any one session. The intention is that the fearful situation becomes associated with being in a relaxed state and, as a result, anxiety is diminished.

Emotive imagery

Emotive imagery is another fear-reduction method that closely resembles systematic desensitisation. First employed by Lazarus and Abramovitz, it involves the association between each situation on the fear hierarchy with imagined scenes which 'arouse feelings of self-assertion, pride, affection, mirth and similar anxiety-inhibiting responses' (1962: 191). Typically, the child's usual hero images (e.g. a famous footballer) or activities that are greatly desired (e.g. driving a speedboat) are elicited, imagined and then related to items in the fear hierarchy by means of a narrative. As with systematic desensitisation, as anxiety is gradually inhibited in each of the lower-level items, the procedure is repeated until the highest item can be considered without undue anxiety.

Although desensitisation and relaxation approaches are recommended widely by clinicians particularly with primary-aged children whose refusal is marked by extreme phobic reactivity (King *et al.* 1995), such methods have yet to be supported by controlled research studies (Kratochwill and Morris 1991).

Shaping and contingency management

Contingency management procedures are based upon behavioural principles whereby the influence of events taking place before and after specific behaviours is highlighted and subsequently modified to effect desired behavioural change. For school refusal, this approach involves maximising rewarding experiences for being in school and minimising the rewards for remaining at home during the school day. Common elements include the reduction of parental or sibling attention when the child is at home, the removal of pleasures such as the use of television and computer during school time and during evenings and weekends.

Shaping refers to a procedure where the child's behaviour is gradually modified by means of contingent reinforcement, until a desired result is achieved. This may involve a number of steps: for example, rewards for undertaking homework at home, progressing to undertaking homework in a friend's house, undertaking homework in a classroom with a parent after school hours, attending school for one lesson each day, attending for half a day, and so on. At each step, the child's successful behaviour is reinforced by praise and attention and by those more tangible rewards that are deemed appropriate.

Modelling

This approach is based upon the premise that an individual may acquire behavioural dispositions as a result of the process of observing another individual. A popular approach for many child phobias, it involves the child observing a model (e.g. the therapist, peer or significant other) engaging in the behaviour that is feared. This may take place either by means of live modelling or through film and imagination. The child observes the model successfully handling the situation with no adverse consequences. Subsequently, the child is asked to imitate the performance of the model. As a result, the child's anxiety is reduced and appropriate skills acquired.

It is important to note, however, that many of the studies reported in the literature deal with less complex social situations than those relating to school attendance. Typically, these studies concern a fear of animals (often dogs) dental or medical procedures. Although modelling techniques have also proven valuable in work with children who lack social skills/confidence (King *et al.* 1995), many fearful situations (e.g. showering in public, going to the toilet, performing in PE) are not easily modelled. Furthermore, controlled studies of the effectiveness of this technique for cases of school refusal are very few (Kratochwill and Morris 1991).

Social skills training

Closely allied to modelling approaches, social skills training involves assisting the child to perceive and understand the behaviour of others and to respond in a more appropriate and skilled fashion. In relation to school refusal, such training is geared to help the child manage interpersonal situations more effectively, so reducing anxiety about evaluation by peers and/or teachers. Social skills training typically includes such skills as listening, non-verbal and verbal expression, recognising the position of others and self-assertion.

Cognitive behavioural therapy (CBT)

Underlying many cognitive therapy approaches is the assumption that patterns of thinking and self-statements about one's ability to cope with potentially challenging situations result in the maintenance of adverse emotions and unpleasant physical sensations and inappropriate, maladaptive patterns of behaviour. A range of approaches has been designed to tackle such faulty thinking, among the most popular being rational-emotive therapy (Ellis 1984), cognitive therapy (Beck 1976) and self-instruction training (Meichenbaum and Goodman 1971). Cognitive behaviour therapy (CBT) involves combining such approaches with behavioural techniques and a plan of action.

With regard to school refusal, such approaches operate on the basis that the child perceives an aspect of school attendance as dangerous (usually because it is considered that harm may result to the child at school or to the caregiver at home). The child does not consider himself or herself to be capable of managing the situation and as a result anxiety/fearfulness increases. By remaining at home, the problem is avoided, anxiety is reduced and school refusal is reinforced.

CBT approaches involve the clinician and child in an investigation of unhelpful, inappropriate and unrealistic beliefs that are subsequently challenged and, hopefully, replaced by new understandings. During this process the child is helped to identify and monitor self-statements that lead to anxiety or fearfulness. Maladaptive thoughts (e.g. 'My classmates will laugh at me if I answer a question incorrectly') are contrasted with competing, more positive conceptions (e.g. 'Everyone makes mistakes from time to time; other children are unlikely to take much notice of me') and the child is shown how these may alternatively result in anxiety production or reduction. Subsequently, a plan of action detailing steps to be taken in achieving a return to school is drawn up.

Although CBT has become increasingly popular with clinicians, research evaluations of its effectiveness with school refusers are few and it is unclear whether such approaches are more effective than other forms of intervention. While King et al. (1998) found gains for the approach, in comparison with a control group receiving no therapeutic input, Last et al. (1998) found an education support group to be equally as effective. A further study of children with social phobia, rather than a more specific fear of school, found that CBT, in conjunction with a social skills training programme, resulted in significant reduction of anxiety compared to those on a waiting list (Spence et al. 2000). In a detailed study of eight students, Kearney and Silverman (1999) found that the four who received behavioural interventions, closely linked to the particular functions served by their refusal, made considerably greater gains than those receiving relaxation therapy and cognitive therapy. When this latter group were subsequently provided with prescriptive behavioural interventions, gains became evident.

Family therapy

This technique is outlined in greater detail in Chapter 2 so will be only briefly discussed here. In the case of school refusal, the problem is often not seen as merely residing in the child, or even in the mother–child relationship, but rather as a product of faulty family functioning. Kearney and Silverman (1995) describe five differing types of family of school refusers: enmeshed and overdependent; coercive and marked by conflict; detached with little interaction among family members; isolated, with little interaction with people outside of the family; healthy families with a child with an individualised psychopathology. According to these writers, each of these types of family will require different forms of therapeutic intervention. Such interventions will also be heavily influenced by the theoretical form of family therapy to which the therapist subscribes.

It should be noted that while assessment of family functioning and some form of family work are universally advocated, it is rare that family therapy, in isolation, is seen as the preferred mode of treatment. In a recent survey of treatment approaches operated by a large sample of American psychologists, Kearney and Beasley (1994) found that work with families tended to focus upon parent training and contingency management (see Chapter 8); family therapy did not register as a specific treatment. It is possible, however, that a rather different picture would have emerged if psychiatrists and social workers, rather than psychologists, had been canvassed. To date, however, no large-scale studies of the efficacy of family therapy for school refusers have been published.

Medication

Drug treatment, usually in the form of antidepressants or tranquillisers, is frequently employed in the United States as one element of intervention programmes. Perhaps the most widely employed form of medication in the United States is imipramine hydrochloride, an antidepressant that can reduce panic attacks (Last and Francis 1988). Although these writers state that the advantages of using this drug as an adjunct to behaviour therapies are 'extraordinarily clear', a note of caution is introduced by King et al. (1995), who point to the existence of a number of side-effects including rare incidents of damage to the heart and more common symptoms of nausea, weight loss and allergic reactions (see also Waters 1990). Often medication is prescribed in addition to therapy. Bernstein et al. (2000), for example, found that imipramine, together with cognitive behavioural therapy was superior to a placebo for reducing depression and increasing school attendance. In Britain, the use of medication for school refusal is far more controversial. In a recent review Murphy and Wolkind (1996: 148) looked at the evidence for the use of antidepressants for school refusal and concluded that: 'given the availability of safer psychological therapies, antidepressant treatment is not generally recommended'.

Combining methods to create individual programmes

Kearney and Silverman (1999) argue that practitioners should assess the particular needs that are served by school refusal and suggest that these are usually typified by one of four categories (see Figure 3.1). Such an assessment can provide clear guidance as to appropriate intervention. Kearney *et al.*'s suggestions are outlined below.

Where school refusal is predominantly the result of a *strongly phobic reaction to being in school*, intervention would normally involve the gradual reduction of anxiety or fear by means of some form of desensitisation. In essence, the goal is to assist the child to be able to think of, and subsequently attend, school with progressive reduction in emotional reaction.

Where school refusal is primarily a *means of avoiding social and/or evaluative situations*, modelling, role play and social skills training techniques are widely advocated. In addition, counselling which aims to change the nature of the child's perceptions, thoughts and beliefs (cognitive therapy) is advocated.

Where the problem results primarily from a *desire to obtain caregiver attention*, parent training focusing upon the use of contingent use of attention and the use of reward systems is advocated (see Chapter 8 for further details).

Where school is refused because *home has more attractions* (for example, television, staying in bed, playing computer games), family therapy and the systematic use of rewards and sanctions (contingency contracting) are suggested. In such situations, there may often be conflict between family members on the appropriate way of dealing with the problem (typically, one family member advocating a 'get tough' line, another arguing for a need to be sympathetic and indulgent). Such conflict often provides the child with attention and an inconsistent parenting regime. The systematic and contingent use of rewards may include the use of computer/TV, pocket money, outings, toys. Sanctions for non-attendance may involve the removal of such incentives and limitations placed upon evening and weekend activities. There is some evidence to suggest that this particular function for school refusal is less susceptible to intervention, perhaps because it often involves several overlapping difficulties (Evans 2000).

It is important to recognise, however, that the above approaches should not be limited to particular categories and that in many cases school refusal may result from a combination of factors. As with all problems, interventions should be closely tailored to the needs and dispositions of the individual child in a flexible and sensitive fashion.

The role of the school in intervention

The majority of published studies and reviews have been produced by American researchers (often with a medical background) who have little expertise or professional involvement in educational matters. The focus for these writers is usually the child and family system and school is often taken as a given to which the child should accommodate. It is perhaps for this reason that the literature makes little reference to examining the ways by which the school can help a child to overcome a reluctance to attend. It is clear, however, that school settings where bullying, truancy or disruption proliferate, where there is rigid streaming that can result in the child being placed in a class containing a significant proportion of disaffected, alienated peers, where teacher–pupil relationships are impersonal or generally hostile, where toilets and other public areas are not closely monitored by staff, are all likely to be important factors in contributing to school refusal. In such cases operating at the level of the child and the immediate family may prove insufficient for resolving non-attendance.

The role of teachers is crucial both in identifying difficulties at an early stage and in providing as supportive and as facilitative a school environment as possible. Early signs of persistent school refusal may include occasional absences, excessive anxiety and frequent complaints about feeling unwell. Some children may seem preoccupied with concerns about home and the well-being of family members, others may seem hypersensitive to seemingly trivial incidents in school. Given widespread agreement that a swift return to school increases the likelihood of successful reintegration, it is essential that teachers are alert to possible present or future cases of school refusal and, where the child's needs cannot be catered for by school-based personnel, readily seek the assistance of support agencies at an early stage. Where teachers, particularly those in senior management, and education social workers have a sound understanding of school refusal and appropriate intervention techniques, however, much of the early diagnostic and treatment work can be undertaken before other services become involved. Thus, training teachers in skilled and effective management of school refusal can lead to a reduction in the referral rate of school refusers to psychologists and psychiatrists (Blagg and Yule 1984).

Unlike truancy, the child's absence may be explained by parents on the grounds of minor medical ailments such as head or stomach aches. In such cases school registers will indicate absence on medical grounds and scrutiny of attendance patterns by education welfare services may not identify the existence of a problem until a later, and potentially more intransigent, stage. Here, the vigilance of the school nurse may also prove particularly valuable.

In cases of school refusal, teachers also have an important role to play in managing the school environment. This may involve making short-term modifications to the child's timetable, ensuring that opportunities for the child to be unsupported in threatening situations (e.g. break- and lunchtimes) are reduced, that inquisition of the child about recent absences is minimised and that the child has ready access to teachers should additional guidance, support or counselling be required.

Blagg (1987) outlines a number of school-based considerations that are important for an effective return to school:

1   *Academic-related concerns.* Does the child need help to catch up with work that has been missed? Will individual tutorials by specialist teachers be necessary? Does the child have learning difficulties that will need to be

addressed? Will it be possible to set up a graduated reintegration package where, initially, only some lessons will be attended? Will the child remain in school at other times?

2   *Peer-related concerns.* Are measures necessary to ensure that victimisation, in the form of bullying or taunting, does not take place? Does the child require a means of avoiding potentially threatening break- and lunch-time settings? Are teachers aware that the child may need to have a low profile in the classroom (e.g. by avoiding situations where they are required to read aloud or answer questions in front of their classmates)?

3   *Teacher-related concerns.* Does the child have a particular anxiety about one or more teachers? Is it appropriate to change the child's class in order to accommodate specific teacher- (or peer-)related anxieties or can the problem be resolved through other means?

It is essential that the school can provide a suitably quiet area where the child can begin the school day and be based when not in class. At the early stages of reintegration it is possible that the child may show signs of panic or anger and it is advisable that an area free from onlookers is reserved for dealing with such difficulties. A trusted teacher who greets the child at the beginning of the school day and prepares him or her for entry to the classroom can help to minimise potential difficulties, as can the involvement of close friends who are sympathetic to their classmate's difficulty. At an early stage, plans should be drawn up to prevent any slips or relapses once the child begins to attend regularly again (Kearney 2001).

It is important that teachers recognise that children's seemingly irrational fears are meaningful rather than dismissing them as attention-seeking or fanciful. It should be recognised that even where a child's physical discomfort does result from psychological rather than organic causes, the adversity of the experience is no less real or unpleasant. Nevertheless, while demonstrating a sensitivity to the child's feelings, it is unwise to engage in lengthy and repeated discussion with the child about these symptoms as this may have a reinforcing effect.

Where school refusal is seen as genuine by teachers, school-based factors that contribute to the problem are often de-emphasised in favour of a focus upon the excessive child–parent dependency of separation anxiety theories (King *et al.* 1995). Some teachers may fail to recognise the effect their interpersonal style has upon the highly sensitive child and find references to this, however sensitively handled, by senior colleagues or support professionals to be demeaning or inaccurate.

It is also important to be sensitive to wider, whole-school influences. A number of practitioners (Hersov 1985; Blagg 1987; King *et al.* 1995) have noted that school refusal is associated with high staff and student absenteeism rates, low levels of achievement, large class sizes, high levels of indiscipline, low staff morale, a management style characterised by authoritarianism and rigidity, and teachers who are themselves authoritarian, anxious or eager to obtain student approval. Despite such considerations, it is rare that a change of school is recommended in the literature. In cases where children do change school difficulties often recur but are now compounded by the child's unfamiliarity with teachers and peers. A change of school is usually only advisable where the child's school refusal is wholly related to a specific educational context that is unlikely to be successfully modified. Even then, anxiety may be displaced to the new setting (see case study, Stacey, below).

Stacey, a thirteen-year-old girl, had displayed anxiety about attending her local secondary school after a child in another class had been murdered in front of her schoolmates by an intruder. Concurrently, she had also been subject to bullying by other girls who had teased and tormented her. After periods of sporadic attendance, marked by frequent arguments, crying fits and somatic complaints, absence became almost total. Stacey's mother (a single parent with no other children), believing that school was not recognising the nature of her daughter's difficulties, arranged for her daughter to transfer to another secondary school several miles away. As there had been no difficulties in primary school, it was anticipated that Stacey's problems would be left behind her.

At first, Stacey settled happily into her new school and enjoyed good relations with her new schoolmates. There was no recurrence of the bullying and she liked her new teachers. After four months, however, she began to become increasingly anxious before school each morning and her sleep pattern became disturbed. After six months she stopped attending school totally. Investigation by the school's educational psychologist suggested that Stacey's difficulties did not relate to a specific feature of her new school; rather, the earlier trauma had continued to haunt her. A graduated return programme, involving attendance at some lessons and, at other times, the provision of work in a quiet room, was established and appeared initially to be succeeding. After a few weeks, however, this programme failed as Stacey's mother unexpectedly withdrew her daughter from school with the stated intention of educating her daughter at home. Mother stated that she did not have the emotional strength to continue to insist that Stacey attend school each day and could no longer cope with the stress that was being experienced at home. She then declined to have any further involvement with clinical support services.

In the light of the discussion above, this case study illustrates two important points:

1   The unwillingness of the staff at the first secondary school to demon-
    strate a recognition of, and sympathy towards, Stacey's difficulties alienated
    the family, reduced the mother's commitment to seeking a school-based
    solution and delayed the involvement of appropriate support agencies.
2   A change of school may not resolve a problem even if its origins are
    clearly located in the original setting.

Immediate or gradual return to school?

A major issue in school refusal is whether the child should be forced to
return immediately or through a more graduated procedure, perhaps after a
period at a specialised off-site education unit. Clearly, prolonged absence
from school increases the difficulty of reintegration:

> With each day out of school more lessons are missed, difficulties in
> keeping up with other children mount, work accumulates, the embar-
> rassment in finding suitable excuses for teacher and children increases,
> and the advantages of 'staying away from it all' become greater every
> day. Return to school becomes progressively more difficult. These sec-
> ondary factors . . . very often overshadow the (original) cause and make
> it difficult to isolate the precipitating events. They may form a barrier
> to effective treatment.
>
> (Glaser 1959: 219)

Kennedy (1965) argues that forced procedures (technically known as *in vivo*
flooding) are appropriate for school refusal, particularly for acute cases where
onset is rapid and there has been no prior history of similar problems. The
advantage of such an approach is that return to school can be immediately
reinforced, opportunities for the child's non-attendance to be reinforced by
being at home are minimised, and the problem is not compounded by the
factors noted by Glaser above. Such an approach, however, can prove highly
stressful for both child and parents and may be perceived as unethical
by some parties. In addition, the programme may require a high level of
ongoing supervision from support agencies that proves to be unavailable.

One of the strongest advocates of forced-return approaches is Blagg
(1987) who outlines a detailed programme focusing upon each of the steps
necessary for establishing a return to school. This outline provides helpful
and practical guidance, particularly for those practitioners with limited
experience of school refusal. Topics covered include: preparing the child,
parents and teachers for return; establishing what changes are necessary
at school and at home; establishing an effective system for ensuring the child
arrives at school each day (initially, with one or more escorts); and establishing monitoring and follow-up procedures. Although forced-return approaches

require that the child remain in school all day, it is accepted that the child's placement on the normal school timetable may be introduced in a step-by-step fashion.

In contrast, gradual-exposure approaches involve returning the child to school initially for those situations that cause minimal anxiety. Gradually the period in school is increased until full attendance is achieved. Often an emphasis is put upon attending for the last part of the day in order that the natural reinforcer of going home at the end of the school day is operative. This approach is generally less stressful than full forced return for the child and family, although the risks of the child's non-attendance being reinforced by spending more time at home are greater.

Blagg and Yule (1984) compared the relative efficacy of differing intervention techniques for a sample of sixty-six children who were refusing school. Thirty children received behaviour therapy consisting of contingency contracting and enforced return to school (*in vivo* flooding), twenty received home tuition for two hours a day and psychotherapy on a fortnightly basis at a child guidance clinic. The remaining sixteen were hospitalised, received regular therapy inputs and tranquillisers as appropriate. At a one-year follow-up, the return to school group demonstrated significantly improved attendance with 93.3 per cent of the sample having been judged as successfully returning to school, while the hospitalised and home tuition groups had made very little progress (37.5 per cent and 10 per cent success rates respectively). In examining attendance rates at follow-up, it was discovered that 83 per cent of the forced-return group were attending school more than 80 per cent of the time, while only 31 per cent of the hospitalised group and none of the home-tuition group reached this level.

What form of intervention is the most effective?

Despite the relatively detailed literature on intervention with school refusers, it is widely noted that the vast majority of publications refer to individual or multiple case studies that, while potentially informative to clinicians (see, for example, Kearney, 2002b), have not been subject to experimental control. Often, the nature of the children's difficulties is inadequately discussed so that it is unclear to what extent problems are related to separation anxiety rather than to school-based factors. There is also no indication of the extent to which there is evidence of severe emotional difficulties, such as clinical depression. Where the outcomes of interventions have been examined (e.g. Blagg and Yule 1984), it has been assumed that school refusers are essentially alike, a proposition that does not appear to be justifiable. A further difficulty in judging the efficacy of treatment results from the use of a number of techniques in combination (e.g. systematic desensitisation, contingency management and drug therapy). As a result, it is difficult to ascertain the unique contribution of each.

Provision for school refusers

Legal considerations

Under the 1969 Children and Young Persons Act those of statutory school age who failed to receive an appropriate education could be placed in the care of the local authority. This resulted in many chronic non-attenders (both truants and school refusers) being placed in foster or children's homes. Many children's homes provided education on the premises and, thus, the legal requirement that the child received education was met. Such establishments often catered for delinquent, conduct-disordered children and in the minds of many professionals these homes were often more appropriate for truants than school refusers. It is perhaps for this reason that legal proceedings were more likely to be pursued where the child was perceived as an unwilling truant rather than as psychologically unable to attend school.

The introduction of the Children Act in 1989 removed the use of care orders solely on the grounds of non-school attendance. In their place Section 36 created a new education supervision order that provides a framework for education welfare services to work with the child and the family. Where the child's parents can demonstrate that they are doing everything they can to encourage the child to return to school, the supervision order does little more than ensure a continued forum for the continuance of professional support (see Robertson, (1996), for further details).

It is possible for parents to provide education in the home setting, either by the employment of a home tutor or by educating their child themselves. The relevant local education authority must be satisfied as to the suitability of the education and will inspect the nature of the arrangements. Although this may be a highly attractive proposition to parents struggling with a highly anxious child (see case study, Stacey, above), and the quality of the child's learning could be high given the availability of appropriate tutors, it is questionable whether such an option would maximise such a child's future adult functioning.

The role of support services

In most cases of prolonged absence from local authority schools, the first point of contact for school staff will be the education welfare officer (EWO), sometimes known as an education social worker (ESW), who is often attached to a patch of schools in a defined geographical area. The EWO has particular responsibility for screening school registers and intervening in cases of poor school attendance at an early stage. Depending upon local circumstances, those whose absence appears to stem from fearfulness, anxiety or depression may be considered to require more specialised help and would then be likely to be referred to one or more support agencies, usually the

LEA educational psychology service, the district health child and family psychiatry or child guidance services or the local authority social services department. In some cases, parents will seek specialist referral to these services themselves, usually via the school or the family doctor.

Many of these services incorporate a variety of professionals, psychologists, psychiatrists, social workers, occupational therapists, nurses and child therapists. Most of the techniques outlined in this chapter may be undertaken by any of these professionals, although emphases will differ. It is likely, for example, that the educational psychologist would have a greater role in addressing important school-based factors (e.g. exploring how the child may be assisted with academic difficulties) whereas the child psychiatrist would be more likely to be closely involved in working with medical colleagues and in prescribing medication. Given the differing perspectives that can be held by professionals involved in tackling school refusal, it is essential that close liaison exists and opportunities for the provision of conflicting advice are minimised. As Blagg (1987) notes, a failure to achieve such liaison can result in the anxious parent becoming even more confused and unsure how to proceed. Furthermore, it may help the resistant parent to ignore any recommendations for action. Blagg recommends that educational psychologists, by virtue of their educational and clinical expertise, are best placed to coordinate multi-professional involvement, although recent changes in psychologists' work patterns have made this more problematic. Particular stresses result from the pressure upon educational psychology services to undertake increasing numbers of statutory assessments of children with special educational needs and the widespread use of time-contracting, by which educational psychologist time is allocated to each school on a pro rata basis. These factors often reduce the educational psychologist's availability and flexibility in responding to individual cases. There may be little time for intensive, ongoing casework and this may preclude the psychologist from monitoring the child's progress and intervening where necessary on a sufficiently intensive basis.

Provision alternative to school

Home tuition

In the United Kingdom many local education authorities provide home tuition for school refusers. This may involve a visit to the home by a peripatetic support teacher for one or two sessions per week with periodic review by an education social worker or educational psychologist. Given that Blagg and Yule's (1984) study found home tuition with psychotherapy to be a highly unsuccessful technique (to such an extent that the authors queried whether this might have even inhibited spontaneous remission), there must be serious doubts as to the efficacy of such an approach. Where such provision is complemented by local authority support services working actively to ensure a return to school, the prognosis may be more favourable (see, for example, Tansey 1995).

Pupil referral units

A number of local education authorities have established off-site provision, pupil referral units, which cater for children with various difficulties that preclude them from attending mainstream school on a temporary or permanent basis. Although the majority of units cater primarily for children whose disruptive behaviour has resulted in exclusion from school, they may include children with other needs: for example, school refusers or pregnant schoolgirls. Usually, these units each address specific difficulties as it would generally be inappropriate to group together highly aggressive, disruptive children with those whose difficulties are very different (Department for Education 1994). There has been little systematic research to examine the effectiveness of such units with school refusers.

Hospitalisation

Inpatient treatment for school refusal is rare in the United Kingdom although part-time placement in child psychiatry department day units is more widely employed. Usually, inpatient treatment is associated with more severe symptoms, particularly depression, and greater incidence of family disruption and dysfunction (Borchardt et al. 1994).

Berg (1991) states that while it may be difficult to get the child to accept admission to hospital, once achieved, emotional upset usually improves and a graduated return to school can be planned. The relatively generous availability of psychiatric staff permits support in escorting the child to school and in the provision of a range of appropriate therapies. Murphy and Wolkind (1996) support the use of hospitalisation where other approaches have failed, the child is becoming increasingly anxious or depressed and/or parents have effectively lost control of their child. They add, however, that potential dangers of this procedure are that hospitalisation can increase the likelihood that the child becomes scapegoated for all the family's problems and is emotionally or physically excluded. In return, the hospitalised child may feel rejected by the family and hostile to its members.

Outcomes

As noted above, the likelihood of a positive outcome appears to be related to the severity of the disorder, the age of onset, and the immediacy of treatment intervention. In addition, susceptibility to treatment is greatly reduced where the refusal has persisted for two or more years (Kearney and

Tillotson 1998). Studies of adults suffering from neurotic disorders (particularly agoraphobia) indicate that a significant number were school refusers as adolescents (e.g. Berg *et al.* 1974). A number of studies have followed up school refusers in adulthood (e.g. Berg and Jackson 1985; Flakierska *et al.* 1988, 1997). In general, these suggest that approximately one-third of cases continues to experience severe emotional disorders and/or problematic social relationships into adulthood, although it should be noted that samples often contain children who were hospitalised – usually the most severe cases.

References

Atkinson, L., Quarrington, B. and Cyr, J.J. (1985). School refusal: the heterogeneity of a concept. *American Journal of Orthopsychiatry* 55, 83–101.

Beck, A.T. (1976). *Cognitive Therapy and the Emotional Disorders.* New York: International Universities Press.

Berg, I. (1970). A follow-up study of school phobic adolescents admitted to an inpatient unit. *Journal of Child Psychology and Psychiatry* 11, 37–47.

Berg, I. (1991). School avoidance, school phobia and truancy. In M. Lewis (ed.) *Child and Adolescent Psychiatry: A Comprehensive Textbook.* London: Willliams and Wilkins.

Berg, I. and Jackson, A. (1985). Teenage school refusers grow up: a follow-up study of 168 subjects, ten years on average after inpatient treatment. *British Journal of Psychiatry* 119, 167–8.

Berg, I., Nichols, K. and Pritchard, C. (1969). School phobia – its classification and relationship to dependency. *Journal of Child Psychology and Psychiatry* 10, 123–41.

Berg, I., Marks, I., McGuire, R. and Lipsedge, M. (1974). School phobia and agoraphobia. *Psychological Medicine* 4, 428–34.

Bernstein, G.A., Borchardt, C.M., Perwein, A.R., Crosby, R.D., Kushner, M.G., Thuras, P.D. and Last, C.G. (2000). Imipramine plus cognitive-behavioral therapy in the treatment of school refusal. *Journal of the American Academy of Child and Adolescent Psychiatry* 29, 24–30.

Blagg, N. (1987). *School Phobia and its Treatment.* London: Croom Helm.

Blagg, N. and Yule, W. (1984). The behavioural treatment of school refusal – a comparative study. *Behaviour Research and Therapy* 22, 119–27.

Bools, C., Foster, J., Brown, I. and Berg, I. (1990). The identification of psychiatric disorders in children who fail to attend school: a cluster analysis of a non-clinical population. *Psychological Medicine* 20, 171–81.

Borchardt, C.M., Giesler, J., Bernstein, G.A. and Crosby, R.D. (1994). A comparison of inpatient and outpatient school refusers. *Child Psychiatry and Human Development* 24(4), 255–64.

Broadwin, I.T. (1932). A contribution to the study of truancy. *American Journal of Orthopsychiatry* 2, 253–9.

Department for Education (1994). *Circular 11/94: The Education by LEAs of Children Otherwise than at School.* London: DFE Publications.

Elliott, J.G. (1999). Practitioner Review: School refusal: issues of conceptualisation, assessment and treatment. *Journal of Child Psychology and Psychiatry* 40, 1001–12.

Ellis, A. (1984). *Rational-emotive Therapy and Cognitive Behaviour Therapy.* New York: Springer.

Evans, L.D. (2000). Functional school refusal subtypes: anxiety, avoidance and malingering. *Psychology in the Schools* 37, 183–191.

Flakierska, N., Linstrom, M. and Gillberg, C. (1988). School refusal: a 15–20-year follow-up study of 35 Swedish urban children. *British Journal of Psychiatry* 152, 834–7.

Flakierska, N., Linstrom, M. and Gillberg, C. (1997). School phobia with separation anxiety disorder: a comparative 20–29 year follow-up study of 35 school refusers. *Comprehensive Psychiatry* 38, 17–22.

Galloway, D. (1983). Truants and other absentees. *Journal of Child Psychology and Psychiatry* 24(4), 607–11.

Glaser, K. (1959). Problems in school attendance: school phobia and related conditions. *Pediatrics* 23, 371–83.

Hersov, L. (1977). School refusal. In M. Rutter and L. Hersov (eds) *Child Psychiatry. Modern Approaches*. Oxford: Blackwell.

Hersov, L. (1985). School refusal. In M. Rutter and L. Hersov (eds) *Child and Adolescent Psychiatry. Modern Approaches*. 2nd edn. Oxford: Blackwell.

Johnson, A.M. (1957). School phobia. *American Journal of Orthopsychiatry* 27, 307–9.

Johnson, A.M., Falstein, E.I., Szurek, S.A. and Svendsen, M. (1941). School phobia. *American Journal of Orthopsychiatry* 11, 702–11.

Kearney, C.A. (1995). School refusal behaviour. In A.R. Eisen, C.A. Kearney and C.E. Schaefer (eds) *Clinical Handbook of Anxiety Disorders in Children and Adolescents*. Northvale, NJ: Aronson.

Kearney, C.A. (2001). *School Refusal Behavior in Youth: A Functional Approach to Treatment and Assessment*. Washington, DC: American Psychological Association.

Kearney, C.A. (2002a). Identifying the function of school refusal behavior: a revision of the School Refusal Assessment Scale. *Journal of Psychopathology and Behavioral Assessment* 24, 235–45.

Kearney, C.A. (2002b). Case study of the assessment and treatment of a youth with multifunction school refusal behavior. *Clinical Case Studies* 1, 67–80.

Kearney, C.A. and Beasley, J.F. (1994). The clinical treatment of school refusal behavior: a survey of referral and practice characteristics. *Psychology in the Schools* 31, 128–32.

Kearney, C.A. and Silverman, W.K. (1990). A preliminary analysis of a functional model of assessment and treatment of school refusal behavior. *Behavior Modification* 14, 340–66.

Kearney, C.A. and Silverman, W.K. (1993). Measuring the function of school refusal behaviour: the School Refusal Assessment Scale. *Journal of Clinical Child Psychology* 22, 85–96.

Kearney, C.A. and Silverman, W.K. (1995). Family environment of youngsters with school refusal behavior. *American Journal of Family Therapy* 23(1), 59–72.

Kearney, C.A. and Silverman, W.K. (1999). Functionally based prescriptive and nonprescriptive treatment for children and adolescents with school refusal behavior. *Behaviour Therapy* 30, 673–93.

Kearney, C.A. and Tillotson, C.A. (1998). School attendance. In D. Watson and M. Gresham (eds) *Handbook of Child Behavior Therapy* (pp. 143–61). New York: Plenum Press.

Kennedy, W.A. (1965). School phobia: rapid treatment of fifty cases. *Journal of Abnormal Psychology* 70, 285–9.

King, N., Ollendick, T.H. and Tonge, B.J. (1995). *School Refusal: Assessment and Treatment*. Massachusetts: Allyn and Bacon.

King, N., Ollendick, T.H., Murphy, G.C. and Molloy, G.N. (1998). Relaxation training with children. *British Journal of Educational Psychology* 68, 53–66.

Kovacs, M. and Beck, A.T. (1977). An empirical-clinical approach toward a definition of childhood depression. In J.G. Schulterbrandt and A. Raskin (eds) *Depression in Childhood: Diagnosis, Treatment, and Conceptual Models*. New York: Raven Press.

Kratochwill, T.R. and Morris, R.J. (eds) (1991). *The Practice of Child Therapy*. New York: Pergamon Press.

La Greca, A.M. and Stone, W.L. (1993). Social Anxiety Scale for Children Revised: factor structure and concurrent validity. *Journal of Clinical Child Psychology* 22, 17–27.

Last, C.G. and Francis, G. (1988). School phobia. In B.B. Lahey and A.E. Kazdin (eds) *Advances in Clinical Child Psychology*, vol. II. New York: Plenum.

Last, C.G., Hansen, M.S. and Franco, N. (1998). Cognitive-behavioral treatment of school phobia. *Journal of the American Academy of Child and Adolescent Psychiatry* 37, 404–11.

Last, C.G., Francis, G., Hersen, M., Kazdin, A.E. and Strauss, C. (1987). Separation anxiety and school phobia: a comparison using DSM-III criteria. *American Journal of Psychiatry* 144, 653–7.

Lazarus, A.A. and Abramovitz, A. (1962). The use of 'emotive imagery' in the treatment of children's phobias. *Journal of Mental Science* 108, 191–5.

Meichenbaum, D.H. and Goodman, J. (1971). Training impulsive children to talk to themselves: a means of developing self-control. *Journal of Abnormal Psychology* 77, 115–26.

Murphy, M. and Wolkind, S. (1996). The role of the child and adolescent psychiatrist. In I. Berg and J. Nursten (eds) *Unwillingly to School*. 4th edn. London: Gaskell.

Ollendick, T.H. (1983). Reliability and validity of the Revised Fear Survey Schedule for Children (FSSC-R). *Behaviour Research and Therapy* 21, 685–92.

Ollendick, T.H. and Mayer, J.A. (1984). School phobia. In S.M. Turner (ed.) *Behavioral Theories and Treatment of Anxiety*. New York: Plenum.

Pilkington, C. and Piersel, W.C. (1991). School phobia: a critical analysis of the separation anxiety theory and an alternative conceptualization. *Psychology in the Schools* 28, 290–303.

Reynolds, C.R. and Paget, K.D. (1983). National normative and reliability data for the Revised Children's Manifest Anxiety Scale. *School Psychology Review* 12, 324–36.

Robertson, I. (1996). Legal aspects. In I. Berg and J. Nursten (eds) *Unwillingly to School*. 4th edn. London: Gaskell.

Smith, S.L. (1970). School refusal with anxiety: a review of sixty-three cases. *Canadian Psychiatry Association Journal* 15, 257–64.

Spence, S.H., Donovan, C. and Brechman-Toussaint, M. (2000). The treatment of childhood social phobia: the effectiveness of a social skills training-based, cognitive-behavioural intervention, with and without parental involvement. *Journal of Child Psychology and Psychiatry* 41, 713–26.

Tansey, K. (1995). This can't be my responsibility: it must be yours! An analysis of a reintegration programme for a school refuser. *British Journal of Special Education* 22(1), 12–15.

Trueman, D. (1984). What are the characteristics of school phobic children? *Psychological Reports* 54, 191–202.

Waters, B. (1990). Pharmacological and other treatments. In B.J. Tonge, G.D. Burrows and J.S. Werry (eds) *Handbook of Studies on Child Psychiatry*. Amsterdam: Elsevier.

Chapter 4

Attention deficit disorder and hyperactivity and similar difficulties

Children who present with difficult and disruptive behaviour are a major concern both to parents and schools. Children with these difficulties who are also restless find it difficult to settle to tasks, have poor impulse control and have for some years been distinguished as perhaps presenting a different problem from that of merely poor behaviour.

Over the years labelling of this group of children has undergone many changes with terms such as hyperactivity, hyperkinesis and attention deficit becoming almost interchangeable as different views and emphases have held sway. Unfortunately, the usefulness of such concepts has become devalued, not only because of this confusion of labelling, but because the terms have come into common parlance where they have been applied to any child whose behaviour is difficult, and who in certain settings demonstrates a resistance to comply with tasks.

Terms in use

Over the years, various features and difficulties have been associated with this condition but there are three elements of key importance.

- Attention deficit is a pattern of behaviour in which the child shows only a brief concentration to tasks imposed by adults, and over any period of play the young person will often change activities quite rapidly. This is increasingly seen as the core feature of this problem.
- Overactivity (often called hyperactivity, and sometimes called hyper-kinesis) is an increased tempo of physical activity. The commonest element is fidgeting, but it may take the form of not being able to sit still for more than a few moments, or of restlessly pacing up and down the room. It is important to realise that this is a true increase of physical activity, as has been demonstrated when the physical movements of these young people are compared to resting levels (Porrino et al. 1983).
- Impulsiveness is where a child will act upon a wish or desire without thought to its consequence. In some situations this can take the form of

quite dangerous behaviour (such as running into roads), but most often it is a pattern of breaking rules without thought as to what might happen as a result.

Diagnostic considerations

The confusion over labelling has recently become clearer. The Government guidance on the appropriateness of the diagnosis of attention deficit hyperactivity disorder (ADHD) (National Institute for Clinical Excellence 2000), and the wealth of research looking at the origins of such symptoms, has allowed the diagnosis of ADHD to become established, and the details of the diagnostic criteria for this condition are set out in Figure 4.1.

The proposal that problems with maintaining attention are at the heart of the difficulties is an attractive one, and much research effort has been concentrated on trying to delineate the mechanism. The attraction comes in the way that the observed symptoms would be logically explained by a difficulty in regulating the wealth of sights, sounds and information which press in upon all of us. If our filtering mechanisms should falter it must have a profound effect upon our functioning.

However, it has been pointed out (Taylor 1995) that attention problems could take several forms – problems with controlling attention, selecting what to attend to, sustaining attention, or not attending intently enough. Determining the exact nature of the deficit is clearly important, and there is increasing evidence that these children have a difficulty in processing information (Leung and Connolly 1994), and so a key mechanism may be the child's difficulty in inhibiting responses to the inappropriate elements of this information deluge (Schachar and Logan 1990). Whatever the processing difficulty, it is now clear that the core problem is a fault with one of the main chemical transmitters within the brain, specifically dopamine (Swanson et al. 1998). It is also becoming clear that the core syndrome is probably hereditary in nature (Faraone et al. 1992), and that ADHD tends to run in families (Faraone et al. 1996).

When diagnosing ADHD, a careful clinical assessment needs to determine if the symptoms and impairments observed might not be better explained by a different diagnosis. At present the Continuous Performance Test is the most accurate method of distinguishing ADHD, but its greatest accuracy is in excluding the diagnosis rather than confirming it (Riccio et al. 2001).

Alternative causes of concentration problems

Probably the commonest reason for children to present with restless, inattentive behaviour is weakness in the parenting regime. Such difficulties usually arise when the child shows a great deal of willfulness, and the parental response has been inconsistent, or simply been one of 'giving in

A *EITHER* Six (or more) of the following symptoms of *inattention* have persisted for at least six months to a degree that is maladaptive and inconsistent with developmental level:

- often fails to give close attention to details or makes careless mistakes in schoolwork, work or other activities
- often has difficulty sustaining attention in tasks or play activities
- often does not seem to listen when spoken to directly
- often does not follow through on instructions and fails to finish schoolwork, or chores (not due to oppositional behaviour or failure to understand instructions)
- often has difficulty organising tasks and activities
- often avoids, dislikes or is reluctant to engage in tasks that require sustained mental effort (such as schoolwork or homework)
- often loses things necessary for tasks or activities (e.g. toys, schoolwork, pencils, books)
- is often easily distracted by extraneous stimuli
- is often forgetful in daily activities

OR Six (or more) of the following symptoms of *hyperactivity/impulsivity* have persisted for at least six months to a degree that is maladaptive and inconsistent with developmental level:

- often fidgets with hands or feet or squirms in seat
- often leaves seat in classroom or in other situations in which remaining seated is expected
- often runs about or climbs excessively in situations in which it is inappropriate (in adolescents this may be subjective feelings of restlessness)
- often has difficulty playing or engaging in leisure activities quietly
- is often 'on the go' or often acts as if 'driven by a motor'
- often talks excessively
- often blurts out answers before questions have been completed
- often has difficulty waiting turn
- often interrupts or intrudes on others (e.g. butts into conversations or games)

B Some hyperactive-impulsive or inattentive symptoms that caused impairment were present before seven years of age.

C Some impairment from the symptoms is present in two or more settings.

D There must be clear evidence of clinically significant impairment in social or academic functioning.

E The symptoms do not occur exclusively during the course of another condition.

Figure 4.1 Attention deficit disorder (DSM-IV)

for a quiet life'. Management of these types of problems are discussed in Chapter 8.

Reactive attachment disorder

As the knowledge of developmental issues has increased there is a growing awareness that the impact of early bonds with parents is more far reaching than perhaps has been realised in the past (See Chapter 1). If the early bonds are damaged then the child finds it hard to form meaningful attachments, and in severe cases this is known as reactive attachment disorder (RAD). A description of the pattern of behaviour shown by these children usually includes:

- being demanding, difficult and resistant;
- ambivalent about, and prone to produce conflict, in close relationships;
- being not very good at giving and receiving comfort and affection;
- having poor peer relationship skills, with no close or sustained peer friendships;
- at various times feeling unloved, unwanted, rejected;
- having low self-confidence and self-esteem;
- having a tendency to blame others when things go wrong;
- being not very good at coping with change;
- being impatient and easily frustrated – leading to anger, rage, temper;
- having poor impulse control, no sense of danger, little concentration;
- underachieving academically and being disruptive in the classroom;
- behaving badly without apparent remorse.

And there are usually elements of

- physical aggression towards their parents;
- jealous, possessive, spiteful behaviour;
- feeling despair or being depressed;
- lying excessively;
- stealing from their family, or outside the home;
- having issues about food;
- abusing alcohol and/or drugs;
- self-harm.

It can be seen from this description that reactive attachment disorder gives a pattern which can be mistaken for ADHD if the underlying cause is not recognised. Medications used to treat ADHD can reduce the symptoms of restlessness and to some degree impulsivity, but the degree of improvement is often quite muted unless the core problems are addressed. The treatment of RAD is complex and often involves many agencies, with work being required for many years before appreciable improvement is noted.

Pervasive developmental disorder

Another set of conditions that can show features which mimic ADHD are the pervasive developmental disorders (PDD). This refers to the group of conditions which includes both autism and autistic-like disorders, such as

Asperger's syndrome. In some circles the term 'autism spectrum disorder' (ASD) is preferred. Whatever the term, the nature of these disorders is defined by three areas of deficit:

- difficulties in reciprocal social interaction;
- impaired communication;
- restricted, repetitive behaviour and interest.

No child will show all of these characteristics, and some show only one or two symptoms in each key area. The diagnostic criteria are reasonably precise for autism and asperger's syndrome and, where features exist but are insufficient for these diagnoses, the youngster is said to have PDD. In addition to elements of the three central themes these youngsters can show difficulty in attachments and show unusual responses to loud sounds or textures in foods. They also often are very restless and find it difficult to focus, with a distractibility that can be indistinguishable from a child with ADHD. Indeed it is sometimes only when the restless behaviour has been reduced that the symptoms suggestive of a PDD emerge and become evident.

Treatment of the pervasive development disorders is beyond the scope of this text, but the inattentive and physical restless components of the disorder do respond reasonably well to medication, and can have a place in the overall programme of intervention for a youngster. Their desire for predictability and routine means these children do best in an organised environment where rules and expectations are clear and consistent. The use of positive behavioural support strategies for these children is often effective, but it is important to remember that programmes should be designed on an individual basis, because children vary greatly in their abilities. In particular these children do not tend to respond to programmes which have escalation of sanction. So for example a boy with PDD who is late for class will not be more prompt if one detention for lateness is made two detentions on the next occasion. Similarly, such young people have great difficulty generalising from one situation to another. The skills they have learned in school tend not to be transferred to the home or other settings, or even from one class to the next. Thus a careful analysis and personalised programme for such young people is essential if they are to fully benefit from environments such as school.

Organic causes

Often children with concentration problems have in their history elements suggesting developmental delay or birth difficulties, and as well as the disorders described above, it should also be borne in mind that physical problems, such as epilepsy can prompt children to present as being restless and having poor concentration. If any such elements are suspected, then a medical opinion should be sought through the family's or the school's

FORM: Short-acting tablets of 5mg, 10mg or 20mg.

DOSAGE: Very individual but average is 5–20mg morning and lunchtime.

DURATION OF ACTION: Rapid acting, the effects become apparent in 15–20 minutes. Its effects last for about 4 hours.

EFFECTS: It specifically improves concentration and memory. If these are major sources of difficulty then there may also be improvement in the control of frustration and anger.

POSSIBLE SIDE-EFFECTS:

- Nervousness and insomnia.
- Reduced appetite and associated weight loss, and if this becomes a problem the drug must at least be stopped on weekends, and if possible stopped completely.
- A few children initially have abdominal pain, nausea and vomiting but these generally fade over time.
- Occasionally headaches, drowsiness, dizziness.
- If the young person has tics, these can get worse.
- A few children become irritable or tearful.
- On very rare occasions a young person can develop anaemia.

PRECAUTIONS: As with any powerful drug it should only be used if the benefits are marked. It is usually helpful if at least once a year there is a period without the medication.

Figure 4.2 Medication for attention deficit disorder – methylphenidate (Ritalin/Equasym)

doctor. The assessment will involve various neurological tests, and probably an electroencephalogram (EEG), which records the electrical activity of the brain. If anything is found, then it may be necessary to offer medication or other treatments which are specific for the problem detected.

Shane was a six-year-old boy who had a three-year history of being unable to settle to any game or task. He frequently destroyed his toys, and would lash out at other children if they thwarted him in any way, and was particularly vindictive towards his younger brother. He was a very poor sleeper, and his mother described a sense of total exhaustion in trying to control him.

Soon after Shane's birth his mother had become pregnant with his younger brother, and as a single parent this had placed great pressure on her coping resources. Shane's early development was not problematic but his acquisition of speech had been very slow and he had had a significant amount of speech therapy when he was four years old.

An EEG revealed abnormal spikes throughout the record, indicating seizure activity. Shane's mother was relieved that a physical cause had been found because she believed that many of the professionals she had met blamed her for Shane's difficult behaviour. He was prescribed anticonvulsants and over the next six weeks Shane's behaviour dramatically

improved. At three-month follow-up his mother reported that his behaviour had greatly improved, though he could still be cruel towards his
younger brother at times.

It is also important to remember that as many as 40 per cent of the children
under five years of age who initially appear to have ADHD actually have
developmental language disorders (Kube *et al.* 2002). The recognition of
such an underlying problem is clearly important. As in this particular case,
the family often feels great relief that the problem has turned out to be
a physical one, and not a reflection of their parenting. In all such cases,
however, it is important not to lose sight of the influence that family issues
can still be exerting. If a family has struggled with a difficult young person
for some time they will have developed mechanisms of responding which, if
they continue, may, in themselves, keep prompting problems. All types of
treatment, therefore, need to include a close examination of family dynamics
if the full benefit of a treatment regime is to be realised.

Association with conduct disorder

One of the features which has been inextricably linked with this disorder
since its first description is conduct disorder. This is a disorder characterised
by a pattern of antisocial behaviour where there may be episodes of stealing,
lying and truanting. Of course, there are many reasons which can account for
the onset of conduct disorder, but the one that is most established is that
of persisting family difficulties (Loeber and Stouthamer-Loeber 1986). However, the frequency with which attention problems and conduct disorder
occur together has prompted much research into whether there is a link
between the two.

It seems clear that if the features of hyperactivity are evident by three
years of age, then this is a strong predictor of conduct disorder in later
childhood (Stevenson *et al.* 1985), especially in boys where there is hostile
parenting by mothers (Morrell and Murray 2003). If the hyperactivity does
not emerge until eight or nine years of age, however, the likelihood of
conduct disorder is no greater than in the general population (Fergusson *et
al.* 1993). All of these children are, however, at risk of educational failure
which tends to reaffirm that the early-onset, pervasive subtype of attention deficit is distinct from those where most of the difficulties appear in
educational settings.

The conclusions from the research into this area are that the two problems
of attention deficit and conduct disorder tend to coexist, rather than one
being the direct consequence of the other. However, if attention deficit is
present, this does increase the likelihood of conduct disorder occurring
especially if there is also psychosocial adversity, such as poverty or marital

violence (Schachar and Tannock 1995). It is also worth noting that conduct and attention deficit disorders seem to have an intensifying effect on each other, so the problems which occur when both are present are greater than the problems which either attention deficit or conduct disorder exerts on its own (McArdle *et al.* 1995).

Martin was a seven-year-old boy presenting with violent outbursts towards his younger sister and a continuous refusal to comply with his mother's wishes. In the evenings she found it hard to prevent him destroying toys, which he did when he became frustrated in any way. Martin was always difficult to settle to bed, constantly demanding his mother's attendance and the routine had therefore become that Martin would sleep in his mother's bed. The day was always punctuated with battles – over dressing, washing, what to have for breakfast, and so on. This picture contrasted starkly with that seen in school where Martin was settled, performing well and presented no behavioural difficulties to the staff. Such a stark contrast between two environments points to a problem within relationships, and it became evident over time that Martin's mother was struggling with a significant depressive illness which had prevented her from establishing a clear and consistent pattern of management with him.

Treatment of this depressive illness, and a series of sessions focusing upon management, allowed Martin's mother to establish a clear and decisive parenting approach. With its introduction Martin said he now felt happier, and that he could cope with no longer being allowed to sleep in his mother's bed.

Martin's case illustrates the importance of assessing a child's behaviour in several settings. A pattern of behaviour problems specific to one area is a strong indication not of attention deficit but that there are issues within that setting that the child is reacting to.

Prevalence

Differences in diagnosis between Europe and North America explain why there has been as much as a twenty-fold difference in the rate of children identified with attention deficit between the two continents in the past (Taylor 1994). However, as the acceptance of ADHD as a diagnosis has been increasing in the UK the rates are gradually equalising, and the previous estimate in Britain of between 1 and 3 per cent of the population (McArdle *et al.* 1995), is gradually moving to the 3–5 per cent prevalence derived from multiple international studies (Wilens *et al.* 2002). The other major shift in the understanding of prevalence is to do with gender. In younger children it has been a consistent finding that ADHD is four times more likely in boys (Ross and Ross 1982), but studies in adolescence show an equal ratio (Cohen *et al.* 1993). This discrepancy emerges because the girls tend not to show the markedly disruptive behaviour which bring the boys to professional attention. Indeed it is now proposed that instead of being seen as a disorder that is limited to males during middle childhood, ADHD it should be conceptualised as a chronic disorder that persists into adolescence and adulthood for both sexes (Willoughby 2003). This also means that in some families one of the parents may have ADHD symptomatology, and the impact that this might have in terms of the routine of life, and in particular marital discord, is beginning to emerge (Minde *et al.* 2003).

Intervention

The evaluation of what is the most helpful way to deal with such children has been made more difficult by the different types of definition that have been used. However, as the diagnosis becomes more generally accepted, the research evidence gives clearer pathways of intervention. If there is a suspicion that there is a problem with attention deficit the first need is to confirm that the types of symptom described in Figure 4.1 are present, and to what degree. Within school it is common to compare children with their peers to make such judgements, and a qualitative difference with the rest of the children on the areas mentioned is a good starting point. The picture can be obtained not only by asking detailed questions about the child's history and performance in other settings, but by using one of the many questionnaires which specifically identify attention deficit symptoms – such as the Revised Ontario Child Health Study Scales (Boyle *et al.* 1993), the Child Behaviour Checklist (Achenbach and Edelbrock 1991) or the Strengths and Difficulties Questionnaire (Goodman 1994).

In such cases it is also worthwhile carrying out an assessment of how long the child can stay on everyday tasks, such as reading, drawing, watching television, playing computer games. This type of information gives a good insight into whether staying with a task is a persistent problem.

With confirmation that this is a case of attention deficit disorder the next stage is to determine into which subtype it falls. Information about the child's present difficulties, when they started, and the child's educational functioning help to determine whether the problems are present in just one setting, such as school, which gives a strong clue that issues within that setting are likely to be at the heart of the difficulties that are being seen.

At this stage professional help can then be sought. The family doctor can arrange for a referral to the local child psychiatry service, or the school's doctor can be approached to advise about the best way of further assessing the child. If the issues have a strong school theme, then the educational psychologist for the school is going to be a valuable source of help. If the problems are particularly family focused, then social services or the health visitor can also be approached for help and advice.

If the major focus of concern, and indeed the reported history, is one of conduct/oppositional-type problems then these behaviours need to be examined and their origins understood. For some, sometimes referred to as 'adrenaline junkies', it is the thrill and excitement of the misdeeds, while for others the problems may be driven by a need to challenge parental authority as part of the adolescent process. In many there are clearly longstanding problems with control by the family. Having gained such an understanding, intervention should be focused upon bringing about change, and this often has a significant component of behavioural management. Social services may already be involved if these problems are of a significant degree, and often these services have a range of strategies that they can offer to help with such problems.

Distinguishing between ADHD and the other causes of concentration problem is of importance, not only to ensure the correct intervention programme, but also to help in estimating the potential improvement that can be expected. For example, a problem which has its origin in parenting difficulties will need a careful family assessment to detail the themes and issues which are contributing to the problem behaviour. This may indicate that a course of family therapy is appropriate, or there may be evidence that the principal carer is suffering from a depressive illness which demands treatment in its own right. By contrast, developmental delays, a desire for predictable routine and a problem that is evident in various settings suggests a pervasive developmental disorder, and so the first step in responding to such children is to ensure that this is excluded.

Dietary approach

The interest in how diet influences behaviour had a significant boost from the work of the team at Great Ormond Street Hospital in the mid-eighties (Egger *et al.* 1985). This work showed that hyperactive behaviour could, in some young people, be significantly influenced by diet. The work also highlighted the difficulties there are in finding an effective approach to assessing and treating such children. In particular the work showed that each child had a unique pattern of allergies, so no universal diet could be offered, and that each young person was allergic to more than one item, with the result that simply stopping one or two things was unlikely to be helpful.

The only way to carry out a successful assessment is therefore to minimise food item intake over a test period and monitor the response. This is called an oligoantigenic diet because, by having so few food items, the number of problem items (antigens) that the young person might face is minimised. More recently the influence of diet on behaviour has been emphasised again

(Gesch *et al.* 2002), and specific clinics which offer this as a main method of intervention are beginning to emerge.

Medication

Stimulants

Medication, and, in particular, the use of central nervous system stimulants, has been the area to receive most research attention over the recent past. The drug most commonly used is methylphenidate (usually known as Ritalin), but sometimes dexamphetamine (known as Dexedrine) is prescribed. These drugs, which are part of the amphetamine family, change the level of brain chemicals and have been clearly demonstrated to help children to concentrate (Vitiello *et al.* 2001). However, they are sometimes drugs of abuse, and are potentially addictive (see Chapter 9). There is no evidence that children prescribed these medications develop addiction to them (Spencer *et al.* 1996b), but it has been estimated that about 2 per cent of high school children in the United States use methylphenidate when it is not prescribed for them (Klein-Schwartz and McGrath 2003), although it does appear that the slow-release form is far less attractive in this regard (Jaffe 2002).

As with all drugs, the stimulant medications do have side-effects. Children can often have difficulty sleeping and for a small minority the medication makes them more irritable and restless. Other side-effects may be a dry mouth, sweating, palpitations, headaches and pains in the stomach. It was suggested that if the drug is taken for a long period it may interfere with a child's growth (Gittelman and Mannuzza 1988), but it is now clear that any shortness of stature is probably due to the genetic make-up of the child and not his or her treatment (Spencer *et al.* 1996a). As was mentioned in Chapter 2, drug prescribing for children has been relatively rare in the United Kingdom, and this has been as true for ADHD as for any other emotional or behavioural problem. However, the evidence of the efficacy of stimulant medication in ADHD is now very strong (Spencer *et al.* 1996b). The most significant study in this regard was carried out in several centres in America (MTA Cooperative Group 1999), and showed that methylphenidate is more effective than behavioural treatment alone (Vitiello *et al.* 2001). The most obvious improvements tend to be a reduction in the overactivity and impulsivity which the child shows, as well as an improvement in overall attention levels (Wilens and Biederman 1992), and increases in academic productivity, improved cognitive functioning and recall (O'Toole *et al.* 1997), as well as improvement in overall classroom performance (Du Paul *et al.* 1994). In addition many children report an improvement in their social interaction (especially with peers), and an increase in the sensitivity in perceiving communications (Whalen *et al.* 1990). An especially interesting phenomenon is the way that methylphenidate suppresses aggressive outbursts

(Murphy *et al.* 1992), and this perhaps illustrates how difficulties with attention and concentration may fuel more general behaviour problems. It also helps to reinforce that the improvements that may arise in such areas through medication must be recognised and capitalised upon to ensure that improvements are maximised in all areas of a child's life.

If medication may be of assistance, the speed of action of methylphenidate allows a very rapid trial of its value to be made. It is, of course, important for families to understand the nature of the drug being used, and Figure 4.2 shows a typical information sheet which should be given to the family of any young person who is receiving the medication.

One of the major drawbacks to stimulant medication use has been the need to regularly take tablets through the day to maintain the improved concentration levels. Children often feel embarrassed to take medication at school, and sometimes families have to make elaborate arrangements around giving daytime doses if schools do not wish to have responsibility for giving medication through the day. These difficulties have prompted the development of single-dose medications, which are usually referred to as slow-release or sustained-release, depending upon their pharmacological profile of action. Although helpful, they are not always as effective as immediate-release preparations (Swanson *et al.* 2003), and some children often prefer to return to the original regime, despite its drawbacks, because they feel less benefit in their classroom activities.

Other medications

In some cases the poor concentration and restlessness may also be associated with a picture of sadness and misery. This combination of hyperactivity and signs of depression prompted some practitioners to examine the effects of prescribing the tricyclic-type of antidepressant for young people with hyperactivity. Studies which have used antidepressants have demonstrated their value in reducing the symptoms of ADHD, especially in adolescents (Wilens *et al.* 1993). However there are several significant side-effects associated with this medication and so it tends to be a second choice. A different type of antidepressant, Bupropion, has also been shown to be effective for ADHD in children with ADHD (Daviss *et al.* 2001). Better known perhaps as an aid to stop smoking, it appears as effective as methylphenidate, but again tends to be suggested when stimulants are inappropriate.

Several other drugs have been suggested as being of value in children with concentration difficulties, but it is probably worth mentioning two others. Clonidine is a medication which was initially developed for managing high blood pressure. In children it has been shown to reduce the symptoms of ADHD, but also helps some children with tics (Steingard *et al.* 1993). Since it is common for tic problems, such as Tourette's syndrome, to be associated with ADHD this double efficacy is sometimes valuable (Tourette's Syndrome

Study Group, 2002). In addition this medication has also been found to be helpful if aggressive themes are particularly evident (Connor *et al.* 2000), but perhaps the family of medications that are proving to be of most help in such situations are the atypical antipsychotic medications (Schur *et al.* 2003). The effectiveness of these medicines to reduce the concentration difficulties specifically is not great, but their impact on wider behavioural difficulties means they can be very helpful in combination.

The medication which will perhaps have the greatest impact in the next few years is atomoxetine. It is a form of antidepressant, and is the first medication to be given a licence for the treatment of ADHD in adults (Michelson *et al.* 2003). Studies in children have shown it to be a very effective agent (Spencer *et al.* 2002), and it appears to cause fewer problems with appetite reduction, and there is a lower incidence of insomnia. As a new medication there will need to be far more evaluation before its role in the general management of ADHD is understood, but these early studies are promising.

Behavioural techniques

Behavioural techniques have a part to play in helping a young person attend to tasks, and gradually increase the period that attention can be sustained. They are also helpful in curbing some of the conduct elements which may be part of the picture. The principles outlined in Chapter 7 would apply equally to this type of problem. However, the emphasis where the child has attention problems is upon trying to improve attention and to increase the child's general sense of self-esteem and self-worth. It is also worth remembering that such young people often don't fully register instructions, or information generally. It is therefore important that instructions and information are regularly repeated, with information being given in various ways, such as saying it, writing it down, and perhaps using diagrams or pictures.

As a starting point it is important with any task to recognise what the child's limit of sustained attention is, and to tailor activities to fit within that time-span. To achieve this, it may be necessary to take the task and divide it into small segments which the young person can definitely manage. Having set this to a realistic level, expecting them to complete the task becomes important not only to ensure that there is a sense of achievement, but to avoid the excuse of poor attention being used simply to avoid work.

Children with attention deficit need structure and routine. They should be helped to make schedules and break assignments down into small tasks to be performed one at a time. It may be necessary to ask them repeatedly what they have just done, how they might have acted differently, and why others react as they do. Especially when young, these children often respond well to the strict application of clear and consistent rules.

Family conflict is one of the most troublesome consequences of attention deficit. Especially when the symptoms have not yet been recognised and the diagnosis made, parents blame themselves, each other, and the child. As they become angrier and impose more punishment, the child becomes more defiant and alienated, and the parents become still less willing to accept the child's excuses or promises. A father or mother with adult attention deficit sometimes compounds the problem. Constantly compared unfavourably with his or her brothers and sisters, the child with attention deficit may become the family scapegoat, blamed for everything that goes wrong. When attention deficit is diagnosed, parents may feel guilty about not understanding the situation sooner, while other children in the family may reject the diagnosis as an excuse for attention-getting misbehaviour.

To avoid constant family warfare, parents need to learn to distinguish behaviour with a biological origin from reactions to the primary symptoms or responses to the reactions of others. They should become familiar with signs indicating imminent loss of self-control by a child with attention deficit. A routine with consistent rules must be established; these rules can be imposed on young children but must be negotiated with older ones and with adolescents. The family should have a clear division of responsibility, and the parents should present a united front. It helps to write down the rules, and it is important to praise good behaviour immediately. Role-playing may help a child with attention deficit to see how others see him. Family therapy or counselling, parent groups, and child management training are sometimes useful.

Most children with attention deficit are taught in the regular classroom, but their pattern of difficulties presents a challenge to the teachers who work with them because they often need some special approaches to help them learn. For example, the teacher may seat the child in an area with few distractions, provide an area where the child can move around and release excess energy, or establish a clear set of rules and rewards for appropriate behaviour. Sometimes just keeping a card or a picture on the desk can serve as a visual reminder to use the right school behaviour, like raising a hand instead of shouting out, or staying in a seat instead of wandering around the room. The regular repetition of instructions or writing instructions on the board can be helpful, as can closely monitoring the child's own recording, and offering quiet study areas. It is also very helpful to offer short study periods broken by activity (including permission to leave the classroom occasionally), and to use brief directions which are often repeated. Teaching the child how to use flashcards, outlines and underlining can all keep the attention focused on the task. Even simple structures such as giving lists of the books and materials needed for the task may make it possible for disorganised, inattentive children to complete the work. Many of the strategies of special education are simply good teaching methods. Telling students in advance what they will learn, providing visual aids, and giving written as well as oral instructions are all ways to help students focus and remember the key parts of the lesson. Timed tests should be avoided as much as possible because the child will tend to underperform under such pressure. Other children in the classroom may show more tolerance if the problem is explained to them in terms they can understand.

Children with attention deficit often need to learn techniques for monitoring and controlling their own attention and behaviour. For example, children may be taught several alternatives to use when they lose track of what they are supposed to do. These strategies may involve looking for instructions on the chalkboard, raising a hand, waiting to see if they remember, or quietly asking another child. The process of finding alternatives to interrupting the teacher can make the child feel more self-sufficient and create an atmosphere of cooperation. With fewer interruptions there is also an increase in praise and a reduction in reprimands. It helps if the teacher can frequently stop to ask children to notice whether they are paying attention to the lesson or if they are thinking about something else, and to record their answer on a chart. As students become more consciously aware of their attention, they begin to see progress and feel good about staying focused. These young people are quite capable of learning, but their hyperactivity and inattention make learning difficult.

Rewards for success are key, and they may be something as simple as the opportunity to run around for five minutes – which is not only a reward but also a release that will help the child settle to the next segment. Gradually extending the time of each segment shapes the young person's behaviour, and begins to create a more durable concentration span. Encouraging the young person to do regularly things they are good at, such as sport, helps to give a strong sense of success. This prevents the child from feeling a total failure because tasks requiring concentration are difficult.

Outcome

Although the overactivity tends to fade in adolescence, the attention problems often persist, with up to half of affected children still showing difficulties related to hyperactivity in adulthood (Mannuzza *et al.* 1993). Indeed it is increasingly clear that ADHD is as much a problem within adulthood as amongst children (Willoughby 2003), although the presentation is a mixture of concentration difficulties and disorders such as depression rather than the restless, fidgety picture seen in children. To be diagnosed as present in adulthood the symptoms must have started in childhood, and it appears that the children at most risk are those with family adversity and poor peer relationships. However, it does not seem that the severity of the attention problems themselves predicts the likelihood of long-term difficulties (Taylor 1995).

Conclusion

There has been a vast amount of effort that is being put into answering the fundamental questions around attention deficit and hyperactivity and it is becoming clear that the core problem is chronic disorder that is probably genetically influenced. The fact that other disorders mimic the symptomatology has, until recently, tended to confuse the picture. The condition remains very important to understand because as well as the concentration difficulties, young people who have concentration problems are very prone to have conduct problems and educational failure. Indeed, it is common to find that despite average cognitive abilities, these young people fare academically less well than their peers (Wilson and Marcotte 1996). For example, work in New Zealand (Fergusson and Horwood 1992) has shown that at twelve years of age the child's level of attention deficit directly influences his or her level of reading achievement. There can therefore be no doubt that this is a very important condition to understand, not only because it is common, but because of the profound effect it has upon young people's lives.

Sources of further help

www.rcpsych.ac.uk/info/mhgu/newmhgu5.htm
www.addiss.co.uk
www.mentalhealth.org.uk/page.cfm?pagecode=PMAMAD
www.nimh.nih.gov/publicat/adhdqa.cfm
www.nimh.nih.gov/publicat/autismmenu.cfm

References

Achenbach, T.M. and Edelbrock, C.S. (1991). *Integrative Guide to the 1991 CBCL 4–18, YSR and TRF Profiles*. Burlington: University of Vermont.

Boyle, M.H., Offord, D.R., Racine, Y., Fleming, J.E., Szatmari, P. and Sanford, M. (1993). Evaluation of the Revised Ontario Child Health Study Scales. *Journal of Child Psychology and Psychiatry* 34, 189–213.

Cohen, P., Cohen, J. and Kasen, S. (1993). An epidemiological study of disorders in late childhood and adolescence. I. Age and gender-specific prevalence. *Journal of Child Psychology and Psychiatry* 34, 851–67.

Connor, D.F., Barkley, R.A. and Davis, H.T. (2000). A pilot study of methylphenidate, clonidine, or the combination in ADHD comorbid with aggressive oppositional defiant or conduct disorder. *Clinical Pediatrics* 39, 15–25.

Daviss, W.B., Bentivoglio, P. and Racusin, R. (2001). Bupropion sustained release in adolescents with comorbid attention-deficit/hyperactivity disorder and depression. *Journal of the American Academy of Child Adolescent Psychiatry* 40, 307–14.

Du Paul, G., Barkley, R. and McMurray, M. (1994). Response of children with ADHD to methylphenidate: interaction with internalizing symptoms. *Journal of the American Academy of Child and Adolescent Psychiatry* 33, 894–903.

Egger, J., Carter, C., Graham, P. and Gumley, D. (1985). A controlled trial of oligoantigenic treatment in the hyperkinetic syndrome. *Lancet* I, 540–5.

Faraone, S.V., Biederman, J. and Chen, W.J. (1992). Segregation analysis of attention deficit hyperactivity disorder: evidence for a single gene transmission. *Psychiatric Genetics* 2, 257–2.

Faraone, S.V., Biederman, J., Mennin, D. and Gershon, J. (1996). A prospective 4-year follow-up study of children at risk of ADHD. *Journal of the American Academy of Child and Adolescent Psychiatry* 35, 1449–59.

Fergusson, D.M. and Horwood, L.J. (1992). Attention deficit and reading achievement. *Journal of Child Psychology and Psychiatry* 33, 375–85.

Fergusson, D.M., Horwood, L.J. and Lloyd, M. (1993). Confirmatory factor models of attention deficit and conduct disorder. *Journal of Child Psychology and Psychiatry* 32, 257–74.

Gesch, C.B., Hammond, S.M. and Hampson, S.E. (2002). Influence of supplementary vitamins, minerals and essential fatty acids on the antisocial behaviour of young adult prisoners. Randomised, placebo-controlled trial. *British Journal of Psychiatry* 181, 22–8.

Gittelman, R. and Mannuzza, S. (1988). Hyperactive boys almost grown up: III. Methylphenidate effects on ultimate height. *Archives of General Psychiatry* 45, 1131–4.

Goodman, R. (1994). A modified version of the Rutter Parent Questionnaire including extra items on children's strengths. *Journal of Child Psychology and Psychiatry* 35, 1483–94.

Jaffe, S.L. (2002). Failed attempts at intranasal abuse of Concerta. *Journal of the American Academy of Child Adolescent Psychiatry* 41(1), 5–6.

Klein-Schwartz, W. and McGrath, J. (2003). Poison Centers experience with methylphenidate abuse in pre-teens and adolescents. *Journal of the American Academy of Child Adolescent Psychiatry* 42(3), 288–94.

Kube, D.A., Petersen, M.C. and Palmer, F.B. (2002). Attention deficit hyperactivity disorder: comorbidity and medication use. *Clinical Pediatrics* 41, 461–69.

Leung, P.W.L. and Connolly, K.J. (1994). Attention difficulties in hyperactive and conduct disordered children: a processing deficit. *Journal of Child Psychology and Psychiatry* 35, 1229–45.

Loeber, R. and Stouthamer-Loeber, M. (1986). Family factors as correlates and predictors of juvenile conduct problems and delinquency. In M. Tonry and N. Morris (eds) *Crime and Justice: An Annual Review of Research*, vol. VII. Chicago: University of Chicago Press.

McArdle, P., O'Brien, G. and Kolvin, I. (1995). Hyperactivity: prevalence and relationship with conduct disorder. *Journal of Child Psychology and Psychiatry* 36, 279–303.

Mannuzza, S., Klein, R.G., Bessler, A. and Malloy, P. (1993). Adult outcome of hyperactive boys: educational achievement, occupational rank and psychiatric status. *Archives of General Psychiatry* 50, 565–76.

Michelson, D., Adler, L. and Spencer, T. (2003). Atomoxetine in adults with ADHD: two randomized, placebo-controlled studies. *Biological Psychiatry* 53, 112–20.

Minde, K., Eakin, L., Hechtman, L., Ochs, E. and Bouffard, R. (2003). The psychosocial functioning of children and spouses of adults with ADHD. *Journal of Child Psychology and Psychiatry* 44, 637–46.

Morrell, J. and Murray, L. (2003). Parenting and the development of conduct disorder and hyperactive symptoms in childhood: a prospective longitudinal study from 2 months to 8 years. *Journal of Child Psychology Psychiatry* 44, 489–508.

MTA Cooperative Group (1999) A 14 month randomised clinical trial of treatment strategies for attention-deficit/hyperactivity disorder. *Arch. Gen. Psychiatry* 56, 1073–86.

Murphy, D., Pelham, W. and Lang, A. (1992). Aggression in boys with ADHD: methylphenidate effects on naturalistically observed aggression, response to provocation and social information processing. *Journal of Abnormal Child Psychology* 20, 451–66.

National Institute for Clinical Excellence (2000). *Guidance on the Use of Methylphenidate (Ritalin/Equasym) for Attention Deficit/Hyperactivity Disorder (ADHD) in Childhood).* London: NICE.

O'Toole, K., Abramowitz, A., Morris, R. and Dulcan, M. (1997). Effects of methylphenidate on attention and nonverbal learning in children with ADHD. *Journal of the American Academy of Child and Adolescent Psychiatry* 36, 531–8.

Porrino, L.J., Rapoport, J.L., Behar, D., Sceery, W., Ismond, D. and Bunney, W.E. (1983). A naturalistic assessment of the motor activity of hyperactive boys: I. Comparison with normal controls. *Archives of General Psychiatry* 40, 681–7.

Rapport, M.D., Carlson, G.A., Kelly, K.L. and Pataki, C. (1993). Methlyphenidate and desipramine in hospitalized children: I. Separate and combined effects on cognitive function. *Journal of the American Academy of Child and Adolescent Psychiatry* 32, 333–42.

Riccio, C.A., Reynolds, C.R. and Lowe, P.A. (2001). Diagnostic efficacy of CPT's for disorders usually first evident in childhood or adolescence. In *Clinical Applications of Continuous Performance Tests* (pp 190–257). New York: Wiley.

Ross, D.M. and Ross, S.A. (1982). *Hyperactivity: Current Issues, Research and Theory.* New York: Wiley.

Schachar, R. and Logan, G.D. (1990). Impulsivity and inhibitory control in development and psychopathology. *Developmental Psychology* 26, 1–11.

Schachar, R. and Tannock, R. (1995). Test of four hypotheses for the comorbidity of attention deficit hyperactivity disorder and conduct disorder. *Journal of the American Academy of Child and Adolescent Psychiatry* 34, 639–48.

Schur, S.B., Sikich, L., Findling, R.L., Malone, R.P., Crismon, M.L., Derivan, A. and Macintyre Ii, J.C. (2003). Treatment recommendations for the use of antipsychotics for aggressive youth (TRAAY). Part I: a review. *Journal of the American Academy of Child and Adolescent Psychiatry* 42, 132–44.

Simeon, J.G., Ferguson, H.B. and Fleet, J. (1986). Bupropion effects in attention deficit and conduct disorders. *Canadian Journal of Psychiatry* 31, 581–5.

Spencer, T., Biederman, J., Harding, M. and O'Donnell, D. (1996a). Growth deficits in ADHD children revisited: evidence for disorder-associated growth delays? *Journal of the American Academy of Child and Adolescent Psychiatry* 35, 1460–9.

Spencer, T., Biederman, J., Wilens, T. and Harding, M. (1996b). Pharmacology of ADHD across the life cycle. *Journal of the American Academy of Child and Adolescent Psychiatry* 35, 409–32.

Spencer, T., Heiligenstein, J.H. and Biederman, J. (2002). Results from 2 proof-of-concept, placebo-controlled studies of atomoxetine in children with attention-deficit/hyperactivity disorder. *Journal of Clinical Psychiatry* 63, 1140–7.

Steingard, R., Biederman, J., Spencer, T., Wilens, T. and Gonzalez, A. (1993). Comparison of clonidine response in the treatment of attention deficit hyperactivity disorder with and without comorbid tic disorders. *Journal of the American Academy of Child Adolescent Psychiatry* 32, 350–3.

Stevenson, J., Richman, N. and Graham, P. (1985). Behaviour problems and language abilities at three years and beavioural deviance at eight years. *Journal of Child Psychology and Psychiatry* 26, 215–30.

Swanson, J.M., Sunohara, G.A. and Kennedy, J.L. (1998). Association of the dopamine receptor D4 (DRD4) gene with a refined phenotype of attention deficit hyperactivity disorder (ADHD) a family based approach. *Molecular Psychiatry* 3, 38–41.

Swanson, J., Gupta, S. and Lam, A. (2003). Development of a new once-a-day formulation of methylphenidate for the treatment of attention-deficit/hyperactivity disorder: proof-of-concept and proof-of-product studies. *Archives of General Psychiatry* 60, 204–11.

Taylor, E. (1994). Syndromes of attention deficit and overactivity. In M. Rutter, E. Taylor and L. Hersov (eds) *Child and Adolescent Psychiatry: Modern Approaches.* Oxford: Blackwell.

Taylor, E. (1995). Dysfunctions of attention. In D. Cicchetti and D.J. Cohen (eds) *Developmental Psychopathology.* New York: Wiley.

Taylor, E., Scharchar, R., Thorley, G. and Weiselberg, M. (1987). Which boys respond to stimulant medication? A controlled trial of methylphenidate in boys with disruptive behaviour. *Psychological Medicine* 17, 121–43.

Taylor, E., Sandberg, S., Thorley, G. and Giles, S. (1991). *The Epidemiology of Childhood Hyperactivity.* Maudsley Monographs no. 33. Oxford: Oxford University Press.

Tourette's Syndrome Study Group (2002). Treatment of ADHD in children with tics: a randomized controlled trial. *Neurology* 58 (February), 527–36.

Vitiello, B., Severe, J.B. and Greenhill, L.L. (2001). Methylphenidate dosage for children with ADHD over time under controlled conditions: lessons from the MTA. *Journal of the American Academy of Child Adolescent Psychiatry* 40, 188–96.

Whalen, C., Henker, B. and Granger, D. (1990). Social adjustment processes in hyperactive boys: effects of methylphenidate and comparison with normal peers. *Journal of Abnormal Child Psychology* 18, 297–316.

Wilens, T.E. and Biederman, J. (1992). The stimulants. *Psychiatric Clinics of North America* 15, 191–222.

Wilens, T., Biederman, J. and Spencer, T.J. (2002). Attention deficit/hyperactivity disorder across the lifespan. *Annual Review of Medicine* 53, 113–31.

Wilens, T.E., Biederman, J., Geist, D.E. and Steingard, R. (1993). Nortriptyline in the treatment of ADHD: a chart review of 58 cases. *Journal of the American Academy of Child and Adolescent Psychiatry* 32, 343–9.

Willoughby, M.T. (2003). Developmental course of ADHD symptomatology during the transition from childhood to adolescence: a review with recommendations. *Journal of Child Psychology and Psychiatry* 44, 88–106.

Wilson, J.M. and Marcotte, A.C. (1996). Psychosocial adjustment and educational outcome in adolescents with a childhood diagnosis of ADHD. *Journal of the American Academy of Child and Adolescent Psychiatry* 35, 579–87.

Wolraich, M.L., Hannah, J.N., Pinnock, T.Y., Baumgaertel, A. and Brown, J. (1996). Comparison of diagnostic criteria for attention-deficit hyperactivity disorder in a county-wide sample. *Journal of the American Academy of Child and Adolescent Psychiatry* 35, 319–24.

Chapter 5

Eating disorders

Introduction

Eating is one of the fundamental requirements, along with breathing, necessary to sustain life. If a person does not breathe for some minutes death occurs very quickly; for someone not eating, although it may take several weeks, the fact of death is no less inevitable. Perhaps this is why, throughout the animal kingdom, feeding is such a major part of the daily routine and has become in some species a part of ritual. In primates in particular, feeding routines have assumed particular importance, and are regularly used to placate aggressors. In humans mutual feeding has also evolved as a major mechanism for showing affection or sexual interest (Morris 1967).

This may go some way to explain why children's problems with eating can so quickly become emotionally charged, and can so often become an area of persisting conflict and difficulty. The high level of concern which feeding problems can provoke provides an excellent mechanism for children to manipulate adult views and achieve their own desires over the expressed wishes of their parents.

Infant feeding

The newborn infant has no capacity to feed itself, and can only respond to danger or discomfort by crying. The main caregiver, usually the mother, has to respond to these signals if the baby is to be reassured. Feeding is an integral part of this process, and so if it becomes disrupted in any way, the impact for both mother and child can be quite profound.

Chatoor and Egan (1987) considered the way that such problems arose and their system of classification is very useful not only for offering some structure, but for giving a direction in how to improve the situation. In the first two months of life the baby is learning the mechanics of feeding, and so it is most likely that feeding problems at this very young age are physical ones. They may be mechanical in that the baby cannot coordinate the movements necessary for effective feeding, or they may be medical – for instance, colic or respiratory problems that make sucking a problem. The main focus then for a young infant with difficulties in feeding is the mechanics of the process, and the nature of the difficulties can usually be determined by means of a careful medical review.

Between two and six months the infant begins the crucial process of developing a specific emotional attachment to the primary caregiver. Therefore, problems arising in this age group usually reflect problems in this developing relationship. The commonest cause is for the mother to be depressed, or simply worn out with the childcare routine. The responses to the young person are then poorer, or in the worst case non-existent, and the child becomes fretful and upset. If matters continue, the baby may start to reduce its demands and become remote and self-stimulating, but usually the response is to demand attention by escalating resistance, and so force the mother to interact, albeit in an irritated and perhaps punitive way. These sorts of interaction are very commonly seen in children who present as being very small, and apparently undernourished – the non-organic failure to thrive syndrome (NOFTS). When in a different environment they usually have insatiable appetites, and characteristically put on significant weight and growth spurts during periods when not in their parent's care. If the resistance becomes extreme then the conflict between parent and child can become very marked, and this is sometimes described as infantile anorexia (Chatoor et al. 1997). It has been found that problems with feeding at a young age can, if persistent, lead to the young person having significantly poorer intellectual functioning than his or her peers (Puckering et al. 1995).

About 25 per cent of children will experience some type of feeding difficulties during infancy or early childhood, and this rate can be even higher in children with developmental disabilities. However, very few of these will be of a nature that requires excessive concern, or professional intervention. For children who are simply very selective in their choice of food, as long as the child is choosing nutritious foods, they can be allowed to choose what to eat. Sometimes they may want to eat a particular food again and again for a while, and then not want to eat it at all. The child should be encouraged to explore new foods on their own but insistence should be avoided as it tends to make resistance greater. Parents should be sensitive to the visual appeal of the food and try to offer only small amounts. They should not insist on a clean plate and avoid the use of bribes, threats or punishments.

If a child is refusing to eat on a regular basis it is important not to fight this. Many parents become very concerned when their toddler refuses to eat. They worry that their child may not get the nutrition needed or that this is a sign of illness. Many worry that the child may be punishing them. If the child doesn't want to eat, parents should accept the refusal and not show any upset. If the child is seeking attention, parental disapproval fills that need, and makes it more likely that the defiance will continue. Wherever possible, meals should occur at predictable times and be made a pleasant experience.

However, parents should not try to achieve this by allowing the child to watch TV or play with toys at the table – it needs to be clear that the meal-time is for eating. It is often helpful if the family sit together to eat, and use the same seats at the table. This type of family gathering provides good role models to the child of how to behave at mealtimes. The texture of food is sometimes a reason for the child not liking certain foods. In such cases it can help to alter the texture of a rejected food, perhaps offering vegetables raw instead of cooked.

Anorexia nervosa

Anorexia nervosa is a condition which has been known for some time, but was first formally identified by Gull in 1873. It has, however, become far better known in recent years as the image of being thin has become the one to which youth has increasingly been urged to aspire. This idealised image is experienced by the young at a time when they are searching for a personal identity, and trying to navigate the difficult route from childhood to becoming an adult. As has been mentioned in Chapter 1, one way that adolescents cope with these pressures is to seek conformity with stereotypes, and peer-group expectations. It is perhaps not surprising, then, that becoming totally focused on body image is a mechanism that some young people use to cope with these difficult pressures. In one survey 40 per cent of teenage girls and 10 per cent of teenage boys were dieting significantly, and for 7 per cent of the girls (and 1 per cent of the boys) this was extreme (Patton *et al.* 1997).

Anorexia nervosa rarely emerges before puberty, and if a younger child is showing problems with weight loss and a reluctance to eat, it is very important that all physical illnesses are carefully excluded before any attempt to diagnose anorexia nervosa is made. In these younger children it is easy for bowel problems to masquerade as anorexia, and caution is therefore very important. The key factor for diagnosis in this age group, as in all others, is the presence of distortion in how the young person sees his or her body.

Anorexia nervosa affects 0.1–0.2 per cent of the adolescent population (Whitaker *et al.* 1990), and occurs in girls ten times more commonly than in boys (Lucas *et al.* 1991). In younger children the problem is quite rare, but here the proportion of boys is as great as 30 per cent (Jacobs and Isaacs 1986). One of the interesting questions to ask is whether the pressures of modern life are resulting in anorexia occurring ever more frequently. From his detailed analysis of the literature, Fombonne has concluded that the rate of occurrence of anorexia nervosa is not increasing over time, which offers some reassurance about the future (Fombonne 1995a).

Anna, at fifteen years of age, was a girl who greatly enjoyed tennis. In the winter her relative inactivity caused her to put on weight and several people within school began calling her 'Pug'. This made her quite distressed, and she determined to lose the extra weight.

Over the next few weeks she embarked upon a severe diet which involved eating low-fat yoghurt for breakfast and lunch and a salad for tea. On occasions Anna would 'cheat' by eating biscuits or chocolate, and afterwards she felt so guilty that she would sometimes not eat for two days to remove this 'weight'.

After three months her periods had stopped and she was 15 per cent below the weight that was typical for her height and age. When seen in individual sessions Anna could not accept that she was thin and was worried that if she began eating again she would rapidly become overweight. Family reassurance did not seem to help ease this anxiety for her. Using a cognitive therapy approach (see Chapter 2), Anna was gradually able to develop new ways of thinking about her weight. Having achieved this it was then possible slowly to change her dietary regime so that it maintained her at a weight appropriate to her height. As part of this programme, she began keeping a diary which listed her positive qualities as well as the nice things which people had said about her on that day. Three times a week she would read recent entries and over the next few months she confirmed that she was now seeing herself in a different light. Two years on, Anna continues to maintain her weight appropriately, and plays tennis for her university.

The problems presented by Anna are relatively clear, although for many young people with anorexia there are underlying problems of which the unwillingness to eat is merely an external manifestation.

This case illustrates the importance of recognising the key elements which lead to a diagnosis of anorexia nervosa. A desire to be slim, a wish to diet, a feeling of being overweight do not in themselves confirm that the young person has anorexia. The diagnosis requires that the young person has a dread of being overweight which is accompanied by an unshakeable belief that she is too large, even if to the objective observer the young person is in fact very thin. This distortion of body image is the key element in determining that anorexia nervosa is present, and if it is absent, then other possible causes of the problem should be considered.

In addition to this key element the young person is usually very thin, and in girls the periods have stopped. In about a third of cases there is also a soft, downy hair on the arms, legs and face, but this is a symptom arising because of the starvation; it is not part of the anorexia nervosa itself.

In the midst of the illness the young person diets very severely, and is very knowledgeable about food; this will tend to be a constant theme of the young person's conversation. Such young people are often good cooks, and will take delight in cooking for others, though they themselves maintain a

Table 5.1 Physical problems which can occur in anorexia nervosa

Symptom	%
Heart abnormalities, especially slowing of heart rate	87
Hypotension (low blood pressure)	85
Kidney abnormalities (giving changes in kidney function)	70
Thinning of spinal bone	50
Anaemia	30
Nutritional hepatitis	30
Stomach ulcers	16
Pancreatitis	occasional

Source: Sharp and Freeman (1993)

strict dietary regime. Indeed, once established, being able to maintain the strict regime is often a major source of pleasure for the young person, and in more reflective moments he or she may well recount how good it felt to be able to resist a particular food or treat. For some, the diet is not sufficient, and there may also be a punishing exercise regime, which is often justified as part of a health drive. In some the weight loss is assisted by taking large quantities of laxatives on a daily basis, or regularly vomiting after meals.

In the midst of the illness such dieting may be the only source of self-praise and when considering other aspects of their life they may view themselves with scorn or even disgust. They often stop meeting friends or taking part in social occasions and generally seem more solitary and preoccupied. In day-to-day things they often are more irritable and bad tempered, with an air of gloominess which can lead people to think that they are becoming depressed (Strober 1991).

The cessation of menstruation is the first sign of the significant impact which the starvation is having, but if the severe dieting is prolonged, damage can occur to important body organs (see Table 5.1) such as the liver and kidneys (Sharp and Freeman 1993). If the dieting is at all prolonged, there is also a thinning of the bones (Mehler 2003). This osteoporosis is also seen in older women whose periods have stopped and so is probably due to the drop in oestrogen levels rather than a direct consequence of starvation (Biller *et al.* 1989).

Rachel's parents had been concerned about her for many months. They knew that she ate very little, and her mother believed that her periods had stopped at least six months ago. Rachel had refused professional help, but had finally agreed when her favourite aunt, with whom Rachel felt an affinity, insisted that she must see someone.

The dietary history Rachel gave indicated that she was eating only 450 calories a day, and when she was weighed it was found that her weight was 40 per cent below the weight that was typical for her height and age. After much discussion she agreed to be admitted to hospital on a voluntary basis, and over the next few days more details of her routines emerged. She had been eating almost nothing but low-fat yoghurt and salad for some months, and over the same period she had been pursuing a very intensive fitness regime which involved jogging daily and swimming four times per week.

Rachel could recite the calorific value of almost every food item, and described her greatest pleasure as cooking Sunday lunch for the family. The ward staff commented that in her first few days in hospital she kept very active, and never seemed to stay still for a moment.

Although finishing meals was expected as part of the programme, increasingly Rachel did not finish her meals when junior nurses supervised them. These nurses said that Rachel had told them how frightened and upset she felt whenever she was expected to eat. They felt sorry for Rachel and felt that they were being cruel in insisting that she ate.

After three weeks Rachel's weight gain was minimal, and a search revealed the remains of meals outside of the room window, and within the room the staff found plastic bags filled with food behind furniture, and even in the springs of a chair.

Boys tend to develop similar symptoms (Oyebode *et al.* 1988), but they usually prove to have much greater underlying psychological problems (Fairburn and Harrison, 2003).

The causes of anorexia nervosa

As the concerns about anorexia nervosa have grown, so have the attempts to explain why some adolescents develop such a potentially profound problem. Family and twin studies suggest there is an important genetic influence in developing anorexia nervosa (Fombonne 1995b). However, for many, the origins of anorexia nervosa are to be found in the young person's own struggle with the pressures of maturity (Crisp 1980). The cessation of periods, the maintaining of the angularity of youth, and the delay in other secondary sexual characteristics are all certainly consequences of starvation. This type of theory is given added credence because many girls with anorexia nervosa tend to dress in a childish manner, perhaps emphasising their desire to avoid becoming an adult. In clinical samples a fear of growing up is certainly a common feature if the anorexia began before fourteen years of age, whereas in older girls it is a desire to be thin which dominates their thinking (Heebink *et al.* 1995).

This difference in emphasis between the two age groups is also reflected in the response to therapy. For those in whom the problem started at a young age, family therapy which focuses upon relationships and maturation tends to be most successful, whereas for those in whom the problem started late in adolescence, the best response tends to be achieved by an individual psychotherapy approach (Russell *et al.* 1987).

Whatever the usual cause, it is clear that certain groups are particularly prone to developing the problem. Ballet dancers in particular show rates far in excess of the general population, as do models (Garfinkel and Garner 1982; Strober 1991). This is perhaps not surprising when one considers the tremendous pressure on such people to stay 'in shape' and avoid getting fat. It is interesting to speculate, though, whether these groups are merely experiencing an intense version of what everyone with anorexia experiences or whether the problem is of a different sort – a necessary routine which has become so habitual that it becomes a goal in its own right. With the interest which this problem prompts being so high, it will not be too long before answers to these conundrums are found.

In recent years there has also been increasing interest in whether there is a genetic basis for eating disorders such as anorexia nervosa. Although the findings are not yet unequivocal, the evidence does suggest that there is a clear, and perhaps substantial, familial contribution in the emergence of eating disorders (Fairburn and Harrison 2003).

Intervention

The general approach to intervention is now quite established (Yager *et al.* 2000), and the first stage of any intervention process is to recognise that a problem is developing. With the modern emphasis upon slimness it can be difficult for families, or other concerned adults, to realise that there is a cause for concern. The first worry is usually the marked thinness of the young person, but it can also be a concern that the diet seems too severe. Asking about eating is usually dismissed, and it is often only when considerable weight has been lost, and there can be no doubt about the matter, that professional help is sought. The first requirement is then to seek a referral to the local psychiatry service.

After gaining an understanding of the history of the problem, and the issues which are sustaining it, the first aim of intervention is to limit further weight loss. The programme which has traditionally been used for this is based on behavioural principles. The exact make-up of the programme varies depending upon the philosophy of the institution, but most would expect that if the young person is 35 per cent below the ideal body weight for height and age, then a hospital admission is indicated. If the young person with anorexia nervosa does not wish to be admitted to hospital, then, if the illness is severe enough, they can be compulsorily detained using the powers available under the Mental Health Act (1981). To do this it has to be evident that the illness is adversely affecting the young person's ability to make rational decisions. It must be remembered, however, that each case is judged on its merits, and diagnosing that someone has anorexia nervosa does not automatically mean that they can be admitted to hospital against their will.

Whether in hospital or not, the first aim is to bring the body weight back to a more normal level. It is important to have a clear idea of the usual food intake because the new regime must very slowly increase from that level to one which is gradually producing a weight gain. The increase in weight is usually quite frightening to the young person and so the process demands great tact, care and lots of reassurance that they will not be made fat. It is sometimes helpful in these early stages to give a sedative medication, which can help reduce the intense feelings of panic that many feel as the weight chart slowly climbs. This gradual gaining of weight is accompanied by agreed rewards and, supplementing this, there needs to be a continuous educational and support programme to reduce the concern about the steady weight gain.

In the early stages the young person will usually talk of nothing but food and weight targets, and it is important to establish a sequence of meetings where this is not the focus, but rather the focus is upon their life and their aspirations for the future. These become the kernel of the individual psychological programme which gathers momentum as the weight concerns reduce. This psychological support may take many forms from formal psychotherapy to approaches based upon problem-solving. All, however, use the young person's own feelings and ideas, and in the process specific events which may have initiated the problem may be uncovered.

As already mentioned, the family's role both in the origin of the difficulties and in their solution may prove pivotal. Most families find exploration of their intimate workings very difficult, but without major shifts in attitude and approach relapse is very likely. One of the first major works in this area was by Minuchin and his team who explored family structures and functioning in what he described as 'psychosomatic families' (Minuchin *et al.* 1978). He described a pattern in which families were quite overinvolved, with a feeling that the family members were very enmeshed with each other. He also found that, typically, conflict between members of the family was avoided, and that if there was marital conflict it was very common for the young person to become caught in the middle of it.

A somewhat similar pattern of findings was noted by Selvini-Palazzoli in her work with anorexic girls in Italy (Selvini-Palazzoli 1974). She also noted that secret alliances between family members were often present, as was a strong expectation that family members would preserve the outward appearance of a settled family life. Although some of the conclusions from such work have been eroded over time, the basic approach to family issues still remains (Humphrey 1994). Understanding the family's functioning remains a fundamental requirement of any intervention programme, especially in the younger patient. The type of family work that is undertaken is largely dictated by the philosophy of the unit treating the young person, but often it has a systems theory basis (see Chapter 2).

Alongside the dynamic exploration of family issues, it is important that a consistent approach is agreed with the parents towards eating. In milder weight-loss situations this may be the only direct management of the eating, and its success is necessary for any lasting progress. The home regime is based upon agreed menus, and a constant expectation that plates will be cleared. The steady increase in amounts offered is still necessary, and using large dinner plates can help with the illusion that the quantity is small. A single exchange item on each menu is permitted, otherwise the meals are as agreed, and the adults of the family stay with them until all is eaten. Resisting excuses and ploys, and maintaining a solid insistence, is not only necessary to maintain the weight, but is often the first indication of a major shift in how the family functions.

Any concerned adult can offer the opportunity to listen to worries or concerns, but if they become food- or weight-orientated, these discussions should be diverted by saying 'those are issues to discuss with your specialist'. Within school, projects on anorexia may be sought out, and may offer the opportunity to ventilate certain feelings or ideas. It is important that the illness does not become too dominant, however, because maintaining a wide range of interests and having success in different arenas are crucial to the recovery process. Gently steering into new tasks, highlighting success and praising positive progress can all help in reducing the drive to be thinner.

There is no medication which specifically helps young people overcome this problem, and so the role of medication in anorexia nervosa is limited to two situations. The first is to help with the initial difficulties over establishing a weight-gain programme; the second is where the anorexia nervosa is occurring alongside a depressive illness. In the latter cases the use of antidepressants may offer some assistance (Kaye *et al.* 2001), but the psychological efforts to understand the problem's origins, and establish solutions, are still the major element of the intervention.

Outcome

Although the general approach to anorexia nervosa has been established for several years, the outcome is still very variable. This is because recovery is determined far more by how successful the psychological efforts have been than whether an appropriate weight was achieved. In general over half of the girls will achieve a reasonable weight and see their periods restored, but boys have a much poorer course (Steinhausen *et al.* 1991). On average 50 per cent of sufferers take six years or more to recover after their first treatment, while the average for those who also use purgatives can be eleven years (Herzog *et al.* 1997), and the likelihood of full recovery diminishes over time, with relapses occurring in 30 per cent of those who do not complete their full treatment programme (Strober *et al.* 1997).

It used to be thought that the earlier that the illness started the poorer the outcome (Walford and McCune 1991), but it is now clear that the age of onset is not associated with having a more severe illness, or one that tends to recur (Zipfel *et al.* 2000). Indeed, it appears that developing the disease as an adult is a predictor of much poorer outcome in the longer term (Ratnasuriya *et al.* 1990).

The disruption to the onset of full puberty prompted by the illness does influence the child's physical development (Russell 1985). Although most recover their weight, they are three times more likely to suffer chronic health problems (Wentz *et al.* 2000), and the nature of these problems can be quite significant (see Table 5.1) with, for example, osteoporosis being quite a common problem in later life, but unlike many of the other complications, it may persist regardless of the overall treatment outcome (Mehler 2003). In the long term, women who have suffered from anorexia do not find it harder to become pregnant, but they do seem to suffer from a greater frequency of complications with their pregnancy, such as prematurity, or requiring a caesarian section (Bulik *et al.* 1999).

Perhaps most worrying of all is the fact that despite the best efforts of clinicians and families about 2 per cent of young women who have anorexia nervosa die during the first year of their illness (Nielsen *et al.* 1998), sufferers have an overall mortality rate of 20 per cent, and over a life time the suicide rate for women with anorexia is some fifty times greater than the norm (Herzog *et al.* 2000). This level of mortality makes anorexia nervosa a condition that, when recognised, must be treated with the greatest of professional respect.

Bulimia nervosa

Bulimia nervosa is a variation of anorexia nervosa which was initially distinguished as a separate problem by Russell in 1979. He described a group of girls who had an intense fear of becoming fat, but, unlike typical anorexic girls, most of this group were not extremely thin. This group was also distinctive because their dietary routine was not extremely restrictive, but rather had episodes when they would eat a very large quantity of food, and afterwards they would vomit, use large amounts of laxatives, or exercise to an extreme degree to prevent the binge meal causing them to put on weight. It is worth mentioning that eating problems do not always present as clearly anorexic or bulimic, and that this group of atypical eating disorders can be quite challenging to manage because they tend to be severe and long-lasting (Fairburn and Harrison 2003).

Bulimia tends to begin well after puberty, and occurs in about 1.2 per cent of adolescent and young adult women (Fairburn and Beglin 1990), and

0.2 per cent of boys (Patton *et al.* 1999). It can occasionally occur in girls before they start their periods, but this is unusual (Schmidt *et al.* 1992). The evidence for a genetic influence is strongly suggestive but not yet proven (Fairburn and Harrison 2003), however there is a strong link to family substance misuse (Lilenfeld *et al.* 1998). In most cases there are clear influences from adverse life events (Fombonne 1995b), with a significant minority of the girls suffering from bulimia reporting that they have been victims of sexual abuse (Pope and Hudson 1992). There is also a subgroup of girls with bulimia who show significant alcohol and drug misuse (Dansky *et al.* 2000) and self-harming tendencies (Paul *et al.* 2002).

Amanda was seventeen years of age and during a school field trip a teacher became worried because Amanda seemed to spend long periods in the toilet after each meal. The teacher wanted to send Amanda home, but Amanda said that this had been happening for some time and that she had a stomach problem. As the week progressed Amanda began to confide in the teacher and in response to the teacher's obvious concern Amanda confessed that she in fact made herself sick after meals. Amanda considered herself to be ugly, and felt fat. She had tried many types of diet and had had slimming pills from her doctor, but couldn't seem to lose weight.

In the last year she had started to be sick after meals, and felt much happier after she had been sick, because she knew this food would not add to her weight problem. After much discussion Amanda agreed to be referred to a specialist clinic.

Initially, Amanda found it hard to talk about her eating problems, but eventually described how upset she was about her appearance, and how desperately she wanted to be thinner. She explained how sometimes the desire to eat became overwhelming, and on these occasions she would literally eat everything in the kitchen. She described how on these occasions she would even eat packets of butter as though they were some sort of ice-cream bar. Afterwards she had to be sick, and then could rest. At other times she felt the need to be sick only after large meals, and said that she was taking thirty laxative tablets a day to help keep her weight down.

In many regular bulimics the vomiting has created a characteristic pattern of enamel erosion on the teeth and enlarged salivary glands in the cheeks. The frequent vomiting also exposes the oesphagus to stomach acid and so is likely to provoke ulcers, and in rare cases it may cause the oesphagus to rupture (Overby and Litt 1988).

Intervention

Identifying a problem of bulimia nervosa can be very difficult. Hearing someone being sick may be the only clue, because otherwise there are few outward signs to notice. Therefore, it is the young person's declaration that there is a problem which tends to be the first indication. A referral to the local psychiatric services is the usual route of response, but experienced counsellors or community psychiatric nurses may be other avenues of help. The first task is to distinguish bulimia from anorexia nervosa, since the treatment emphasis is quite different. In trying to assist young people with bulimia various approaches have been used, but this has now been refined into three broad thrusts. The first takes the form of trying to understand the problems which are prompting the difficulties, and seeking solutions to them either through environmental change (such as changing house or job), or through the inner understanding given by psychotherapy. The second is to seek behavioural change which aims to extinguish the symptoms. This is usually through cognitive therapy (discussed in Chapter 2) which engages the patient in a careful examination of how the problem is viewed and thought about. When used in bulimia nervosa, the focus of cognitive therapy is upon seeking thoughts that are closely associated with the episodes of vomiting, and then seeking alternatives to reduce the urge to be sick.

The third avenue is the use of medication. Work in various centres has produced evidence that certain antidepressants can reduce episodes of bulimia and the preoccupation with body size (Goldstein *et al.* 1995). A review of this work concludes that psychological treatment and antidepressants do not differ in remission rates, but dropout rates are lower with psychological treatment. A combination of antidepressants and psychological treatment is now seen as the best way of intervening with this condition (Bacaltchuk *et al.* 2001).

The family's role in helping to resolve the problems depends upon whether direct family themes, such as conflict or abuse, are seen to be underlying the behavioural pattern. The use of family therapy can sometimes deal with such issues in a way that allows the young person to escape what feels like an oppressive atmosphere. If such themes are not dominant, then the family role tends to be one of support – both in terms of offering time for quiet reflection, and in terms of routine and structure. If it is clear that the hour after mealtimes is a particularly difficult time, then restructure routines so that there is no opportunity to vomit. This can be achieved by chores, playing board games or even taking a walk together. Such plans work best when agreed with sufferers, and this also allows them to be challenged if they try to excuse themselves.

Within other settings, such as school, assistance in breaking patterns is harder to organise. Keeping occupied is the most important requirement: empty time is dangerous time. A routine of going to clubs or assisting with the library can be quite powerful, but direct help means that the problem has to be shared, and that specific things are asked of the adult. It is unusual for school staff even to know that one of their students has bulimia, and so positive help tends to be very uncommon.

Friends can be a great source of help. They can be asked to be vigilant and close friends can be empowered to be quite forceful in stopping trips to the toilet unaccompanied. These types of intrusion are, however, only of value if the young person wants them, and they are part of a structured plan. As isolated measures they offer little, and if not sought by the sufferer, they can ruin relationships, and make matters worse by deepening the sense of isolation.

Outcome

Bulimia has been identified as a separate condition now for some years, and over this time there has been a steady flow of studies pointing to the value of psychological intervention, particularly cognitive behaviour therapy. However, if this approach fails there are few alternative therapeutic approaches that appear to offer any chance of success (Mitchell *et al.* 2002). Overall, about two-thirds of the women receiving therapy are reported to have fully recovered ninety months after treatment concluded (Herzog *et al.* 2000). In contrast to anorexia nervosa, it appears that women with bulimia nervosa tend to recover better the earlier the onset. It also seems that the seriousness of the initial psychological problems does not help to predict how good the recovery will be (Johnson-Sabine *et al.* 1992), although complications such as self-harming do (Paul *et al.* 2002).

If bulimia is developed in adolescence, when it emerges is increasingly seen as important. While developing bulimia early in adolescence is associated with a twenty-fold increase in risk for adult bulimia nervosa, developing it in late adolescence is associated with a thirty-five-fold increase in risk for adult problems (Kotler *et al.* 2001). Despite these increased risks, many do manage to put their eating problems behind them, but in those who do not there continue to be symptoms typical of a wide variety of different psychological problems (Collins and King 1994).

Conclusion

Eating is a crucial part of every person's life, and any disruption to it is potentially life threatening. It is therefore not surprising that disruption to eating, by whatever mechanism, provokes extreme concern from family and professionals alike. The research in the areas described here shows a steady move towards understanding what is the most effective way to intervene in such situations, hopefully giving the young person the best chance of minimising the impact of the eating disorder upon future life.

Sources of further help

www.askdrsears.com/html/4/t040200.asp
www.edauk.com
www.anorexia-uk.co.uk
www.mentalhealth.org.uk/html/content/bkannerv.cfm
www.nimh.nih.gov/publicat/eatingdisorder.cfm
www.eating-disorders.org.uk
www.anad.org

References

Bacaltchuk, J., Hay, P. and Trefiglio, R. (2001). Antidepressants versus psychological treatments and their combination for bulimia nervosa. *Cochrane Database Systematic Review* 4, CD003385.

Biller, B.M.K., Saxe, V. and Herzog, D.B. (1989). Mechanisms of osteoporosis in adult and adolescent women with anorexia nervosa. *Journal of Clinical Endocrinology and Metabolism* 68, 548–54.

Bulik, C.M., Sullivan, P.F., Fear, J.L., Pickering, A., Dawn, A. and McCullin, M. (1999). Fertility and reproduction in women with anorexia nervosa: a controlled study. *Journal of Clinical Psychiatry* 60, 130–5.

Chatoor, I. and Egan, J. (1987). Etiology and diagnosis of failure to thrive and growth disorders in infants and children. In J. Noshpitz (ed.) *Basic Handbook in Child Psychiatry*. New York: Basic Books.

Chatoor, I., Hirsch, R. and Persinger, M. (1997). Facilitating internal regulation of eating: a treatment model for infantile anorexia. *Infants Young Child* 9,12–22.

Collins, S. and King, M. (1994). Ten year follow up of 50 patients with bulimia nervosa. *British Journal of Psychiatry* 164, 80–7.

Crisp, A.H. (1980). *Anorexia Nervosa: Let Me Be*. London: Academic Press.

Dansky, B.S., Brewerton, T.D., Kilpatrick, D.G. (2000). Comorbidity of bulimia nervosa and alcohol use disorders: results from the national women's study. *International Journal of Eating Disorders* 27, 80–190.

Fairburn, C.G. and Beglin, S.J. (1990). Studies of the epidemiology of bulimia nervosa. *American Journal of Psychiatry* 147, 401–8.

Fairburn, C.G. and Harrison, P.J. (2003). *Lancet* 361, 407–16.

Fombonne, E. (1995a). Anorexia nervosa: no evidence of an increase. *British Journal of Psychiatry* 166, 462–71.

Fombonne, E. (1995b). Eating disorders: time trends and possible explanatory mechanisms. In M. Rutter and D.J. Smith (eds) *Psychosocial Disorders in Young People: Time Trends and Their Causes*. Chichester: John Wiley.

Garfinkel, P. and Garner, D. (1982). *Anorexia Nervosa – A Multidimensional Perspective*. New York: Brunner.

Goldstein, D.J., Wilson, M.G. and Thompson, V.L. (1995). Long term Fluoxetine treatment in bulimia nervosa. *British Journal of Psychiatry* 166, 660–6.

Gull, W.W. (1873). Anorexia hysterica (apepsia hysterica). *British Medical Journal* 2, 527–9.

Heebink, D.M., Sunday, S.R. and Halmi, K.A. (1995). Anorexia nervosa and bulimia nervosa in adolescence: effects of age and menstrual status on psychological variables. *Journal of the American Academy of Child and Adolescent Psychiatry* 34, 378–82.

Herzog, W., Schellberg, D. and Deter H.-C. (1997). First recovery of anorexia nervosa patients in the long-term course: a discrete-time survival study. *Journal of Consulting and Clinical Psychology* 65, 169–77.

Herzog, W., Greenwood, D.N., Dorer, D.J., Flores, A.T. and Ekeland, E.R. (2000). Mortality in eating disorders: a descriptive study. *International Journal of Eating Disorders* 28, 20–6.

Humphrey, L.L. (1994). Family relationship. In K.A. Halmi (ed.) *Psychobiology and Treatment of Anorexia Nervosa and Bulimia Nervosa*. Washington, DC: American Psychiatric Press.

Kotler, L.A., Cohen, P., Davies, M., Pine, D.S. and Walsh, B.T. (2001). Longitudinal relationships between childhood, adolescent and adult eating disorders. *Journal of the American Academy of Child & Adolescent Psychiatry* 40(12), 1434–1440.

Jacobs, B. and Isaacs, S. (1986). Pre-pubertal anorexia nervosa: a retrospective controlled trial. *Journal of Child Psychology and Psychiatry* 27, 237–50.

Johnson-Sabine, E., Reiss, D. and Dayson, D. (1992). Bulimia nervosa: a follow up study. *Psychological Medicine* 22, 951–9.

Kaye, W.H., Nagata, T. and Weltzin, T.E. (2001). Double-blind placebo-controlled administration of fluoxetine in restricting- and restricting-purging-type anorexia nervosa. *Biological Psychiatry* 49, 644–652.

Lilenfeld, L.R., Kaye, W.H. and Greeno, C.G. (1998). A controlled family study of anorexia nervosa and bulimia nervosa-psychiatric disorders in first-degree relatives and effects of proband comorbidity. *Archives of General Psychiatry* 55, 603–10.

Lucas, A.R., Beard, C.M. and O'Fallon, W.M. (1991). Fifty year trends in the incidence of anorexia nervosa in Rochester, Minnesota: a population-based study. *American Journal of Psychiatry* 148, 917–22.

Mehler, P.S. (2003). Osteoporosis in anorexia nervosa: prevention and treatment. *International Journal of Eating Disorders* 33, 113–26.

Minuchin, S., Rosman, B. and Baker, L. (1978). *Psychosomatic Families. Anorexia Nervosa in Context*. Cambridge, MA: Harvard University Press.

Mitchell, J.E., Halmi, K. and Wilson, G.T. (2002). A randomized secondary treatment study of women with bulimia nervosa who fail to respond to CBT. *International Journal of Eating Disorders* 32, 271–81.

Morris, D. (1967). *The Naked Ape: A Zoologist's Study of the Human Animal*. London: Jonathan Cape.

Nielsen, S., Moller-Madsen, S., Isager, T., Jorgensen, J. and Pagsberg, K. (1998). Standardised mortality in eating disorders – a quantitative study summary of previously published and new evidence. *Journal of Psychosomatic Research* 44, 413–34.

Overby, K.J. and Litt, I.F. (1988). Mediastinal emphysema in an adolescent with anorexia nervosa and self-induced emesis. *Pediatrics* 81, 134–6.

Oyebode, F., Boodhoo, J.A. and Schapira, K. (1988). Anorexia nervosa in males: clinical features and outcome. *International Journal of Eating Disorders* 7, 121–4.

Patton, G.C., Carlin, J.B., Shao, Q. and Hibbert, M.E. (1997). Adolescent dieting: healthy weight control or borderline eating disorder. *Journal of Child Psychology and Psychiatry* 38, 299–306.

Patton, G.C., Selzer, R., Coffey, C., Carlin, J.B. and Wolfe, R. (1999). Onset of adolescent eating disorders: population based cohort study over 3 years. *British Medical Journal* 318, 765–8.

Paul, T., Schroeter, K., Dahme, B., Nutzinger, D.O. (2002). Self-injurious behavior in women with eating disorders. *American Journal of Psychiatry* 159, 408–11.

Pope, H. and Hudson, J. (1992). Is childhood sexual abuse a risk factor for bulimia nervosa? *American Journal of Psychiatry* 149, 455–63.

Puckering, C., Pickles, A., Skuse, D. and Heptinstall, L. (1995). Mother–child interaction and the cognitive and behavioural development of four-year-old children with poor growth. *Journal of Child Psychology and Psychiatry* 36, 573–95.

Ratnasuriya, R.H., Eisler, I., Szmukler, G.I. and Russell G.F.M. (1990). Anorexia nervosa: outcome and prognostic factors after 20 years. *British Journal of Psychiatry* 158, 495–502.

Russell, G.F.M. (1979). Bulimia nervosa; an ominous variant of anorexia nervosa. *Psychological Medicine* 9, 429–448.

Russell, G.F.M. (1985). Premenstrual anorexia nervosa and its sequelae. *Journal of Psychiatric Research* 19, 363–9.

Russell, G.F.M., Szmukler, G.I., Dare, C. and Eiser, M.A. (1987). An evaluation of family therapy in anorexia nervosa and bulimia nervosa. *Archives of General Psychiatry* 44, 1047–56.

Schmidt, U., Hodes, M. and Treasure, J. (1992). Early onset bulimia nervosa – who is at risk? *Psychological Medicine* 22, 623–8.

Selvini-Palazzoli, M. (1974). *Self Starvation: From Individual to Family Therapy in the Treatment of Anorexia Nervosa.* New York: Aronson.

Sharp, C.W. and Freeman, C.P.L. (1993). The medical complications of anorexia nervosa. *British Journal of Psychiatry* 162, 452–62.

Steinhausen, H.Ch., Rauss-Mason, C. and Seidel, R. (1991). Follow up studies of anorexia nervosa: a review of four decades of outcome research. *Psychological Medicine* 21, 447–54.

Strober, M. (1991). Family-genetic studies in eating disorders. *Journal of Clinical Psychiatry* 52 (suppl. 10), 9–12.

Strober, M., Freeman, R., Morrell, W. (1997). The long-term course of severe anorexia nervosa in adolescents: survival analysis of recovery, relapse, and outcome predictors over 10–15 years in a prospective study. *International Journal of Eating Disorders* 22, 339–60.

Walford, G. and McCune, N. (1991). Long term outcome of early onset anorexia nervosa. *British Journal of Psychiatry* 159, 383–9.

Wentz, E., Gillberg, I.C., Gillberg, C. and Rastarn, M. (2000). Ten-year follow-up of adolescent-onset anorexia nervosa: physical health and neurodevelopment. *Developmental Medicine & Child Neurology* 42, 328–33.

Whitaker, A., Johnson, J., Shaffer, D. and Rapoport, J. (1990). Uncommon troubles in young people: prevalence estimates of selected psychiatric disorders in a non-referred psychiatric population. *Archives of General Psychiatry* 47, 487–96.

Yager, J.Y., Andersen, A., Devlin, M., Egger, H., Herzog, D. and Mitchell, J. (2000). Practice guidelines for the treatment of patients with eating disorders (revision). *American Journal of Psychiatry* 157 (supplement 1).

Zipfel, S., Lowe, B., Reas, D.L., Deter, H.-C. and Herzog, W. (2000). Long-term prognosis in anorexia nervosa. *Lancet* 355, 721–2.

Chapter 6

Traumatic and stressful situations

General considerations

It is an interesting observation that while some people can cope with adversity without experiencing great distress others become stuck in remembrance, misery and fear. It is not fully understood why there should be such a variation in reaction, but it does seem that in general adverse life events are linked to the development of psychiatric illness in adolescence. These effects are relatively non-specific in that such adverse events do not predict what type of psychiatric illness the teenager may develop or how severe that illness may prove. The work in this area does show that some children are protected from the harmful effects of negative life events by their own inner strengths (Goodyer 1993), while others can be assisted to develop such resilience through appropriate therapeutic measures (Place et al. 2002).

A key factor in trying to predict how a traumatic event might be dealt with is the child's age. At about two years of age the toddler can distinguish individuals and begin to recreate experiences in play. Through this the child can recognise that events have occurred but cannot set them in any context. This means that at this age a child can't anticipate events or consequences very easily because the context that would act as a warning is missing. By the age of three years the child's play is becoming more sophisticated and is starting to become the medium through which the child seeks to gain an understanding of the world. With this development also comes a fundamental change of thinking as the child begins to shed the belief that the world is governed solely by their actions.

Around the age of four years the child develops the ability to recognise alternative ways of proceeding and can favour one over another, which is the beginning of the child recognising that there can be alternative origins for problems other than the child's own action. By six years of age this ability is so fully developed that the child is then able to relate the causes of events to origins which the child recognises he or she can't influence. The importance of this developmental sequence is that a child younger than five years of age is likely to view any traumatic event as something that they caused to occur.

The death of a parent, for instance, will be linked to some fleeting thought about wishing them dead, or a sequence of abuse will be seen by the child as something that they are responsible for. Such an attribution can be a major source of guilt for a child, and act as the stimulus for the development of a variety of psychological difficulties at the time, and into the future.

Specifically stressful situations

Bereavement

As with all other aspects of coping with stressful events, the age at which children are asked to cope can have a crucial impact on how they deal with stressful events. Following bereavement, children younger than five years of age see death as reversible and so the person has simply gone somewhere else, and may perhaps return one day. This belief is simultaneously reassuring to the child and disconcerting for adults, who may feel that the child's lack of marked distress is because 'they don't care' or because 'it hasn't sunk in yet'. In fact neither of these is the case – the child simply believes the person is elsewhere, a fact which is not a cause for distress.

By the age of seven years the child can recognise that death is an ending and is permanent. As a result, in children of this age the loss of a loved one can have quite an impact, for the child can recognise the loss but does not have the emotional experience or maturity with which to deal with it. In children over seven years of age, therefore, the sense of loss can provoke reactions which approximate those seen in adults. Immediately upon learning of the loss there is a sense of shock and disbelief. The young person often appears dazed, but in the following days there is the emergence of misery, and possibly an attempt to withdraw from company. There is usually a deterioration in sleep patterns and concentration, and eating habits change. There are broadly two patterns that young people may display in the weeks following the death of significant figures in their lives. The first is where the child may find it so difficult to come to terms with the loss that he or she tries to retain a 'relationship' in some way. This often takes the form of retaining a keepsake, or having feelings that the person is still with them (Silverman *et al.* 1992). Sometimes the child may report seeing or hearing the person, but these events are not of the same quality as the hallucinations seen in major psychotic illnesses. In such young people reunion fantasies are quite common, and this pattern can cause adults to become quite concerned about the child.

The second type of reaction is typically seen after a traumatic death. Children feel overwhelmed by the distress and so seek to avoid any remembrance of it. They will avoid items, or situations, that could act as reminders, and begin to fear that other significant people may also suddenly be taken from them. This can be compounded if they associate the death with some threat or wish that they uttered in anger, for the magical thinking that is so prevalent in the early school years can easily link two such events. This leads children to believe that others may be in danger from their anger, and prompts further withdrawal from social groupings. This pattern of avoidance and withdrawal can significantly distort the grieving process, and if prolonged may need professional intervention.

Commonly, in the aftermath of a significant bereavement, children will lose motivation to do schoolwork, and will often report intrusive thoughts or images associated with the dead person crowding into their minds when they try to work or study. There may be a sequence of minor illnesses, which can be an effective way of obtaining adult concern and care for a child who does not fully understand that being bereaved can obtain such support in its own right.

Over the subsequent weeks these intense emotions give way to a more blunted pattern of sadness and irritability, and sometimes there is the emergence of aggression. If the children are able to share their feelings they often report feeling particularly distressed by remembrances, items that remind them of the person, or dates that have particular significance. Over the subsequent months these features fade and become less frequent, so that by eighteen months most have effectively dealt with their feelings and stop grieving. Very few young people go on to have adult problems as a result of a bereavement (Fristad *et al.* 1993), and the strongest determinant of whether this will occur is the quality of childcare offered in the aftermath of the bereavement (Breier *et al.* 1988). Indeed, some young people take on a more mature perspective as the result of suffering a bereavement and emerge better equipped to cope with future adversity (Balk 1990). This in itself can sometimes be problematic, for if a child with this sense of responsibility feels obliged to assume a parenting role within the family (to allow the parents the space to grieve themselves), then this can, if prolonged, begin to distort the developmental path of the young person.

The other crucial factor which influences a child's reaction to a death is the relationship that existed before the bereavement. The death of a distant relative will prompt little in the way of direct grief, and most of the child's behaviour will be in response to the parents' reactions to the news. If, however, the death is of a parent with whom the child had a close relationship, then the child can feel a keen sense of abandonment and quite a profound bereavement reaction will ensue.

Responses and intervention following bereavement

When children are faced with coping with the loss of a significant adult it is important to consider the child's age. In younger children it is necessary to be prepared for indifference, and perhaps a surprising lack of distress. Indeed, in younger children it is often the adults who need reassurance that the child's reaction is quite age-appropriate, and not a sign that there are deeply repressed feelings that will later cause the young person major problems.

In older children the first need is to establish a supportive and caring environment. It is important to recognise that the child will have questions and strong emotions that must be dealt with. Children may not feel able, or feel they haven't permission, to grieve, or may not know how to respond to the emotions that they are experiencing. The supportive response is to let the child feel that it's acceptable to be upset, and perhaps even confirm that being tearful at such times is a natural reaction. It is also usually helpful if the child attends the funeral. Most children express a desire to attend the ceremony, and research indicates that attendance is generally beneficial to their ultimate adjustment (Weller *et al.* 1988).

Following an intensely distressing bereavement it is important to keep a special watch for a young person who, in the aftermath of a bereavement which has severely touched a parent, becomes a parent to the rest of the family. Initially, this can be seen as helpful – getting other children in the family ready for school or accepting more household tasks so that the parent can rest. To a certain degree such a shift in role can also make a positive contribution to the child's maturation process, but, if too intense, or if the child is too young to assume such responsibility, then their longer-term development may be adversely affected. In the shorter term such a shift in family roles may also limit the amount of grieving which the child can actually do, and so leave unresolved problems which may manifest in other ways – for instance, as physical symptoms such as headaches.

Another way that children may miss out on their own grieving process is if their sense of duty prompts them to make efforts to distract their parents from their grief. This often takes the form of misbehaviour, since this is the most potent way of obtaining parental attention, and certainly is capable of demanding a high priority in their parents' concerns.

Alex presented at eight years of age with a six-month history of being difficult and truculent at home. His mother said he had become defiant and everything had become a battle. Alex's parents saw the behaviour as particularly problematic because their younger child had developed leukaemia some months ago and they felt they had enough worries without having to respond to Alex's tantrums and defiance.

When seen alone, Alex quickly became weepy and distressed, saying that he was very concerned about his brother, but since he had developed his illness his parents spent all their spare time with him, and Alex felt he had no time with them. He said of the last few weeks that 'they aren't crying all the time now, they're too busy shouting at me'.

A further mechanism by which poor behaviour can emerge is if the parents have been so deeply affected by the loss that their parenting abilities have become blunted, or they have lost the motivation to keep insisting upon good behaviour. Looser boundaries and less certain responses to challenge can allow poor behaviour to surface and it often reaches quite a marked level before the parent realises how much things have deteriorated.

Work with adolescents suggests that young people of this age feel better if they can talk about their feelings of loss with their peers (Gray 1989), but many worry that their emotional distress will be too much for their friends to cope with, or may not know how to express how they are feeling. This awkwardness and uncertainty about how to behave tends to drive the young person to withdraw into solitude. This is probably why many teenagers report that their friendships deteriorate in the aftermath of a bereavement (Balk 1990).

If the young person retains good social links and is keeping up with schoolwork, then they are coping well with the situation and do not require outside assistance. As Dyregrov (1991) has outlined, however, there are several elements that are worth pursuing after a bereavement in order to make sure that the grief is dealt with appropriately.

- Ensure that the child gets information on the illness or circumstances of the death. It is important that they understand the situation properly, and to this end the explanations must be concrete and explicit.
- Correct any misunderstandings or wrong information.
- Give the child explicit permission to grieve, and offer opportunities to do so in a safe environment. In younger children features of the death may dominate pictures and play for some weeks after, and this should be accepted as the norm.
- Give information on how people grieve, in particular confirming that it's appropriate to have a range of feelings, not only sadness at the loss, but anger that they have been deserted.
- Re-establish routines as soon as practicable – returning to the familiar and the predictable helps to minimise the fears that the young person's own future is threatened by the loss.
- Help retain peer links, but this should be by offering opportunities not by creating any sense of pressure.
- Reinforce parental strength and control, and ensure that rules are still enforced. This gives the necessary sense of support to the young person, as well as offering the same predictability as existed before the loss.
- Parents should also be encouraged to plan how they will respond to their children so that they can reaffirm that they are solid and dependable.
- Most children benefit from being given the opportunity to say 'goodbye' properly. The younger the child the more concrete this expression tends to be – for example, a young child may wish to place a favourite toy upon the grave.

As well as these typical bereavement processes there are two special situations that are worthy of mention. The first is when the child is witness to a particularly horrific death. In these situations professional help from the local social services department, or through the family doctor, is nearly always necessary if the child is to resolve fully the feelings such an experience provokes. A variation on this theme, which brings with it myriad emotional problems, is the thankfully rare situation when one parent kills another. Although the processes are not very different, specialised assistance, through the agencies mentioned, is necessary (Hendriks *et al.* 1993).

The second situation is when a classmate has a terminal illness, and so it can be seen that a whole class will have to cope with a bereavement. In such a situation it is helpful to prepare the class by giving the information in a structured way, and prompting class members to plan how they will react and respond (Yule and Gold 1993).

Growing up in a violent household

There is increasing concern that growing up in a household where there is violence has a damaging effect upon a child's development. This arises not only because of the direct impact that witnessing or being a victim of violence causes, but indirectly because of the way that the violence prevents effective parenting from being given.

Research in this field has indicated that physically abused toddlers tend to show far more angry noncompliance than their peers, and are easily frustrated in tasks or games (Erickson *et al.* 1989). Older children tend to show disruptive and aggressive reactions (Shields *et al.* 1994). A particularly interesting observation is that boys who have grown up in violent households appear to become more aroused by angry exchanges than peers, and perhaps as a consequence are far more likely to involve themselves in the angry exchanges (Cummings *et al.* 1994). This pattern tends to recur throughout their lives, with exposure to such violence being associated with later increased risks of anxiety, conduct disorder, problems with alcohol, and criminal offending (Fergusson and Horwood 1998). As adults they are also particularly prone to having romantic relationships which are punctuated by violent and abusive episodes (Lavoie *et al.* 2002).

Cicchetti and Toth (1995) have described how growing up in a violent household, or being the victim of any type of abuse, has the potential to distort four areas of a child's functioning:

- emotional regulation;
- attachment;
- sense of self;
- peer relationships.

Emotional regulation comprises the way the young person copes with feelings and, as already pointed out, this can mean exaggerated reactions, or responses which are too quick and ill thought out, to situations of potential aggression. In other situations the emotion may be more the expected ones of misery or distress, but prompted by trivial and unrelated situations, which can give the impression that the young person is moody or suffering from a depressive illness when in fact the problem is a distorted regulatory mechanism.

Attachment to the parent is the first, and perhaps most fundamental, relationship which a child achieves. It helps to establish a pattern of emotions, thoughts and expectations which become the yardstick for all future relationships to be judged by. Abused children have more insecure attachments (Crittenden 1988) and this often means that the toddler finds it difficult to cope with separation, giving a 'disorganised', disorientated quality to the pattern of dealing with the daily separations which are part of any child's life (Carlson et al. 1989). However, if toddlerhood is without major incident, and the negative experiences begin later in life, then the risk of disturbing attachment markedly decreases (Lynch and Cicchetti 1991). As parents, young people who have experienced disturbed attachment have poorer parenting practices, and are more likely to maltreat their own children (Main and Goldwyn 1984). This is largely because, since they have not developed solid attachments in childhood, they find it particularly difficult to develop such attachments with their own children.

The child's sense of self becomes established by the age of two years, and, as already mentioned, with this begins the process of developing a capacity to use play to represent situations, which in turn helps the child understand what he or she is responsible for, and what part others play in bringing events about. If young people have abusive experiences before this age, then this sense of self is distorted. Such children find it harder to engage in the symbolic play so typical of toddlerhood (Alessandri 1991) and they tend to be more aggressive and less competent with their peers. Such young people show a low self-esteem and have less sense of being able to cope (Cicchetti and Toth 1995).

As has already been pointed out in Chapter 1, establishing effective peer relationships is a key developmental issue for all children. Violent experiences can distort this process because such young people have heightened levels of physical and verbal aggression and may respond in this way to friendly overtures and even signs of distress in others (Mueller and Silverman 1989). The other reaction which is commonly seen, and which can significantly disturb peer-relationship development, is a withdrawal from peer interactions and an avoidance of activities where the young person is expected to mix with peers (Rogosch and Cicchetti 1994).

Interestingly, parents who maltreat their children often have high expectations of their performance, and yet they do not provide the support necessary to achieve the goals they set. For instance, they provide less verbal stimulation to their children and do not encourage autonomy, both of which are important in fostering achievement (Trickett *et al.* 1991). In addition, these parents see childrearing as less enjoyable and use more controlling disciplinary techniques than average. Because these children tend to be quite challenging, schools can easily replicate this pattern of management, and with it become identified with the parents. The antipathy which is felt for the parents can, in these circumstances, then be acted out against the school.

In the longer term young people who have grown up in violent households, or experienced significant abuse as children can develop depression (Toth *et al.* 1992), but most commonly they go on to have problems with delinquency (Lewis *et al.* 1989), and to show a violent tendency in their relationships (Malinosky-Rummell and Hansen 1993).

Responding to children who are growing up in a violent household

Helping young people who have experienced a violent upbringing has many similarities to the response offered to children who have been the victims of abuse. The intervention focuses on three areas, the first of which is the family element. It is essential that the functioning of the parental figures is well understood, in particular their own childhood history, and their perceptions, feelings and reactions to the child. If any of these elements show distortion, intervention may need to be offered using either cognitive approaches or family therapy techniques (see Chapter 2). If there are problems within the parent–child interaction then parental depression must be excluded as a cause. If it is truly interactional then play sessions with parent and child can help to establish the necessary rapport and make a contribution to efforts to correct problems with the attachment process (Lieberman *et al.* 1991).

The second element is work with the child. This can only begin once it is clear that the child is now safe from violent or abusive experiences. A child cannot begin to deal with painful issues of this kind unless it is clear that such events are now in the past. To ask a child to explore such issues when they may recur invites them to expose themselves to even greater harm. This is because within any therapeutic process young people must question and challenge their beliefs, ventilate the anger which they have harboured, and perhaps ask difficult questions of their parents. To attempt this when further violence or abuse is possible is dangerous indeed.

If the young person can feel trust and security within the treatment relationship, then these emotions and themes can be explored in a gradual manner. As the process progresses the expressions of emotion become more marked before a gradual subsidence of the difficulties occurs. It is important to be alert to these changes: good therapy makes things worse before it makes them better.

The last element of an intervention programme focuses on the environment in which the child is living. One aspect of this is clearly to remove the potential for further violence or abuse, but there are also the important themes of maintaining routines and allowing the child experiences of success. In addition, positive relationships of all kinds are important in offering alternative experiences to those that are being worked with in the therapeutic alliance.

The importance of intervention is not only due to its effect on immediate disturbances and difficulties, but because it decreases the probability of the young person developing major problems in later life. In particular, effective intervention reduces the likelihood of there being relationship problems in adulthood, as well as reducing the risk of the pattern being repeated when the former victims become parents themselves (National Research Council 1993). However the longer the abuse has been occurring, the more likely there are to be physical changes within the brain (Glaser 2000), which in turn reduces the chances of making a significant impact upon the young person's longer-term functioning.

Being the victim of sexual abuse

Many of the themes relevant to children growing up in a violent household are commonly found in other forms of abusive situation, but being the victim of sexual abuse does carry with it specific issues and reactions which are worthy of separate consideration.

Sexual abuse is a term which can encompass a wide range of inappropriate sexual activity from fondling to full intercourse, with about 5 per cent of reported incidents involving penetrative intercourse (Baker and Duncan 1985). Girls are 2.5 times more likely to be the victim than boys (Finkelhor 1986), and although the child can be any age, it is most common for it to begin between the ages of eight and twelve years (Monck *et al.* 1993). Such abuse occurs irrespective of social status or religious persuasion and in many of the cases the abuse is a repeated act over several years. Most cases are never reported, and it has been estimated that as few as 2 per cent of cases are brought to the attention of the authorities (Russell 1983), with incest with a sibling probably being the most common (Finkelhor 1979), and yet least reported. The type of difficulty experienced by the young person depends on five factors:

- the age and stage of development at the time of the abuse;
- the type of abuse that occurred;
- the sophistication of the young person's own coping mechanisms for dealing with the emotions it provokes;
- the caregiver's reactions and innate mechanisms for coping with the feelings which the abuse raises;

- the environmental factors: for example, does the abuser still see the child?

Generally, sexual abuse results in significant psychiatric impairment in the victims, most typically oppositional defiance, anxiety or depression (Merry and Andrews 1994). By and large, the severity of the abuse, the use of force, and victim's relationship to the perpetrator have all been found to be linked to a poorer outcome, whilst strong family support and parental monitoring tend to reduce the impact (Tyler 2002). It is also interesting to note that when the victim is a boy, the long-term effects may be more severe and more complex in nature than previously thought (Garnefski and Diekstra 1997).

In the immediate aftermath anxiety symptoms tend to be the most evident – evidenced by insomnia, nightmares and somatic complaints, with half of the cases having the severe symptoms associated with post-traumatic stress disorder (PTSD) – re-experiencing the trauma, flashbacks and avoiding situations which might act as reminders (McLeer *et al.* 1988). Indeed, for some children the trauma of the experience can be so great that they try to distance themselves from the events by 'forgetting' that they occurred. This defence against pain is known as denial and can be sustained for quite long periods of time, but for some the memories do return in later life; indeed, it is now becoming increasingly common for adults with psychiatric illnesses to disclose that they have been the victims of sexual abuse as children, raising questions as to the part that such traumas play in the causation of psychiatric illness (Sheldrick 1991).

The other defence mechanism that some children use is dissociation. Here the child escapes into 'another life' where such painful experiences do not occur. There are periods of amnesia, intense daydreaming and going into a trance-like state which can occasionally lead to the child developing multiple 'personalities', each with its own characteristics, a disorder which is very disruptive to functioning when an adult.

Although such defence mechanisms can clearly have a profound effect upon long-term functioning, lesser effects can cause havoc to the self-image of a child. Most victims of abuse see themselves as 'damaged goods' because of their experiences (Sgroi 1982), and this compounds the feelings of depression and misery that are so common for the children to have. This is why so many victims in adult life have marked psychiatric problems such as major depressive illnesses (Livingstone 1987), eating disorders (Pope and Hudson 1992) and drug abuse (Goodwin *et al.* 1990). In addition to such defined problems there are often difficulties in relating to peers (Sgroi 1982) and a trend towards excessive aggression when thwarted or angry (Friedrich *et al.* 1986).

About 16 per cent of children report feelings of arousal within the abusive relationship (Monck *et al.* 1993). The sense of conflict between these feelings and the knowledge of being abused can be a powerful force in creating psychiatric problems.

One of the most consistent observations is the way that sexually abusive experiences distort the child's own sexual functioning, and this seems especially true if the abuse occurred before the age of seven years (McClellan *et al.* 1996). Public masturbation and the tendency to repeat sexually abusive experiences are very common patterns (Monck *et al.* 1993). Infants who have been abused find it difficult to distinguish appropriate displays of affection from the episodes of sexual activity (Yates 1982), leading to abused toddlers showing quite explicitly sexual behaviour. It is important to remember that children learn about sexuality, they are not born with an innate knowledge; so if they are sexually explicit, this is because of what they have seen or experienced.

Sara was four years of age when her nursery became concerned at her sexualised play. She would openly masturbate while playing, and would sit on adults' knees, rocking slowly while making a moaning sound and becoming quite excited. Investigations revealed that Sara had been subjected to repeated sexual abuse from the age of two years of age, as had her elder sister.

It is within the nature of any painful or traumatic event that extreme reactions can take the form of seeking out more similar experiences, or trying to avoid them. So it is with sexual abuse, for as well as sexual acting out the child can react by avoiding sexual situations, and attempting to repress sexual feelings (Finkelhor 1979). While this may not be too problematic in childhood, such a way of coping with the painful experiences can have a profound effect upon adult relationships, especially when they are also influenced by disturbance of gender identity. This disturbance can show itself in girls as a drive to be more masculine in demeanour, and to express a strong preference to become a boy (Cosentino 1993). Similar gender confusion has been noted in abused boys and it is postulated that such confusion may prompt experimentation with homosexuality (Singer 1989).

The age of children can quite markedly influence the pattern seen, because if children are very young, then, as was described earlier, the ability to distinguish whether they caused the abuse is poorly developed and they will tend to accept it as part of routine adult–child interaction. In addition, the belief in the authority of adults means that if the abuse is perceived as wrong, the child is likely to see it as occurring because of the bad things they have done. Such beliefs can form a powerful foundation for children to believe they are bad, unlovable, or worthy of punishment – all strong causes for having major adjustment problems in adult life.

In considering the list on p. 106, it is clear that only the last three factors can be influenced, and so it is important that all three of these aspects are addressed if any meaningful help is to be offered (Cicchetti and Toth 1995). Sexually abused children are often seen within school to be anxious, inattentive and unable to understand classroom expectations. They tend to be unpopular with peers, and show an increased frequency of withdrawal and aggressive outbursts in any interactions they have with them. Typically, they tend to get by because they are highly dependent upon teachers (Erickson *et al.* 1989).

Intervention with children who have been sexually abused

The first requirement of any intervention is to recognise that abuse is occurring. The majority of cases comes to light because of a disclosure by the child, and so an essential first principle is to accept the child's statements when first told. Being the victim of abuse can provoke quite significant behavioural difficulties and so it is dangerous to dismiss a child's report of abuse simply because they have been troublesome in the past.

If one is the recipient of a disclosure of any type of abuse, one should offer a calm and accepting demeanour. Responses should be in a supportive tone, and either a repetition of their last phrase, or simple requests for them to continue. The information must be passed on to the relevant professionals and so any promise to 'keep the secret' must be avoided. Record as accurately and as soon as possible what was said, and then follow the advice about making a referral that is contained in the Child Protection Procedures manual.

The professional network of social workers and police acts on the disclosure by carrying out a careful investigation. The first priority is always to ensure that the child is safe from further abuse, and in half of the families the concern about how supportive the family will be is sufficient for the child to be accommodated away from home (Monck *et al.* 1993).

Upon completion of the assessment there may be legal action in the form of civil proceedings (care order applications and so on) or criminal proceedings against the abusing adult. The timing of therapy has to be considered in the light of such proceedings because any formal intervention needs to occur in the context of a supportive and consistent parenting regime. The sense of control and parental containment enhances the sense of safety that is crucial if children are to surrender their defences and allow themselves fully to explore the emotions and beliefs that are associated with their abuse experiences. The choice of timing is also important in ensuring that the courts, in the case of criminal proceedings, do not feel that therapeutic work has contaminated the child's evidence.

Initial intervention is focused upon ventilating feelings, and this is achieved by repeatedly exploring the events and exposing the associated emotional elements. With such processes the distress should gradually subside and children develop a better understanding of the events and their part within them (Berliner 1990). If the child remains cool and detached despite evidence of traumatic abuse experiences, then it is likely that he or she is trying to cope with the events by dissociation or denial (see above). This is especially likely if the abuse experiences are multiple or occur over a long period. In such situations formal psychiatric help is indicated, and the situation is likely to demand a lengthy intervention.

In most cases a variety of approaches is necessary in order to address the various types of difficulty that abuse can cause. The sexualised components are addressed initially by age-appropriate sex education and establishing with the child what are the age-appropriate ways of dealing with sexual needs and urges (Berliner 1990). Group therapy can help significantly in dealing with children's belief that they are the only ones to whom this has happened, as well as helping to reduce the intensity of behavioural problems (Nekli and Waters 1989). Cognitive therapy has also been shown to offer specific assistance in reducing the difficulties associated with abuse (Cohen and Mannarino 1996). In addition, work with the abuser, and the wider family, is usually occurring at the same time and is primarily looking to understand why it occurred and exploring how such abusive behaviour can be prevented in future.

It is important within this process not to lose sight of parental distress, since the success of such programmes can be strongly influenced by how well the parents are coping (Cohen and Mannarino 1996).

There are three potential solutions to the problem of ensuring that in future the child has a safe and supportive environment:

- reintegration back into a complete family; however, this is possible in only about 15 per cent of cases (Bentovim *et al.* 1988);
- remaining with the non-abusing parent: this is the commonest solution;
- being accommodated with an alternative family: this is the solution when the family's support and protection is deemed inadequate.

Outcome for sexually abused children

The studies carried out among adults reveal the potential that exists for sexually abusive experiences in childhood to prompt major psychiatric difficulties in adult life. In particular there is concern that abused children may become abusing adults, and a great deal of therapeutic effort is focused upon trying to break this cycle. It is clear that the present intervention programmes are effective at reducing the symptoms which show themselves after disclosure of abuse (Monck *et al.* 1993), but female sexual abuse victims continue to experience more relationship problems and more problems in sexual functioning (Rumstein-McKean and Hunsley 2001). Sexual offending usually begins in adolescence (Butler and Seto 2002), with the mean age being about fourteen years of age (Salter *et al.* 2003), and it is probable that about 12 per cent of childhood victims of sexual abuse go on to become abusers themselves (Salter *et al.* 2003). Becoming a perpetrator seems to be particularly likely if the initial abuser was a female relative (Glasser *et al.* 2001). Finally it is increasingly evident that being the victim of abuse makes the young person far more likely to develop physical health problems (Dube *et al.* 2003) which, combined with the psychological aftermath, clearly presents the young person with considerable challenges to their coping abilities.

Coping with parental separation and divorce

Parental separation is one of the most common traumatic events that a child can face. In fact children who have experienced a separation or divorce are up to three times more likely to have emotional and behavioural difficulties than the average, with children of divorced showing poorer academic achievement, having more conduct and psychological adjustment problems, as well a low self-concept, and poorer social relations than their peers (Amato 2001). However, it is very rarely a single event, for, in the vast majority of cases, there has been ongoing relationship difficulty between the parents before the specific act of separation occurs. Wallerstein and Blakeslee (1989) describe three phases of separation:

1 *Acute*: a highly emotional phase with tense conflict between the parents and one (or even both) may develop depression or even become suicidal. This phase is usually relatively brief, but can last for several years if the couple becomes trapped in a sequence of legal battles, personal recriminations or ploys to try to re-establish the relationship.
2 *Transitional*: the parents begin to distance themselves from each other and establish new relationships. This is a period of excitement but also of uncertainties.
3 *Settlement*: new patterns of living are established and there is no longer direct emotional linkage to the ex-partner.

With the separation of parents come changes in income and perhaps of home and school. As the phases described above indicate, there is also a change in the emotional tenor of the parents, which may lead to psychiatric illness. With the fracture of the previous parenting system and these marked emotional changes in the immediate aftermath of the separation, the parenting offered to the child may diminish. This can become an ongoing problem if the custodial parent does not establish a new equilibrium quickly, or if the search to replace the lost partner detracts too much from the reassertion of appropriate parenting patterns. Equally problematic is if the child becomes a parent's prop through this difficult period, for a dependency on the child can then develop which makes normal development tasks far harder for the child to achieve.

A sadly common consequence of separation is the pattern of ongoing friction between the parents which superficially can be focused upon contact or financial settlements, but in fact is a continuation of their relationship conflict. Within this type of conflict there can be competition for the affection and allegiance of the child which can take many forms, few of which are helpful to the child's development.

Michael was six years old when his parents separated. Michael's mother was very bitter at her husband's departure and the way that he had 'deserted the family'. She resisted any idea of ongoing contact between Michael and his father because she feared he would 'pick up his habits and his ways'. The court imposed regular contact at a neutral venue and before each meeting Michael's mother would remind him that his father was 'a bad man'. After the visits she would closely question Michael about his father's present lifestyle, whether he had a new partner and so on.

A situation such as this imposes major stress upon the child. Not only is there a need not to upset the parent who looks after you, but any suggestion of liking the other parent is seen as disloyalty. Equally, the contact sessions cannot be enjoyed for their own sake because of the danger of fuelling the battle by some inadvertent comment.

Coping with the separation and divorce is actually the final stage of the process which has entangled the family in ongoing friction and emotional upheaval, usually for a lengthy period. Indeed, such marital friction is more damaging to a child than the separation itself, especially for boys where such problems usually prompt acting-out behaviour (Cherlin *et al.* 1991). The elements described in the section on violent households (see above) are equally relevant here, as are the concerns about how the friction might affect the future functioning of the child.

Faced with the distress of parental separation, children react as they would to any very painful situation. Initially, the dominant feeling is one of their present world collapsing, and a sense of anxiety, perhaps even dread of the future. Their grief at the loss of their family is usually compounded by concern at the distress shown by their parents, and bewilderment as their loyalty to both parents is challenged. Pre-school children resist separation, become more demanding, cry frequently, and may 'lose' acquired routines such as table manners or developmental skills such as toileting. Sleep disturbances are common, as is behaving more aggressively towards parents, siblings and peers. In this age group it is not the parental separation itself that seems to be the determining factor; rather it is related to factors within the mother such as her income, level of education, her childrearing beliefs, and the level of intrinsic depression she is showing (Clarke-Stewart *et al.* 2000). Thus in this young age group it is more to do with how the parent manages the effects of separation that determine its long-term effects, rather than the separation itself.

When the separation occurs at a time when the children are just established in school, they have vivid concerns as to whether the departed parent will continue to care for them and they show open grief at the separation. Children of this age find it difficult to understand the complexities of the situation and often seek to resolve the hurt by trying to reunite the parents.

Jeanette was seven years old at the time her parents separated. To that point there had been no concern about her development or functioning, but in the weeks following the separation her behaviour in school deteriorated and she became more challenging towards her mother within the home. These episodes of refusal to comply were only stopped by Jeanette's father coming to the home and 'taking charge'. Jeanette told her father that she liked it when he came back to the house and she would stop being naughty if he moved back permanently.

When the separation occurs just before puberty, the child's ability to understand the issues is greater and the child's own reactions are more complex. However, overall, the reaction is still rather black and white and is often typified by anger at the 'bad' parent for causing the separation, and an intense commitment to care for the 'hurt' one. Such commitment can interfere with peer relationships and school performance, as these elements are given second place to being with the parent that 'needs them'.

Parental separation during children's adolescence complicates a time when they are endeavouring to cope with their own emotional storms brought on by this developmental stage. The additional stress of the separation tends to intensify the existing emotional features and can precipitate the emergence of acting-out behaviour, depression or even suicidal feelings. At this age, the concrete thinking of the child is giving way to a more abstract and complex understanding of situations which can often lead to the adolescent reaching a strongly held view as to how the events leading up to the separation should be interpreted.

Although in general boys appear to fare somewhat worse than girls in the aftermath of parental separation (Block *et al.* 1981), when adolescence is reached girls of separated parents do experience greater difficulty than the average in separating from their mothers (Kalter *et al.* 1985). A good relationship with one or both parents predicts a better outcome (Emery 1982), and a helpful supportive adult outside the family can offer additional benefit in helping the child cope with the stresses within the family (Lussier *et al.* 2002). However, overall, it is how parents cope with the trauma of separation and divorce that is the major determinant of how children will cope (Guidubaldi and Perry 1985), and to what extent they will carry a fear of failed relationships into their adult lives.

Assisting the process of coming to terms with parental separation

The first strand of intervention is to endeavour to establish an amicable and flexible atmosphere between the separating parents to minimise the child's sense of being 'in the middle'. Successful resolution of the family law issues of custody, contact and maintenance is crucial to setting the tone in which the child's future functioning will be determined. There are six tasks that children must achieve if they are to minimise the impact of parental separation (after Wallerstein 1983):

*   acknowledge the reality of the separation;
*   distance themselves from parental conflicts and distress, and re-establish normal routines;
*   come to terms with the losses that separation has prompted;
*   resolve their sense of anger and self-blame;
*   accept the permanence of the separation;
*   set realistic goals for future relationships with parents and new parental figures.

Adults in contact with the child can facilitate this process by being available, understanding and supportive, and being so without being drawn into the value judgements about parental behaviour which often dominate the child's thinking in the early stages.

Children trapped in acrimonious separations, or who are reacting badly to the family changes, may require more focused help. This commonly takes the form of group work where the child can share feelings and recognise he or she is not the only one to whom this has happened. In addition, an active group process can help to reduce the intensity of emotional and behavioural problems, as well as improving peer skills. Individual work needs to address the child's beliefs, attitude and feelings about the separation, and examine closely the child's position within the new domestic arrangements. Seeing the family as a whole can also be helpful in dealing with situations where the child is caught between warring parents, but such intervention needs to be finely judged, because a child may be punished by one of the parents if his or her contribution within the session was not seen as supportive enough of the parent's point of view.

Coming to terms with physical illness

In the western world about 5 per cent of children have a significant, handi-capping physical disorder (Pless and Nolan 1991). How such children react to their difficulties is very varied, but the trend is that the more severe the handicap, the greater the risk of the young person developing a psychiatric disorder (Daud *et al.* 1993). However, most young people do cope, and those who seek to cope actively by thinking of other things or using calming self-statements tend to fare much better than those who simply hope things will be all right (Gil *et al.* 1991). When problems do occur, they tend to show themselves either as emotional symptoms or as eating anomalies (Pearson *et al.* 1991).

Paradoxically, although the development of a significant disability obviously has a major impact upon the young person, it is the impact that it has upon the parent which is often the most significant for predicting future psychological difficulties. As a result of coming to terms with their child's disability or illness, the parents may become depressed or overprotective, or lose interest in the child, all of which can have a marked effect upon the child's development. However, if support can be mobilised for the parents through counselling or formal psychiatric help, then the attentiveness to the child can become more average, and hence more healthy for the child (Reynolds *et al.* 1988).

Illnesses or injuries which involve the brain are particularly problematic and evidence suggests that children with epilepsy, for instance, may be up to four times more likely to develop psychiatric problems than the general population, particularly if there are other neurological abnormalities evident (Rutter *et al.* 1970). It is not only the direct impact of the illness which causes the problems, however, for children with epilepsy are also more prone to show an inappropriate level of dependency than their peers (Hoare 1984). In some people it is clear that seizures can be provoked by becoming emo-tional or feeling stressed. This observation has prompted the development of programmes which look to control seizures using psychological methods, and there is evidence that teaching appropriate psychological and behavioural techniques can offer some people a degree of control (Motofsky and Balaschak 1977).

Head injuries may result in a child developing a seizure problem, but such an injury may prompt psychological difficulties even without the emergence of post-traumatic epilepsy. It is possible that even mild head injuries may result in psychological difficulties (Middleton 1989), but the vast majority of such injuries cause problems that are transient and quickly resolved. In severe head injuries, however, up to 50 per cent of victims will show long-term psychiatric problems (Max *et al.* 1998), and this is most likely in those who had some emotional or behavioural difficulties before the injury occurred. The likelihood of future difficulties can also be predicted by how much of the immediate post-accident events the child can't remember. If the period of this post-traumatic amnesia is for the events which have occurred more than a week after the accident then psychiatric difficulties are increasingly likely (Chadwick *et al.* 1981).

Dealing with the emotional aspects of physical illness

In any situation where there is physical illness this must be treated by the appropriate methods. As the above shows, however, it is also important to be aware of the psychological elements that may be occurring, and perhaps contributing, to the picture. The first element of concern should be to help the child cope with the illness and the limitations it imposes. If the illness is a life-threatening one, then a variation of bereavement counselling may be necessary to help the child find some resolution to the questions that such a devastating diagnosis prompts. Such efforts may be concentrated into a brief time-span in the case of acute illnesses, or may have a far more protracted make-up if the illness is one that shortens life expectancy to some degree. The recent interest in cognitive behaviour therapy (See Chapter 2) has led to it being used with adults who are faced with stressful situations, and results suggest that it is more effective than supportive counselling in preventing chronicity of psychological symptoms (Ehlers and Clark 2003), but whether it will demonstrate the same benefits in children is still unclear (Cohen 2003).

In some illnesses the more pressing issue is coming to terms with limitations. For example, diabetes requires a degree of dietary vigilance that other children do not require, or children with cerebral palsy have physical and mobility restrictions that prevent them participating fully in all the activities of their friends. If the illness gives the child an unusual appearance or oddity of action, then feeling self-conscious is to be expected. There may need to be intensive work, however, to ensure such children do not avoid such feelings by isolating themselves, but rather look at their feelings and develop mechanisms, using behavioural and cognitive techniques, that ensure they push through the feelings and maintain an active and full life.

The child's reaction to illness or disability is strongly influenced by the reaction of the family. It is very natural for parents to see a child's distress at being teased by peers as a reason to allow the child to avoid and withdraw. It is far harder to help them find ways of coping so that they can continue and face the situation. As part of any intervention, families must be given appropriate information and education about the illness, its problems and clinical management. It is also necessary that they are advised how to respond to the problems and difficulties which day-to-day living throws up. A pattern of caring and concern has to be balanced with a recognition that some pushing to try to overcome is necessary if the full potential is to be reached.

Part of that process begins by ensuring that parental expectations are realistic. There is great danger in not recognising that certain skills and abilities have been lost, for the child will not achieve and the resulting sense of disappointment erodes everyone's self-esteem. Equally important is to avoid underestimating capabilities, and indeed this is often the more damaging extreme. Most children are far more capable than might appear at first sight, and it is vital that each child lives to the limit of his or her capabilities. A child with epilepsy, for instance, need not have a parent in attendance constantly – trips out with friends are a necessary milestone that even children with epilepsy have to experience at some point. Precautions are important, foolhardiness is to be avoided, but, having taken sensible steps, it is necessary sometimes for the parents to adopt that classical parental role of sitting at home and worrying.

A key element for any child, no matter what the underlying problem or difficulty, is to encourage maximum involvement with peers. So much of a child's learning and experience of life comes from peer interaction that to limit this in any way is to begin to deprive the young person of a significant element of life. With such contact comes the risk of teasing or cruel comments, but it is better for children to learn how to cope with such things than to withdraw and never risk themselves in the world. Adults can help in this process, not only by minimising the opportunity for teasing to occur, but by giving the child mechanisms for dealing with such situations when they arise. Many schools now have anti-bullying programmes and the techniques they teach are just as applicable to children with illness or disfigurement.

With regard to the particular case of problems associated with illnesses affecting the brain, there is a variety of drugs available to control seizure activity. The use of such drugs can sometimes prompt psychiatric problems in their own right (Taylor 1991), and this has led to certain drugs, such as phenobarbitone, falling out of favour. The choice of drug regime is governed by a variety of factors, and needs to be carefully tailored to suit the needs of each individual case. The elements described above for psychological management are especially applicable to families where there is a child with epilepsy, for appropriate usage may help to reduce the rate of seizure activity in its own right.

In children who, after a head injury, are disinhibited, aggressive or emotionally quite volatile the anti-epilepsy drugs such as carbamazepine (Lewin and Sumners 1992) and lamotrigine (Pachet et al. 2003) have proven to be quite helpful. Such treatment, however, must be considered in the context of a strong behavioural management programme which focuses upon rewarding the sought behaviour and minimising the response to difficult or challenging behaviours. These programmes are very difficult for families to carry through and there needs to be a high degree of support from health agencies and social services if they are to be effectively implemented.

In addition to such specific programmes it is important for the adults involved with the child to:

- determine the present level of skills and abilities;
- use this evaluation to establish clear rules and expectations which are very slowly increased over time;
- offer appropriate experiences so that the child can reacquire skills such as pencil control and so on;
- slow the pace of presenting information;
- minimise background distraction;
- recognise that the child may need additional time to complete tasks.

Such a package gives the best chance for children who have suffered setbacks through head injury, or illness, to achieve their maximum potential.

Recovering after a traumatic event

Work with victims of disasters, such as the sinking of a cross-channel ferry (Duggan and Gunn 1995), highlights the sequence of events that people experience when they have been involved in extreme trauma. One of the first studies to look at the effects of intense trauma on children was the Chowchilla study (Terr 1979) which examined twenty-six children who were kidnapped and held in a darkened trailer for twenty-six hours. This very traumatic event affected the children deeply, and it was clear that all children, regardless of their previous adjustment, can demonstrate features of an intense stress reaction if the events are significant enough. However, the child's previous development, relationship with parents, and other stresses within the family all tend to influence how the youngster copes with such events in the longer term (Terr 1983).

In the general population less than 1 per cent can be expected to show the features of a full-blown post-traumatic stress disorder, but up to 15 per cent may show symptoms of distress at any one time (Helzer *et al.* 1987). When faced with a major traumatic episode, children tend to remain quiet, but then show acute distress in the immediate aftermath (Terr 1979). Almost immediately they begin to try to think of some reason why this should have happened to them, a process called 'causal attribution' (Joseph *et al.* 1991). This 'search for a reason' can go on for months and is one of the aspects which tends to become a persistent feature of the child's thinking in later years.

In general, any child over three years of age will have good recall of the events unless they were unconscious or concussed. This will not be the case, however, if there were several traumatic events (see the section on being the victim of abuse earlier in this chapter), or if the single event has a long-lasting effect – such as the death of a parent (Terr 1991).

In the days and weeks following the event(s) images associated with the trauma keep recurring either in quiet moments or when any reminder occurs. Fearfulness quickly becomes a feature of the child's functioning – not only a fear that events may be repeated, but of more mundane elements such as being separated from parents, the dark or the presence of strangers. Sleep is often disturbed by vivid dreams, which are often lifelike re-enactments of the events. Children's play becomes dominated by the events, as do their drawings, and they may demonstrate a need to keep recounting the story. The play elements tend to have an obvious link to the trauma, and become quite monotonous in content. This is especially so for children under the age of three years who cannot fully verbalise their experiences and so play out their feelings and experiences over and over again. In older children intrusive 'flashbacks' occur, which bring with them not only elements of the events but the emotions which are associated with them. Such emotional intensity is very draining, as well as distressing, and so the person usually tries to avoid being reminded of the event and generally may appear emotionally flat. There is some variation in these specific features depending upon the age of the child.

Within months some of the features, especially the emotional elements such as sleeplessness, irritability and the anxious striving to be close to parents, fade, but the re-enacting of events in play tends to persist. This monotonous preoccupation may cause the child either to become increasingly withdrawn or perhaps to victimise others as they have been victimised.

Intervention following traumatic events

Although early intervention to prevent problems is tempting, it is not clear that it has a positive effect (Bisson *et al.* 1997), and indeed it appears to be the presence, or absence, of other factors (such as previous psychological problems and adequate social support) that are more likely to affect the outcome than whether early protective intervention occurred (Bisson and Deahl 1994). There is evidence that if early intervention is required then cognitive behaviour therapy is more effective than supportive counselling in preventing the development of chronic symptoms of post-traumatic stress disorder (Ehlers and Clark 2003), which increases the importance of assessing victims carefully to identify those who would benefit from early intervention.

The early days after traumatic events can be very distressing for all and the impact upon the child may be lessened by the use of drugs – particularly anxiety-reducing medications such as beta-blockers and clonidine. In the longer term the use of groups to help children share their experiences and feelings has proved helpful, especially if they were all exposed to the same event. Such groups need to focus upon the sharing of feelings and reactions, with encouragement offered for each member to speak out, but the leaders also need to remain acutely aware that the degree of trauma experienced by each child is likely to be different.

Although cognitive techniques can be used in the older child to intrude upon the difficult remembrances which can become so much part of the child's routine, it is play therapy which has long been the mainstay of helping traumatised children (Webb 1991). Such an approach can help obtain a greater detail of events, but it is its function of helping children to express their feelings and to understand the emotional context which is the key. In older, more verbal children the move is towards more formal psycho-therapy – with a particular emphasis upon ventilating their feelings, discussing symptoms and their meaning, and looking at what the children are doing 'to cope'. Such processes also allow the 'why me?' question to be addressed. As was indicated earlier, this is a persistently negative theme and its eradication can have a major impact upon reducing symptoms and emotional distress.

Experience with adult victims indicates that by two years after the event little remains, but avoiding things that are reminders of the trauma is still often present (Duggan and Gunn 1995). For a significant minority (12 per cent), however, their problems have increased and they have developed clear psychiatric problems. In the five-year follow-up of the children from Chowchilla (Terr 1983) nearly all found it hard to imagine having a full and happy life, career, and so on, which may indicate how much more such events may blight a child.

Sources of further help

www.rcpsych.ac.uk/info/help/pimh/index.htm
www.nimh.nih.gov/publicat/violencemenu.cfm
www.rcpsych.ac.uk/info/mhgu/newmhgu21.htm
www.aacap.org/publications/factsfam/index.htm
www.rcpsych.ac.uk/info/mhgu/index.htm

References

Alessandri, S.M. (1991). Play and social behaviours in maltreated pre-schoolers. *Developmental Psychopathology* 3, 191–206.

Amato, P.R. (2001). Children of divorce in the 1990s: an update of the Amato and Keith (1991) meta-analysis. *Journal of Family Psychology* 15, 355–70.

Baker, A.W. and Duncan, S.P. (1985). Child sexual abuse: a study of prevalence in Great Britain. *Child Abuse and Neglect* 9, 457–67.

Balk, D.E. (1990). The self-concept of bereaved adolescents: sibling death and its aftermath. *Journal of Adolescent Research* 5, 112–32.

Bentovim, A., Van Elburg, A. and Boston, P. (1988). The results of treatment. In A. Bentovim, J. Hildebrand, M. Tranter and E. Vizard (eds) *Child Abuse within the Family: Assessment and Treatment*. London: John Wright.

Berliner, L. (1990). Clinical work with sexually abused children. In C.R. Hollin and K. Howells (eds) *Clinical Approaches to Sex Offenders and their Victims*. Chichester: John Wiley.

Bisson, J.I. and Deahl, M.P. (1994). Psychological debriefing and prevention of post traumatic stress. *British Journal of Psychiatry* 165, 717–20.

Bisson, J.I., Jenkins, P.L., Alexander, J. and Bannister, C. (1997). Randomised controlled trial of psychological debriefing for victims of acute burn trauma. *British Journal of Psychiatry* 171, 78–81.

Block, J.H., Block, J. and Morrison, A. (1981). Parental agreement–disagreement on child rearing orientations and gender-related personality correlates in children. *Child Development* 52, 965–74.

Breier, A., Kelsoe, J.R., Kirwin, P.D. and Beller, S.A. (1988). Early parental loss and development of adult psychopathology. *Archives of General Psychiatry* 45, 987–93.

Butler, S.M. and Seto, M.C. (2002). Distinguishing two types of adolescent sex offenders. *Journal of the American Academy of Child Adolescent Psychiatry* 41, 83–90.

Carlson, V., Cicchetti, D., Barnett, D., Braunwald, K. (1989). Disorganised/disorientated attachment relationships in maltreated infants. *Developmental Psychology* 25, 525–31.

Chadwick, O., Rutter, M. and Brown, G. (1981). A prospective study of children with head injuries. II. Cognitive sequelae. *Psychological Medicine* 11, 49–61.

Cherlin, A.J., Furstenberg, F.F., Chase-Lansdale, P.L., Kiernan, K.E., Robins, P.K. and Morrison, D.R. (1991). Longitudinal studies of effects of divorce on children in Great Britain and the United States. *Science* 252, 1386–9.

Cicchetti, D. and Toth, S.L. (1995). A developmental psychopathological perspective on child abuse and neglect. *Journal of the American Academy of Child and Adolescent Psychiatry* 34, 541–65.

Clarke-Stewart, K.A., Vandell, D.L., McCartney, K., Owen, M.T. and Booth, C. (2000). Effects of parental separation and divorce on very young children. *Journal of Family Psychology* 14, 304–26.

Cohen, J.A. (2003). Treating acute posttraumatic reactions in children and adolescents *Biological Psychiatry* 53, 827–33.

Cohen, J.A. and Mannarino, A.P. (1996). Factors that mediate treatment outcome of sexually abused preschool children. *Journal of the American Academy of Child and Adolescent Psychiatry* 35, 1402–10.

Cosentino, C.E. (1993). Cross-gender behavior and gender conflict in sexually abused girls. *Journal of the American Academy of Child and Adolescent Psychiatry* 32, 940–7.

Crittenden, P.M. (1988). Relationships at risk. In J. Belsky and T. Negworski (eds) *Clinical Implications of Attachment Theory*. Hillsdale, NJ: Erlbaum.

Cummings, E.M., Henness, K., Rabideau, G. and Cicchetti, D. (1994). Responses of physically abused boys to inter-adult anger involving their mothers. *Developmental Psychopathology* 6, 31–42.

Daud, L.R., Garralda, M.E. and David, T.J. (1993). Psychosocial adjustment in pre-school children with atopic eczema. *Archives of Diseases in Childhood* 69, 670–76.

Dube, S.R., Felitti, V.J., Dong, M., Giles, W.H. and Anda, R.F. (2003). The impact of adverse childhood experiences on health problems: evidence from four birth cohorts dating back to 1900 *Preventive Medicine* 37, 268–77.

Duggan, C. and Gunn, J. (1995). Medium term course of disaster victims: A naturalistic follow-up. *British Journal of Psychiatry* 167, 228–32.

Dyregrov, P. (1991). *Children in Grief. A Handbook for Adults.* London: Jessica Kingsley.

Ehlers, A. and Clark, D. (2003). Early psychological interventions for adult survivors of trauma: a review. *Biological Psychiatry* 53, 817–26.

Emery, R.E. (1982). Interparental conflict and the children of discord and divorce. *Psychological Bulletin* 92, 310–30.

Erickson, M., Egeland, B. and Pianta, R. (1989). The effects of maltreatment on the development of young children. In D. Cicchetti and V. Carlson (eds) *Child Maltreatment: Theory and Research on the Causes and Consequences of Child Abuse and Neglect.* New York: Cambridge University Press.

Fergusson, D.M. and Horwood, L.J. (1998). Exposure to interparental violence in childhood and psychosocial adjustment in young adulthood. *Child Abuse and Neglect* 22, 339–57.

Finkelhor, D. (1979). *Sexually Victimized Children.* New York: Free Press.

Finkelhor, D. (1986). *Sourcebook on Child Sexual Abuse.* New York: Sage.

Friedrich, W.N., Urquiza, A.J. and Beilke, R. (1986). Behavioral problems in sexually abused young children. *Journal of Pediatric Psychology* 11, 47–57.

Fristad, M.A., Jedel, R., Weller, R.A. and Weller, E.B. (1993). Psychosocial functioning in children after the death of a parent. *American Journal of Psychiatry* 150, 511–13.

Garnefski, N. and Diekstra, R.F.W. (1997). Child sexual abuse and emotional and behavioral problems in adolescence: gender differences. *Journal of the American Academy of Child and Adolescent Psychiatry* 36, 323–9.

Gil, K.M., Williams, D.A., Thompson, R.J. and Kinney, T.R. (1991). Sickle cell disease in children and adolescents: the relation of child and parent pain coping strategies to adjustment. *Journal of Pediatric Psychology* 16, 643–63.

Glaser, D. (2000). Child abuse and neglect and the brain – a review. *Journal of Child Psychology and Psychiatry* 41, 97–116.

Glasser, M., Kolvin, I., Campbell, D., Glasser, A., Leitch, I., Farrelly, S. (2001). Cycle of child sexual abuse: links between being a victim and becoming a perpetrator. *British Journal of Psychiatry* 179, 482–94.

Goodwin, J.M., Cheeves, K. and Connell, V. (1990). Borderline and other severe symptoms in adult survivors of incestuous abuse. *Psychiatric Annals* 20, 22–32.

Goodyer, I.M. (1993). Recent stressful life events: their long term effects. *European Journal of Child and Adolescent Psychiatry* 2, 1–9.

Gray, R.E. (1989). Adolescent perceptions of social support after the death of a parent. *Journal of Psychosocial Oncology* 7, 127–44.

Guidubaldi, J. and Perry, J.D. (1985). Divorce and mental health sequelae for children: a two year follow-up of a nationwide sample. *Journal of the American Academy of Child Psychiatry* 24, 531–7.

Helzer, J.E., Robins, L.N. and McEvoy, L. (1987). Post traumatic stress disorder in the general population: findings of the Epidemiologic Catchment Area Survey. *New England Journal of Medicine* 317, 1630–4.

Hendriks, J.H., Black, D. and Kaplan, T. (1993). *When Father Kills Mother. Guiding Children through Grief.* London: Routledge.

Hoare, P. (1984). Does illness foster dependency? A study of epileptic and diabetic children. *Developmental Medicine and Child Neurology* 26, 20–6.

Joseph, S.A., Brewin, C.R. and Yule, W. (1991). Causal attribution and psychiatric symptoms in survivors of the *Herald of Free Enterprise* disaster. *British Journal of Psychiatry* 159, 542–6.

Kalter, N., Reimer, B., Brickman, A. and Chen, J.W. (1985). Implications of divorce for female development. *Journal of the American Academy of Child Psychiatry* 24, 538–44.

Lavoie, F., Hébert, M., Tremblay, R., Vitaro, F., Vézina, L. and McDuff, P. (2002). History of family dysfunction and perpetration of dating violence by adolescent boys: a longitudinal study. *Journal of Adolescent Health* 30, 375–83.

Lewin, J. and Sumners, D. (1992). Successful treatment of episodic dyscontrol with carbamazepine. *British Journal of Psychiatry* 161, 261–2.

Lewis, D.O., Mallouh, C. and Webb, V. (1989). Child abuse, delinquency and violent criminality. In D. Cicchetti and V. Carlson (eds) *Child Maltreatment: Theory And Research on the Causes and Consequences of Child Abuse and Neglect*. New York: Cambridge University Press.

Lieberman, A.F., Weston, D. and Pawl, J.H. (1991). Preventive intervention and outcome with anxiously attached dyads. *Child Development* 62, 199–209.

Livingstone, R. (1987). Sexually and physically abused children. *Journal of the American Academy of Child and Adolescent Psychiatry* 26, 413–15.

Lussier, G., Deater-Deckard, K., Dunn, J. and Davies, L. (2002). Support across two generations: children's closeness to grandparents following parental divorce and remarriage. *Journal of Family Psychology* 16, 363–76.

Lynch, M. and Cicchetti, D. (1991). Patterns of relatedness in maltreated and non-maltreated children: connections among multiple representational models. *Developmental Psychopathology* 3, 207–26.

McClellan, J., McCurry, C., Ronnei, M. and Adams, J. (1996). Age of onset of sexual abuse: relationships to sexually inappropriate behaviors. *Journal of the American Academy of Child and Adolescent Psychiatry* 35, 1375–83.

McLeer, S.V., Deblinger, E. and Atkins, M.S. (1988). Post traumatic stress disorder in sexually abused children. *Journal of the American Academy of Child and Adolescent Psychiatry* 27, 342–53.

Main, M. and Goldwyn, R. (1984). Predicting rejecting of her infant from mother's representation of her own experience: implications for the abused–abusing inter-generational cycle. *Child Abuse and Neglect* 8, 203–17.

Malinosky-Rummell, R. and Hansen, D. (1993). Long term consequences of childhood physical abuse. *Psychological Bulletin* 114, 68–79.

Max, J.E., Koele, S.L., Smith, W.L. (1998). Psychiatric disorders in children and adolescents after severe traumatic brain injury: a controlled study. *Journal of American Academy Child Adolescent Psychiatry* 37, 832–40.

Merry, S.N. and Andrews, L.K. (1994). Psychiatric status of sexually abused children 12 months after disclosure of abuse. *Journal of the American Academy of Child and Adolescent Psychiatry* 33, 939–44.

Middleton, J. (1989). Thinking about head injuries in children. *Journal of Child Psychology and Psychiatry* 30, 663–70.

Monck, E., Bentovim, A. and Goodall, G. (1993). *Child Sexual Abuse: A Descriptive and Treatment Study*. London: HMSO.

Motofsky, D. and Balaschak, B. (1977). Psychological control of seizures. *Psychological Bulletin* 843, 723–7.

Mueller, E. and Silverman, N. (1989). Peer relations in maltreated children. In D. Cicchetti and V. Carlson (eds) *Child Maltreatment: Theory And Research on the Causes and Consequences of Child Abuse and Neglect*. New York: Cambridge University Press.

National Research Council (1993). *Understanding Child Abuse and Neglect*. Washington, DC: National Academic Press.

Nekli, J. and Waters, J. (1989). A group for sexually abused young children. *Child Abuse and Neglect* 13, 369–77.

Pachet, A., Friesen, S., Winkelaar, D. and Gray, S. (2003). Beneficial behavioural effects of lamotrigine in traumatic brain injury. *Brain Injury* 17, 715–22.

Pearson, D.A., Pumariega, A.J. and Seilheimer, D.K. (1991). The development of psychosomatic symptomatology in parents with cystic fibrosis. *Journal of the American Academy of Child and Adolescent Psychiatry* 30, 290–7.

Place, M., Reynolds, J., Cousins, A. and O'Neill, S. (2002). Developing a resilience package for vulnerable children. *Child and Adolescent Mental Health* 7, 162–7.

Pless, I.B. and Nolan, T. (1991). Revision, replication and neglect – research on maladjustment in chronic illness. *Journal of Child Psychology and Psychiatry* 22, 347–65.

Pope, H. and Hudson, J. (1992). Is childhood sexual abuse a risk factor for bulimia nervosa? *American Journal of Psychiatry* 149, 455–63.

Reynolds, J.M., Garralda, M.E. and Jameson, R.A. (1988). How parents and families cope with chronic renal failure. *Archives of Diseases in Childhood* 63, 821–6.

Rogosch, F.A. and Cicchetti, D. (1994). Illustrating the interface of family and peer relations through the study of child maltreatment. *Social Development* 3, 291–308.

Rumstein-McKean, O. and Hunsley, J. (2001). Interpersonal and family functioning of female survivors of childhood sexual abuse. *Clinical Psychology Review* 21, 471–90.

Russell, D.E. (1983). The incidence and prevalence of intrafamilial and extrafamilial sexual abuse of female children. *Child Abuse and Neglect* 7, 133–46.

Rutter, M., Graham, P. and Yule, W. (1970). A neuropsychiatric study in childhood. *Clinics in Developmental Medicine*, nos 35/36. London: Heinemann.

Salter, D., McMillan, D., Richards, M., Talbot, T., Hodges, J., Bentovim, A., Hastings, R., Stevenson, J. and Skuse, D. (2003). Development of sexually abusive behaviour in sexually victimised males: a longitudinal study. *Lancet* 361, 471–6.

Sgroi, S. (1982). *Handbook of Clinical Intervention in Child Sexual Abuse*. Lexington, MA: Lexington Books.

Sheldrick, C. (1991). Adult sequelae of child sexual abuse. *British Journal of Psychiatry* 158 (Suppl. 10) 55–62.

Shields, A.M., Ryan, R.M. and Cicchetti, D. (1994). The development of emotional and behavioral self regulation and social competence among maltreated school children. *Developmental Psychopathology* 6, 57–75.

Silverman, P.R., Nickman, S. and Worden, J.W. (1992). Detachment revisited. The child's reconstruction of a dead parent. *American Journal of Orthopsychiatry* 62, 494–503.

Singer, K.I. (1989). Group work with men who experienced incest in childhood. *American Journal of Orthopsychiatry* 59, 468–72.

Taylor, E. (1991). Developmental neuropsychiatry. *Journal of Child Psychology and Psychiatry* 32, 3–47.

Terr, L.C. (1979). Children of Chowchilla. *Psychoanalytical Study of the Child* 34, 547–623.

Terr, L.C. (1983). Chowchilla revisited. *American Journal of Psychiatry* 40, 1543–50.

Terr, L.C. (1991). Childhood traumas: an outline and overview. *American Journal of Psychiatry* 148, 10–20.

Toth, S.L., Manly, J.T. and Cicchetti, D. (1992). Child maltreatment and vulnerability to depression. *Developmental Psychopathology* 4, 97–112.

Trickett, P.K., Aber, J.L. and Carlson, V. (1991). The relationship of socioeconomic status to the etiology and development sequelae of physical child abuse. *Developmental Psychology* 27, 148–58.

Tyler, T.A. (2002). Social and emotional outcomes of childhood sexual abuse: A review of recent research *Aggression and Violent Behavior* 7, 567–89.

Wallerstein, J.S. (1983). Children of divorce: the psychological tasks of the child. *American Journal of Orthopsychiatry* 53, 230–43.

Wallerstein, J.S. and Blakeslee, S. (1989). *Second Chances: Men, Women and Children a Decade after Divorce*. New York: Ticknor and Fields.

Webb, N.B. (1991). *Play Therapy with Children in Crisis: A Casebook for Practitioners*. New York: Guilford Press.

Weller, E.B., Weller, R.A. and Fristad, M.A. (1988). Should children attend their parent's funeral? *Journal of the American Academy of Child and Adolescent Psychiatry* 22, 559–62.

Yates, A. (1982). Children eroticized by incest. *American Journal of Psychiatry* 139, 482–5.

Yule, W. and Gold, A. (1993). *Wise before the Event: Coping with Crisis in Schools*. London: Calouste Gulbenkian Foundation.

Chapter 7

Noncompliance and oppositional behaviour in young children

Introduction

On one occasion, one of the present authors was visiting the home of an eight-year-old child, Simon, who, although highly intelligent and often friendly with visitors, frequently found himself in conflict with parents and teachers. Seated in the family living room, the child had repeatedly engaged in a variety of attention-seeking behaviours such as waving household materials in front of an open fire, switching television channels with the remote control and jumping on the furniture. When admonished by his mother, he immediately sought to engage her in an argument and clearly delighted in her subsequent inability to manage him.

Simon then pushed his face up to his mother's and said that it was time for his medication for nocturnal enuresis (bedwetting). His mother told him that he was mistaken and asked him to be quiet. Simon then pawed at his mother, grabbed her arm and attempted to lead her to the tablets that were carefully situated on top of a clock hanging on the wall – well out of reach. Simon's mother, who had tried to maintain an air of dignified resignation during the early stages of the interview, became increasingly anxious and, as Simon tried to knock the clock off the wall, it was apparent that she was beginning to be overcome by panic. Eventually, her resolve snapped and she told the boy that he could have the tablets.

Having taken two tablets from the container, Simon's mother asked her son to come and take them from her. Simon pretended not to hear and started to take a renewed interest in the television. During the next few minutes the author witnessed an increasingly agitated mother struggling to get the tablets into the mouth of her son who was furiously clamping his mouth shut to deny her. For Simon, the act of opposing others, and winning, was a major element of his interactions.

This chapter addresses the origins, development and management of oppositional behaviour in young children aged from two to ten years. Oppositional or noncompliant behaviour is common to everyone but is perceived as particularly evident (and problematic) in childhood. The child watching the television who does not 'hear' the call for bed, the child who reacts to the word 'no' by storming upstairs, slamming the doors, the child who won't turn down the volume on the radio are all failing to comply with adult instructions or requests. When does such behaviour become a major problem worthy of professional intervention, a form of child 'tyranny' (Barcai and Rosenthal 1974) or an example of the 'brat syndrome', which Bernal *et al.* characterise as 'a child who often engages in tantrums, assaultiveness, threats etc., which are highly aversive and serve to render others helpless in controlling him' (Bernal *et al.* 1968: 447)?

The current edition of the American Psychiatric Association's *Diagnostic and Statistical Manual – DSM-IV* (1994: 94) states that oppositional defiant disorder (ODD) is 'a recurrent pattern of negativistic, defiant, disobedient and hostile behaviour toward authority figures that persists for at least six months'.

The manual adds that ODD is characterised by the frequent occurrence of at least *four* of the following behaviours:

- losing one's temper;
- arguing with adults;
- actively defying or refusing to comply with the requests or rules of adults;
- deliberately doing things that will annoy others;
- blaming others for his or her own mistakes or misbehaviour;
- being touchy or easily annoyed by others;
- being angry and resentful;
- being spiteful or vindictive.

The manual states that to qualify as ODD, the above behaviours must occur more frequently than is typically observed in individuals of comparable age and at a similar developmental level. Furthermore, they must lead to significant impairment in social, academic or occupational functioning.

The prevalence of severe noncompliance in children varies greatly from one study to another. The APA study states that rates of ODD vary from 2 per cent to 16 per cent depending upon the sample and method of assessment. In 1989 the US Institute of Medicine estimated that 4–10 per cent of children in the United States met the criteria for ODD and/or conduct disorder.

The infant years are marked by a growing sense of individuation and autonomy and, as such, the emergence of oppositional behaviour in the toddler is age-appropriate and largely desirable. Indeed, many parents might become concerned for the well-being of their child if he or she never displayed stubbornness, resistance or negativism. Starting at the age of eighteen to twenty months, oppositional behaviour often peaks between three and four before declining as children approach their sixth birthday. As noted by Haswell *et al.*:

The child's intellectual conquest of the meaning of the word 'no' and the concept of negation, along with the realisation of the self as a separate being with a separate will, makes possible the refusal of others' wills. The struggle for autonomy is thus at the heart of oppositional behaviour as the preschool child grows in mastery and explores her/his growing need for independence. Thus, whereas oppositional . . . behaviour is frustrating for parents . . . it is a normal and crucial aspect of early childhood development.

(Haswell *et al.* 1981: 440)

It is those children whose oppositional behaviour appears particularly intense or long lasting who become the subject of parental and professional concern. Johnson *et al.* (1973), found that noncompliance in a normal sample of children occurred in 26 per cent of the total opportunities for compliance. In contrast, in studies of children described as 'deviant' noncompliance ratios were in the 57–80 per cent range (e.g. Forehand and King 1977). It is important to note, however, that some of these differences may reflect parental desires to heighten their child's deviant status, in order to justify professional intervention.

Gard and Berry (1986), in a review of the literature, argue that oppositional children differ from normal children in that they engage in a range of problem behaviours to a greater degree and intensity. In particular they:

- are exceedingly non-compliant to those in authority;
- refuse to conform to ordinary rules and conventions;
- are perceived as wilful and contrary;
- appear to derive satisfaction in provoking adults;
- may display tantrum behaviours, which may be aggressive and destructive;
- tend to demonstrate poor school performance;
- exhibit an inability to delay gratification and accept frustrations;
- appear to develop serious problems in social relationships;
- tend to have a negative outlook towards themselves and others;
- often lack basic social skills;
- tend not to be as responsive to normal social reinforcement or punishment.

Although some writers have queried the validity of the distinction (Hill 2002), the psychiatric literature differentiates oppositional defiant disorder from conduct disorder, the former being seen as a somewhat less severe difficulty lacking the aggression towards others, the destruction of property and the theft and deceit which are frequently features of conduct-disordered children. Nevertheless, it would appear that the two conditions are very closely related (Rowe *et al.* 2002) and may share a developmental relationship. For a proportion of children, ODD evolves into conduct disorder in adolescence, prior to the appearance of antisocial personality disorder in adulthood (Loeber and Stouthamer-Loeber 1998). Conduct-disordered adolescents who demonstrated symptoms of ODD, and subsequently conduct disorder, in their pre-school years are likely to be more chronically antisocial in later life than those children whose difficulties emerge in adolescence after a normal history of social and behavioural development (White *et al.* 1990). Early onset of behavioural problems has been shown to be the most important predictor of future delinquency, violence and substance abuse (Snyder 2001). Given this scenario, the importance of intervening at an early stage is clear.

Within-child factors

All parents know that some children seem temperamentally more difficult to socialise than others, and differences between children within the same family cannot be sufficiently explained solely by environmental factors. Mounting evidence from studies of both ODD and conduct-disordered children points to a significant genetic component (Hill 2002). However, it is widely accepted that biological characteristics by themselves are unlikely to account for antisocial behaviour; rather, these interact with environmental experiences in establishing deviant behaviour (Plomin and Hershberger 1991) with the latter exerting the greater influence (Dishion *et al.* 1995).

Temperamental (or dispositional) factors are likely to play an important mediating role between the child's genetic make-up, environmental experiences and behaviour. Research suggests that negative temperamental characteristics of infants (e.g. difficultness, unadaptability and negative emotions and feelings) are related to later behavioural difficulties, although this relationship is substantially weaker than key parental and family factors (Bates *et al.* 1991). A promising line of enquiry with respect to conduct-disordered children (e.g. Dodge 1993) concerns the extent to which particularly aggressive and challenging children are less able to recognise and understand social cues and thus respond appropriately. In their comparative study of children with a mixture of conduct disorder and ODD and those developing more normally, Webster-Stratton and Lindsay (1999) found that the former group tended to make more negative attributions, were less able to solve problems and demonstrated fewer social skills when playing with friends.

Although gender differences in ODD are relatively unexamined (Hoffenaar and Hoeksma, 2002) such behaviour tends to be more common in males before puberty, although gender differences tend to disappear subsequently.

Parental and family factors

General behavioural difficulties in young children have been found to be associated with parental conflict leading to divorce (Kazdin 1987), although it is the degree and nature of the parental conflict, rather than divorce per se, which appear to be the most important factors (O'Leary and Emery 1982). It is also widely noted in the literature (Webster-Stratton 1993) that parents of young children with behavioural difficulties tend to encounter a greater incidence of major stressors (unemployment, divorce, poverty) and more minor everyday troubles which can result in depression, impatience, irritability and the adoption of a coercive approach to family relations. It does appear, however, that the impact of negative environmental factors is mediated substantially by the quality of the parenting provided (Murray *et al.*, 1999).

A key issue is whether highly oppositional children are the product of poor parenting or whether the deficiencies in parenting skills often observed in such cases are by-products of the anxiety and tensions which result from having to contend with a difficult child. Similarly, findings that oppositional children tend to have overcontrolling, aggressive, depressed mothers and distant, passive, non-communicative fathers are open to similar questions regarding causality. Research studies have indicated that parents of challenging children tend to exhibit fewer positive behaviours towards their children, are more likely to threaten, criticise, nag and humiliate their children, are less likely to monitor their children's behaviours and don't give them enough time to comply with commands (Forehand *et al.* 1975; Delfini *et al.* 1976; Webster-Stratton and Spitzer 1991).

Most practitioners will recognise a series of behaviours frequently exhibited by parents with oppositional children. Commands are given in an anxious or irritable voice, spoken rapidly. The parent may maintain a tense posture and observant manner and be quick to intervene if the child fails to comply. Alternatively, the parent may deliberately avoid following up a request as noncompliance is expected and, as such, an effort is made to avoid conflict. Some parents signal resignation by distancing themselves from the child, speaking in a flat, toneless fashion and giving directions in the form of questions, 'Don't you think it's time that you went upstairs to bed?' Such questions are often accompanied by defensive postures (e.g. arms and or legs crossed) and an accompanying lack of voice projection.

Patterson (1982) coined the term 'coercive process' to describe a pattern of behaviour in which children come to realise that they can have their desires met, or avoid censure, by increasingly escalating their negative behaviours until their parents capitulate. Although such patterns of interaction occur in all families from time to time, it is considered that a high rate of such exchanges acts as a form of training to interact in a coercive fashion.

In line with this thinking, Gard and Berry's (1986) review of the research literature described the common pattern of interaction shown in Figure 7.1.

Intervention issues

It has been generally found that behavioural approaches to noncompliance are the most effective means of effecting change. These can take the form of:

Parent issues instruction/command.

Child perceives command as aversive/undesirable and responds with noncompliance.

Parent EITHER: withdraws command – this reinforces the child's noncompliance.
OR attempts to reason/persuade the child to comply – again, this reinforces the unwanted behaviour.

Parent fails to persuade child to comply, becomes increasingly frustrated and begins to shout, threaten or physically chastise.

EITHER
child eventually complies – parent's aggressive/aversive behaviour is reinforced and increases the perception that such behaviours are 'the only way to get through to the child'. Child is resentful, and less likely to push parent to the limit subsequently;
OR
increased anger and punishment continue to be ineffective. Child recognises own power to defy parent even when threat is great. Perception of power is reinforcing for the child.

Figure 7.1 Common pattern of interaction

- group parent training;
- individual parent training;
- child's individual behaviour programme;
- child-based social skills and problem solving training;
- behavioural training incorporating some form of family therapy.

Parent management programmes for oppositional and other conduct-dis-ordered children have been subject to more detailed evaluation than any other form of therapy. These studies suggest that such programmes are among the most promising types of intervention (Kazdin 1997; Brestan and Eyberg, 1998). Indeed, there is some evidence that they are also effective when ODD children have associated attentional difficulties (Hartman *et al.* 2003).

With a strong psychological focus, parent training programmes are typ-ically coordinated by social work, psychology or psychiatry services. Often teachers, nursery nurses and other childcare professionals have an important role, either by sharing in the delivery of programmes or by offering encour-agement and support to parents who are struggling to change their child management behaviours.

Group parent training

Although practices vary, the most common model of parent training involves a short presentation by the therapist for approximately thirty minutes for each of the six to ten weeks of the programme. The presentation is then fol-lowed by either large- or small-group discussion depending upon the number of trainers available. Each presentation introduces a particular issue or theme (e.g. how to operate a time-out procedure) which can subsequently be incorporated into a plan of action. In the early stages the presentations serve to provide an understanding of behavioural principles and methods and how parents may react in counterproductive ways. The focus subsequently shifts to the recording and assessment of behaviour and, finally, to issues of intervention.

After each presentation and group discussion, each parent is asked to feed back on the results of the previous week(s) and to consider the implementation of the technique under consideration in the week ahead.

An example parent programme is outlined, below.

Week 1 What is normal behaviour? What is problem behaviour?

This first session provides a gentle introduction to the programme. It introduces parents to the notion that defiance, aggression and other challenging behaviours are common in young children and seeks to help them become less threatened and intimidated by their situation. An important element of this first session is the reduction of feelings of isolation and separateness often encountered by such parents.

Opportunities are provided for parents to talk about the difficulties they encounter with their children and the distress and anxiety that can result. The group leader should be careful not to allow this activity to degenerate into a negative spiral of complaint but, rather, to draw upon the accounts provided to help parents to recognise that their problems are common to others and their frequent feelings of heightened anxiety are a common yet undesirable consequence of child defiance.

The homework task may be to focus upon one aspect of their child's behaviour and to consider how they (and, perhaps, other members of the family) typically respond. Parents are asked to jot this information down in a notebook shortly after an event has taken place. This serves to introduce the idea of systematic recording, an important aspect of behavioural approaches.

Week 2 Measuring and recording behaviour

This session is designed to assist parents to focus more closely upon problematic behaviours and, in particular, to gain a more detailed grasp of when and how frequently these occur. During this session it is hoped that those who believe that their child's problematic behaviours 'take place all the time' may be assisted to gain an accurate picture of the circumstances. Parents are asked to focus upon a particular problem behaviour exhibited by their child and are shown how a simple recording system can be established. An example is provided in Figure 7.2.

Each parent is asked to devise a simple recording chart, similar to that in Figure 7.2, that records the incidence of one or more problem behaviours exhibited by their child. The homework task may be the maintenance of the chart during the forthcoming weeks.

The frequency chart helps parent and therapist to gain a realistic picture of the true frequency of the problem behaviour and the times when this is most prevalent. This serves both to indicate when the potential for difficulty is greatest and as a baseline upon which to gauge the effectiveness of the subsequent intervention.

Week 3 The relationship between behaviour and consequences

Participants are provided with a number of scenarios involving a child's problem behaviour and examples of parental responses. One example would

	Sun	Mon	Tues	Wed	Thur	Fri	Sat
7.00–8.00							
8.00–9.00							
9.00–10.00							
10.00–11.00							
11.00–12.00							
12.00–1.00							
1.00–2.00							
2.00–3.00							
3.00–4.00							
4.00–5.00							
5.00–6.00							
6.00–7.00							
7.00–8.00							
8.00–bedtime							

Week beginning ....

Figure 7.2 Chart demonstrating the number of times each day that a child disobeys parents

be a child crying for sweets in a supermarket, an escalating temper tantrum and, as a result of the public humiliation, immense parental anxiety and eventual capitulation. Parents would be asked to record whether these scenarios reflected their own experience and the extent to which the parental compliance outlined in the scripts reflected their own circumstances.

A key skill is the ability to ignore a child's problematic behaviour while not responding emotionally. Often the parent's continued watchfulness, anxiety or interruption is highly reinforcing to the child and thus maintains the unwanted behaviour. Participants are instructed to ignore the irritation. One of the writers has found the common childhood game of 'Knock Down Ginger' or 'Knocky Nine Doors', where the child rings a doorbell and runs and hides, to be a productive metaphor. Most parents grasp the message that the occupant who rages and yells is more likely to become a frequent victim of the game. (For further details of the use of such strategies with parents, see Beaver, 1996: 193–201.)

A major difficulty concerns when to ignore and when to intervene, as unfamiliar 'ignoring' behaviour can result in the child seeking to restore the usual pattern of interaction by accentuating the problem behaviour to a point where the child, or significant other, is at physical risk. Parents often need guidance as to when they should intervene, how to avoid being too emotionally charged at such times, and how to minimise the rewarding nature of such attention.

The scenarios would provide a contextualised introduction to key behavioural principles, in particular to the concept of reinforcement. From this would be developed the antecedents–behaviour–consequences (ABC) model of behaviour analysis that is common to most behavioural programmes.

John (aged four) is sitting in his front room and is bored. He has repeatedly tried to gain his mother's attention but she keeps shooing him away in order to complete her domestic tasks. John has nothing to do and is uninterested in the television programme he has been instructed to watch. He decides to play with some of his parents' ornaments but clumsily knocks one over and it is destroyed. Mother runs into the room horrified, shouts at her son and gives him a smack. She then takes him into the kitchen with her and gives him the task of helping her to stir the cake mix which she has prepared.

Mary (aged six) is with her father in the supermarket. He is not happy about having to do the shopping and has little patience with his daughter's repeated whining. She usually helps her mother collect items from the shelves but her father wants her to stay by his side and be quiet. At the checkout, Mary demands a chocolate bar from the prominent display.

Father, irritated by the store's cynical promotion, refuses, saying that she will be having dinner shortly. Mary exhibits a major temper tantrum, shouts that she hates her father and then grasps the counter, refusing to budge. Father becomes increasingly embarrassed and has a sense of guilt that he has mishandled the situation. Reluctantly, he purchases the chocolate bar while telling his daughter that she is a very naughty child who doesn't deserve the treat she is to receive.

In both of the scenarios above, it is tempting for parents to focus upon the problem behaviour (carelessness with treasured possessions, the display of a temper tantrum) without considering the events which took place before and afterwards. As the incidents demonstrate, parental handling prior to each event was a contributory factor. More sensitive awareness of each child's frustration and a little imagination may have prevented the incidents from occurring.

One should also consider the extent to which each parent's reaction was likely to increase the likelihood of similar behaviour in the future. Although John's mother may consider a smack and a telling off to be a punishment, she may fail to recognise that, for most children, any attention is better than no attention: 'Attention to a child is like sunshine to a flower.' Subsequently, John is further 'rewarded' by being allowed to help her in the kitchen. Mary's father also rewards his daughter for undesirable behaviour, although in this case with the purchase of the chocolate bar. His public labelling of her as 'naughty' only serves to compound matters, as the internalisation of the label by Mary may result in her becoming more obstructive on future occasions.

Consideration of the events leading up to such incidents (antecedents) and those which follow (consequences) is a cornerstone of all behavioural programmes. Most involve assisting parents to analyse a series of difficult situations in the form of an ABC chart (see Figure 7.3).

Although the above brief extract provides an incomplete picture, it is clear that much useful data are beginning to emerge. There are occasions, for example, when parental responses reinforce John's poor behaviour. At other times his behaviour is not tolerated – possibly when his father is present. In a real-life situation, parents might be asked to consider each situation and consider alternative options. Many of the difficulties appear to arise from sibling conflict. It may be valuable for parents in such situations to consider how such situations can be prevented or minimised.

A homework task for those undertaking a parent training programme might be to complete a simple ABC chart, similar to Figure 7.3 during the forthcoming week. This would form the basis for a group exploration of the above issues.

Antecedents	Behaviour	Consequences
Monday teatime: John and Mary were watching the television. They started to argue about which channel to watch. I told them that I would turn it off if they didn't stop shouting.	John punched Mary and threw his toys around the room.	I sent Mary upstairs to play. John was told to settle down to the television or he'd be sent to bed.
Tuesday breakfast: John fussed over which cereal to eat. He wanted the toy from the bottom of one of the packets.	John refused to eat anything until the toy was retrieved. He 'accidentally' spilled milk over the table.	The toy was retrieved but only after a lot of fuss!
Tuesday evening: John was irritating Mary by running into her bedroom and taking her dolls. Mary scratched his face.	John kicked Mary, hard, and ran screaming into the kitchen where I was washing up.	Both children were told off. I said that I would play with them both later if they stopped arguing.
Wednesday teatime: A fun time! John and Mary told us about some amusing events at school. I couldn't see trouble ahead, although both kids were getting rather excited. John began to get silly and made stupid noises at the meal table. Mary was encouraging him. I told him that if he didn't settle down he would have to go to his room.	He got worse! Eventually his dad had to carry him forcibly to his room to calm down. John was kicking and biting in temper.	When he eventually calmed down, he was allowed to watch television.

Figure 7.3 Extract from a weekly ABC chart

Week 4 Increasing desirable behaviour – how to apply reinforcement

This session would develop from Week 3 by focusing upon how reinforcement can be used to increase desirable behaviour in children. The importance of ensuring that reinforcement follows desired behaviour relatively swiftly, particularly in the initial stages, would be stressed. Differing forms of reinforcement from smiling and approving to more tangible forms such as sweets and pocket money and their impact are discussed and evaluated. The powerful effect of intermittent reinforcement (see Chapter 2) would be described with reference to everyday experiences (e.g. the attraction of fruit machines). Case examples of the use of contingent reinforcement would be presented with the aim of helping participants to grasp the fact that they can be proactive and influential in shaping children's behaviour.

The homework task may be to consider the reinforcers that are, or are potentially, available in the home. Parents would be asked to consider how these may become contingently related to desired behaviours.

Week 5 Decreasing inappropriate behaviour – the role of punishment

The literature indicates that many parents place too great a reliance upon harsh and frequent punishments. The difference between negative reinforcement (where desired behaviour is increased by the removal of an aversive stimulus) and punishment (where an aversive response is designed to reduce a given behaviour) is a distinction that, in the opinion of the present writers, may prove unnecessarily sophisticated and unnecessarily complex for many participants. Thus punishment here is taken as any response that the child may perceive as unwelcome.

The limited role of many punishments in reducing inappropriate behaviour is outlined. Participants are asked to discuss the current operation of punishment in their homes and its effectiveness. The reinforcing effect of parental attention (even if this takes an aversive form) is outlined and parents are helped to greater understanding of the seemingly paradoxical effect of their actions.

The most important means of reducing undesirable behaviour (removing reinforcement, employing a time-out procedure, as illustrated in Figure 7.4) are outlined and the relevance to participants' own situations is highlighted.

Homework for this parent training session involves consideration of how reinforcement and punishment may operate with one's child – the implication being that this will be operationalised in an actual intervention.

Week 6 Communicating with others

This session (which may take place earlier in the programme) provides an opportunity for consideration of the verbal and non-verbal behaviours which signal authority to the child and help to ensure compliance. A focus of the session will be upon the use of eye contact, posture, voice, position, the articulation of simple, straightforward, concrete instructions (rather than taking the form of questions or rationales) and the conveyance of 'I mean it!' messages. Other important issues include the importance of providing verbal alerts (e.g. 'In five minutes you will need to put your toys away and come upstairs for your bath'), supporting the child's desire for autonomy by offering choices where possible, giving the child time to comply with instruction (four–five seconds) and the need to exercise some flexibility in interacting with the child.

The inputs from the group leader(s) may be supported by the use of role-played videotaped interactions. While permitting the parents the opportunity

Time-out is short for 'time-out from positive reinforcement' and usually involves the removal of the child to a location where positive reinforcers (e.g. attention, peer approval, interesting toys and objects) are unavailable. In the home setting this is often a bedroom, a corridor, a corner of a room or a chair. It is important, however, that the particular location is not disturbing to the child (e.g. a dark area in a confined space) and that parents have some opportunity to maintain a degree of vigilance.

Although a highly effective strategy, it is important that it is carried out systematically and in keeping with a predetermined schedule. Most commentators consider a period of from three to fifteen minutes to be sufficient (the longer period being more appropriate for older children) and it is important that parents do not become over-punitive by increasing the period in order to gain a greater sense of control.

McAuley and McAuley (1977: 103) outline a three-stage time-out procedure:

> Stage 1 – the child is commanded to do something or to stop doing something; stage 2 – the child is rewarded if he complies; if he has not complied within a reasonable length of time (which is judged according to the content of the command) then a second command is given with a punishment warning; stage 3 – the child is rewarded if he complies; if he has not complied within a further reasonable time he is sent to time-out.

McAuley and McAuley note that instituting time-out procedures often involves three problems, refusal to go to time-out, refusal to stay in time-out and refusal to leave time-out. With young children, it may be necessary for the parent to use physical means of ensuring that the procedure is followed. The child's frustration may often result in screams, assault and tantrums and it is essential that the parent appears unmoved emotionally throughout this time. In general, timing should not commence until the child is quiet. On the first few occasions this may last for an hour or more and require considerable doggedness and determination on the part of the rapidly tiring parent. Subsequently, however, the child will usually cease such behaviours relatively quickly. If the child refuses to leave time-out, the parent should avoid re-entering a power struggle by attending to such statements which are usually ploys by the child to appear unconcerned by the technique. Close monitoring of the child's behaviour over time should provide a clear indication of the true effectiveness of the intervention.

It is important that the use of time-out is complemented by an attempt to teach the child prosocial behaviours such as how to share with others, or how to tidy away one's toys.

Figure 7.4 Time-out

to distance themselves to some extent, the use of critical incidents can help parents to recognise and reflect upon examples of ineffectual communication that may mirror that in which they engage themselves.

An advantage of introducing this topic in a later session is that the development of group identity and trust may permit opportunities for participants to engage in practical development through role play.

Homework may require participants to reflect upon one or more incidents during the forthcoming week where they have attempted to communicate authority and ensure compliance.

Week 7 Family factors

Many behavioural programmes fail because of inconsistency within the family and the wider social network. This session is geared to help participants recognise how family members may consciously or unconsciously undermine an attempt to introduce a behavioural programme. This may be for many reasons, for example, a sibling's desire to scapegoat, the other parent's assertion that there is no problem to address or grandparental indulgence. This session must be handled skilfully as highlighting such difficulties can result in increasing tension and heightened disharmony within the family that are likely to exacerbate the difficulties encountered. Rather, the aim must be to help participants to gain greater understanding of family dynamics and, in the light of this, to find creative ways of ensuring that the family has ownership of, and commitment to, the programme.

Weeks 8–12 Establishing and operating the programme

By Week 8, participants will have identified those behaviours that are to be addressed, will have data as to their incidence and frequency, have considered the availability of the means of reinforcement and punishment, and have greater understanding of their own and their family's impact upon the child under consideration. The programme's design permits change in parental handling (and, hopefully, the child's behaviour) from its outset, an important element in ensuring continued parental engagement. Week 8, however, is geared to pulling these threads together to produce a more comprehensive and systematic intervention intended to operate over the next few weeks.

Following a 'weight watchers' motivational model, the goals and operation of the programmes are made explicit and each week participants report upon progress. Where difficulties arise, the group works with the parent to modify the programme or redouble his or her efforts. The active support of the group is highly reinforcing and empowering for many parents, particularly those who feel isolated and helpless to effect change.

There has been much consideration in the parent training literature as to the most effective means of providing information. In addition to traditional means of offering advice and guidance, the provision of written materials, telephone contact and audio and videotaped sequences is often seen as helpful. It is widely agreed that some programmes have placed too great an emphasis upon a translation of behavioural principles rather than upon the articulation, modelling and practice of skills. In this respect, the use of video-modelling, whereby parents examine illustrative clips of positive and negative parental handling, has proven helpful (Behan and Carr 2000). Reviews of evaluation studies (e.g. Moreland et al. 1982) would appear to suggest that the modelling of appropriate parental behaviour and the supervision of behaviour rehearsal are key features in ensuring that parents acquire and continue to maintain important skills of using commands, providing attention at appropriate times and operating time-out. One technique that places a premium upon modelling, parent–child interaction therapy, developed by Eyberg, Boggs and Algina (1995) involves the parents interacting with their child in a laboratory setting. Here the parent is asked to put into practice the skills that have been taught earlier. While the parent is interacting with the child, advisers, observing through a one-way mirror, provide extensive coaching by means of a 'bug' in the parent's ear. The intervention gradually shifts to the home context as skills are acquired. Evaluations of this approach have been encouraging (e.g. Funderburk *et al.* 1998; Schuhmann *et al.* 1998).

Many writers have expressed concern at the relatively high drop-out rates of those engaged in parent training: on average 25–30 per cent of those who commence the programme (Forehand *et al.* 1983). It is clear that there are certain categories of parent that are particularly at risk of failing to complete. McMahon *et al.* (1981) found that drop outs from parent training programmes were more likely to be from low socio-economic status groupings, show greater incidence of maternal depression, and tend to offer more commands to their children. Maintenance of initial gains was less likely to occur in families where the mother was isolated or had poor relationships with members of the local community (Wahler 1980). While these mothers had shown an ability to utilise the behavioural techniques during the programme, these were not maintained and they continued to understand their children's behaviour in general, blame-orientated terms. Wahler *et al.* (1981) noted that these mothers' widespread experience of interpersonal dealings marked by conflict and attrition had generalised to their children. In such cases approaches might need to incorporate family therapy approaches which permit consideration of broader intra-familial and extra-familial relationships (Griest and Wells 1983).

In comparison with an individual programme, group training has a number of advantages and disadvantages:

Advantages
1   Because several parents are seen together the approach is relatively cost-effective.
2   Parents value and are encouraged by the knowledge that others are encountering similar difficulties.
3   Group discussion about ideas and practices covered during the training helps to ensure understanding of the material.
4   Parents serve as models for one another.
5   The recording and discussion of individual family outcomes can prove highly motivating and helps to maintain adherence to agreed programmes.

Disadvantages
1 It is rare that the therapist is able to observe or gain accurate measures of actual parent behaviours in the home setting.
2 It is difficult to set up simulation exercises involving guided feedback to parents.
3 It may prove easier for parents to drop out of a group programme.

In general, however, research studies suggest that group training programmes are as effective as individual programmes (Behan and Carr 2000) and, of course, can prove far more cost-effective.

Individual parent training

This employs many of the same principles as group parent training but, operating in clinic and home contexts, permits more tailored intervention to meet the needs of the particular parents. A number of programmes, based upon the work of Forehand and his colleagues (1977, 1981) have incorporated sophisticated simulation techniques in which parents (usually mothers) practise issuing instructions and responding to noncompliance in their young children. In one study (Powers and Roberts 1995), for example, parents were trained in a simulation room equipped with a 'bedroom', 'dining table' and 'play area'. A doll, held by a co-therapist played the child's role. The simulation involved the parent responding to a predetermined script with the lead therapist, situated behind a one-way window, speaking to the co-therapist by means of an ear 'bug'. Findings indicated that parent training undertaken in these clinic-based simulation sessions resulted in significantly improved performance in the home.

Child's individual behavioural programme

Many interventions involve both an individual behavioural programme and an element of parent training (although the training element may often be rather less structured and overt than that described above). In such cases, the focus may be upon examining the pay-offs for the child's negative behaviour and in ascertaining how inappropriate antecedent conditions and typical reinforcements may be amended. In this approach, parental handling and management of the child is shaped primarily through the operation of the programme. Key elements include reducing the child's capacity for negotiation, ensuring that instructions are complied with and taking care that rewards and sanctions are clearly signalled and operate contingently.

Adam, aged eight, was referred to the educational psychologist by his school at parental request. He was perceived by his teachers as being rather idiosyncratic – he would occasionally make funny noises in class, demonstrated some rather unappealing personal habits, was something of a loner and, in his interests and sense of humour, appeared to function as a somewhat younger child. Although he had some learning difficulties – for example, he was only a beginning reader and required additional help from a support teacher – he was generally well behaved in class and responsive to his teachers. On occasions he had been brought to the headteacher for his involvement in minor misdemeanours (e.g. writing on the walls, teasing younger children).

At home, his behaviour was radically different. Here, he was often argumentative, irritating, destructive and refused to respond to his parents' direction. Many of the arguments centred upon requests for sweets, toys and television or refusal to undertake self-help tasks such as washing himself, getting dressed or preparing for bedtime.

Adam's father worked long hours and was often away from home. Although supportive, the demands upon him were such that he was often unable to impact greatly upon the family's functioning. When Father was at home, Adam's behaviour was markedly better and this resulted in Father becoming frustrated at his wife's inability to cope at other times. His mother, a caring, concerned parent, was frequently overwhelmed by the demands of her son, particularly in public settings where his noisy and overbearing manner frequently brought anxious glances from members of the public. Adam's maternal grandparents, while indulging the boy, were exasperated by his behaviour and often fuelled the tension within the family. For them, Adam was a lost cause who was regularly compared unflatteringly with his younger sister (Sasha, aged five) who could 'do no wrong'.

Adam was essentially a good-natured boy with a loving disposition. He would often cuddle his parents and grandparents affectionately and his behaviour appeared to stem primarily from poor social learning rather than from any latent hostility or antagonism towards his family.

The educational psychologist came to the conclusion that a number of therapeutic outcomes were desirable:

1   Adam's behaviour needed to be shaped by a more explicit and contingent use of reinforcement with the aim of encouraging greater compliance.
2   Adam's family (particularly his mother) needed to appear more confident and strong in their interactions with him. In particular, his power in public settings should be eroded.
3   The family needed to work together in a more supportive and collaborative fashion.
4   The family scapegoating of Adam should be reduced. Continued comparison with his younger sibling should cease.

5   The significant influence of the school (in particular, the headteacher) should be drawn upon to add greater weight to the intervention.

Baseline measures of Adam's noncompliant behaviour, completed by Mother, indicated that bickering and non-compliance were almost continuous occurrences. As a result, it was agreed to set up a behavioural programme which would monitor sequences of thirty minutes – a highly intrusive and demanding schedule.

Capitalising upon Adam's love of the *Power Rangers* television characters, Adam and his mother designed a Monopoly-style Power Rangers game board on a large piece of card. Each segment of the pathway represented a thirty-minute time period. There were sufficient segments to cover morning and evening sessions during weekdays and all day on Saturday and Sunday. The number of boxes totalled approximately one hundred.

At the end of each thirty-minute period an entry was made. If the target behaviours were achieved (no arguing with parents, compliance with instructions), Adam drew or coloured in the square. If these were not achieved, a large cross was drawn in the square with a felt pen.

Rewards, in the form of pocket money, sweets, television programmes and other treats, were tied in tightly and explicitly to daily and weekly targets. It was made clear to Adam that there would be no negotiation or debate about parental judgements or the operation of reinforcement. Adam was required to take the chart to school at the end of each week to show his classteacher and headteacher. In addition, the educational psychologist indicated that he would review progress at three-week intervals.

Although somewhat daunted by the schedule, Adam's parents agreed to establish the programme and to adhere to the measures agreed. His grandparents, however, thought that the scheme was 'daft' and was unlikely to be any more effective than earlier attempts to tackle Adam's misbehaviour. This perception provided an opportunity for the psychologist to tackle issues 2 and 3 (see above) and to highlight the importance for the family of maintaining a united and determined position. Reluctantly, the grandparents agreed to 'give it a try'. Discussion focused upon the ways to give instructions, to pause afterwards to permit time for compliance, and to ensure that all verbal and non-verbal messages signalled an air of authority.

The effects of the programme surpassed all expectations. During the next few weeks, Adam's behaviour continually improved to a level which astounded all participants, including the psychologist. The displays of public non-compliance gradually disappeared as Adam's goals shifted to the gaining of public recognition for positive behaviour and the rewards which were contingent upon this.

A crucial factor, somewhat obscured by the demands of the intensive behavioural programme, was the very real change in the family functioning, particularly that of Adam's mother. In interview she stated, 'Whereas before I was often hesitant and anxious in talking to Adam, he now knows that I am determined to see matters through. The new programme and the support of school and the psychologist have made me feel a lot less isolated and, as a result, my confidence has increased.'

This air of self-assurance and confidence that instruction will be complied with are important elements in all interpersonal dealings (see Chapter 8) and are elements that can be overshadowed by behavioural technologies. The change in the way in which Adam was handled may well have been the most important element in the intervention. The complex and detailed behavioural programme may have been the means by which this change could be best effected.

Three months after the programme was completed, a follow-up interview was conducted. As is often the case with such programmes, Adam's behaviour had deteriorated somewhat but by no means to a level commensurate with the original position. Regression to earlier patterns of behaviour is common in many behavioural programmes, although the goal that new patterns of reinforcement and concomitant changes in management will have lasting and positive effects remains. As Adam's mother stated during the follow-up interview, 'Yes, he can still be difficult at times but things are different now. I know that I can handle whatever happens. I'm no longer overwhelmed by feelings of panic. Adam knows that I won't be intimidated as I used to be and that I'll stand my ground. Nevertheless, I think that I'll always find him to be a handful!'

This case study demonstrates the complex interaction between a simple behavioural model, the nature and quality of child–adult communication and the wider family and school contexts within which these operate. In the opinion of the writers, the failure of many behavioural interventions results from a simplistic focus upon a mechanistic technology and a corresponding neglect of key interpersonal/parenting skills and wider family dynamics.

Child-based social skills and problem-solving training

While pioneering parent training, Webster-Stratton and her colleagues note that approximately one-third of children with conduct problems whose parent receive training programmes continue to experience difficulties two years later (Webster-Stratton 1990a). In addition, some parents are unwilling, or unable, to participate in training programmes or apply the guidance received in their daily family life (Webster-Stratton 1990b). For this reason, Webster-Stratton (2001) advocates direct social skills training, problem-solving and anger management of children with ODD and other conduct disorders. Their 'Dinosaur School' curriculum for children aged four to eight years draws upon a coping model that requires the youngsters to discuss and model the use of appropriate social skills. As with Webster-Stratton's parent training programme, videotaped vignettes are employed as one tool to open up discussion and serve as stimuli for drawing up a list of more adaptive alternative responses. In general, it would appear that this approach does lead to fewer behavioural difficulties although it proved less effective where parents were unduly critical of their children or used physical punishments (Webster-Stratton *et al.* 2001).

Behavioural training involving family therapy

As noted in the case study above, it is often necessary to complement the operation of a behavioural programme (whether through a child-focused programme or parent training) with some form of wider family work. This is particularly important where difficulties relating to intra-familial roles, communication and/or tensions serve to exacerbate the child's problems. In many cases it becomes clear that one or more members of the family have their needs satisfied as a result of the child's challenging behaviour (e.g. acting as a convenient scapegoat, drawing attention from marital tensions, permitting displacement of hostility) and thus such individuals may consciously or subconsciously seek to subvert any externally directed initiative. In such circumstances it may prove necessary for the therapist to help the family members gain greater understanding of their roles and relationships with one another.

Outcomes

Although oppositional behaviour in children can be highly distressing and disempowering for parents, the voluminous number of existing studies clearly indicates that where parents (and other key family members) take a full and active part in a structured intervention programme, improvements in the child's behaviour usually occur relatively speedily. Given such programmes, the prognosis for oppositional children appears to be markedly superior than for those whose behaviour is marked by hyperactivity or significant learning difficulty.

Website

www.incredibleyears.com

References

American Psychiatric Association (APA) (1994). *Diagnostic and Statistical Manual of Mental Disorders*. 4th edn. Washington, DC: Author.

Barcai, A. and Rosenthal, N. (1974). Fears and tyranny: observations of the tyrannical child. *Archives of General Psychiatry* 30, 302–96.

Bates, J.E., Bayles, K., Bennett, D.S., Ridge, B. and Brown, M.M. (1991). Origins of externalising behaviour problems at eight years of age. In D.J. Pepler and H.H. Rubin (eds) *The Development and Treatment of Childhood Aggression*. Hillsdale, NJ: Erlbaum.

Beaver, R. (1996). *Educational Psychology Casework: A Practical Guide*. London: Jessica Kingsley.

Behan, J. and Carr, A. (2000). Oppositional defiant disorder. In A. Carr (ed.), *What Works with Children and Adolescents*. London: Routledge.

Bernal, M., Durgee, J., Pruett, H. and Burns, B. (1968). Behaviour modification and the brat syndrome. *Journal of Consulting and Clinical Psychology* 32, 447–55.

Brestan, E.V. and Eyberg, S.M. (1998). Effective psychosocial treatments of conduct-disordered children and adolescents: 29 years, 82 studies, and 5,272 kids. *Journal of Clinical Child Psychology* 27, 180–189.

Delfini, L., Bernal, M. and Rosen, P. (1976). Comparison of deviant and normal boys in home settings. In E. Marsh, L. Hammerlynek and L. Handy (eds) *Behaviour Modification and Families*. New York: Brunner/Mazel.

Dishion, T.J., French, D.C. and Patterson, G.R. (1995). The development and ecology of antisocial behavior. In D. Cicchetti and D.J. Cohen (eds) *Developmental Psychopathology*, vol. 2. Chichester: John Wiley.

Dodge, K.A. (1993). Social-cognitive mechanisms in the development of conduct disorder and depression. *Annual Review of Psychology* 44, 559–84.

Eyberg, S.M., Boggs, S.R. and Algina, J. (1995). Parent–child interaction therapy: a psychosocial model for the treatment of young children with conduct problem behavior and their families. *Psychopharmacology Bulletin* 31, 83–91.

Forehand, R. and King, H.E. (1977). Noncompliant children: effects of parent training on behavior and attitude change. *Behavior Modification* 1, 93–108.

Forehand, R. and McMahon, R.J. (1981). *Helping the Noncompliant Child*. New York: Guilford.

Forehand, R., King, H.E., Peed, S. and Yoder, P. (1975). Mother–child interactions: comparisons of a noncompliant clinic group and a nonclinic group. *Behaviour Research and Therapy* 13, 79–84.

Forehand, R., Middlebrook, J., Rogers, T. and Steffe, M. (1983). Dropping out of parent training. *Behavior Research and Therapy* 21, 663–8.

Funderburk, B.W., Eyberg, S.M., Newcomb, K., McNeil, C.B. Hembree-Kigin, T. and Capage, L. (1998). Parent–child interaction therapy with behavior problem children: maintenance of treatment effects in the school setting. *Child and Family Behavior Therapy* 20, 17–38.

Gard, G.C. and Berry, K.K. (1986). Oppositional children: taming tyrants. *Journal of Clinical Child Psychology* 15(2), 148–58.

Griest, D. and Wells, K. (1983). Behavioral family therapy with conduct disorders in children. *Behavior Therapy* 14, 37–53.

Hartman, R.R., Stage, S.A. and Webster-Stratton, C. (2003). A growth curve analysis of parent training outcomes: examining the influence of child risk factors (inattention, impulsivity, and hyperactivity problems), parental and family risk factors. *Journal of Child Psychology and Psychiatry* 44, 388–98.

Haswell, K., Hock, E. and Wenar, C. (1981). Oppositional behaviour of preschool children: theory and intervention. *Family Relations* 30, 440–6.

Hill, J. (2002). Biological, psychological and social processes in the conduct disorders. *Journal of Child Psychology and Psychiatry* 43, 133–64.

Hoffenaar, P.J. and Hoeksma, J.B. (2002). The structure of oppositionality: response dispositions and situational aspects. *Journal of Child Psychology and Psychiatry* 43, 375–85.

Johnson, S.M., Wahl, G., Martin, S. and Johansson, S. (1973). How deviant is the normal child? A behavioural analysis of the preschool child and his family. In R.D. Rubin, J.P. Brady and J.D. Henderson (eds) *Advances in Behavior Therapy*, vol. 4. New York: Academic Press.

Kazdin, A.E. (1987). Treatment of antisocial behaviour in children: current status and future directions. *Psychological Bulletin* 102, 187–203.

Kazdin, A.E. (1997). Psychosocial treatments for conduct disorder in children. *Journal of Child Psychology and Psychiatry* 38(2), 161–78.

Loeber, R. and Stouthamer-Loeber, M. (1998). Development of juvenile aggression and violence: some common misconceptions and controversies. *American Psychologist* 53, 242–59.

McAuley, R. and McAuley, P. (1977). *Child Behaviour Problems*. London: Macmillan.

McMahon, R.J., Forehand, R. Griest, D.L. and Wells, K. (1981). Who drops out of treatment during parent behavioral training? *Behavioral Counselling Quarterly* 1, 79–85.

Moreland, J.R., Schwebel, A.I., Beck, S. and Wells, R. (1982). Parents as therapists: a review of the behavior therapy parent training literature – 1975 to 1981. *Behavior Modification* 6, 250–76.

Murray, L., Sinclair, D., Cooper, P., Ducournau, P. and Turner, P. (1999). The socioemotional development of 5-year old children of postnatally depressed mothers. *Journal of Child Psychology and Psychiatry* 40, 1259–71.

O'Leary, K.D. and Emery, R.E. (1982). Marital discord and child behavior problems. In M.D. Levine and P. Satz (eds) *Middle Childhood: Developmental Variation and Dysfunction*. New York: Academic Press.

Patterson, G.R. (1982). Coercive Family Process. Eugene, OR: Castalia.

Plomin, R. and Hershberger, S. (1991). Genotype-environment interaction. In T.D. Wachs and R. Plomin (eds) *Conceptualization and Measurement of Organism–Environment Interaction*. Washington, DC: American Psychological Association.

Powers, S.W. and Roberts, M.W. (1995). Simulation training with parents of oppositional children: preliminary findings. *Journal of Clinical Child Psychology* 24(1), 89–97.

Rowe, R., Maughan, B., Pickles, A., Costello, E.J. and Angold, A. (2002). The relationship between DSM-IV oppositional defiant disorder and conduct disorder: findings from the Great Smoky Mountains Study. *Journal of Child Psychology and Psychiatry* 43, 365–73.

Schuhmann, E.M., Foote, R.C., Eyberg, S.M., Boggs, S.R. and Algina, J. (1998). Efficacy of parent–child interaction therapy: interim report of a randomized trial with short-term maintenance. *Journal of Clinical Child Psychology* 27, 34–45.

Snyder, H. (2001). Epidemiology of official offending. In R. Loeber and D.P. Farrington (eds). *Child Delinquents: Development, Intervention and Service Needs* (pp. 25–46). Thousand Oaks, CA: Sage.

Wahler, R.G. (1980). The insular mother: her problems in parent–child treatment. *Journal of Applied Behaviour Analysis* 13, 207–19.

Wahler, R.G., Hughey, J. and Gordon, J. (1981). Chronic patterns of mother–child coercion: some differences between insular and non-insular families. *Analysis and Intervention in Developmental Disabilities* 1, 145–56.

Webster-Stratton, C. (1990a). Long-term follow-up of families with young conduct problem children: from preschool to grade school. *Journal of Clinical Child Psychology* 19, 144–149.

Webster-Stratton, C. (1990b). Stress: a potential disruptor of parent perceptions and family interactions. *Journal of Clinical Child Psychology* 19, 302–12.

Webster-Stratton, C. (1993). Strategies for helping early school-aged children with oppositional defiant and conduct disorders: the importance of home–school partnerships. *School Psychology Review*, 22(3), 437–57.

Webster-Stratton, C. and Lindsay, D.W. (1999). Social competence and early-onset conduct problems: issues in assessment. *Journal of Clinical Child Psychology* 28, 25–93.

Webster-Stratton, C. and Spitzer, A. (1991). Reliability and validity of a parent Daily Discipline Inventory: DDI. *Behavior Assessment* 13, 221–39.

Webster-Stratton, C., Reid, J. and Hammond, M. (2001). Social skills and problem-solving training for children with early-onset conduct problems: who benefits? *Journal of Child Psychology and Psychiatry* 42, 943–52.

White, J., Moffit, T., Earls, F. and Robins, L. (1990). Preschool predictors of persistent conduct disorder and delinquency. *Criminology* 28, 443–54.

Chapter 8

Disruptiveness in schools and classrooms

Introduction

> Most pupils believe that they and their teachers have different interests. In their view, it is his business to exact of them hard service, theirs to escape from it; it is his privilege to make laws; theirs to evade them. He is benefited by their industry, they by their indolence; he is honoured by their obedience, they by their independence. From the infant school to the professional seminary this moral warfare exists.
>
> (*English Journal of Education* 1858: 373; cited in Furlong 1985: 1)

Historical accounts of childhood misbehaviour in school (Pearson 1983) remind us that problem behaviour is no recent phenomenon. Nevertheless, concern about rising misbehaviour in school is currently a worldwide concern. In Britain the perception of rising indiscipline is resulting in an increasing use of formal exclusion of disruptive children from school, resulting in a proliferation of Pupil Referral Units (PRUs) and, reflecting the trend towards more inclusive educational practices, the provision of in-house units (Didaskalou and Millward 2002).

Although labels such as 'emotional and behavioural difficulties' and 'disruptive' may be helpful to educationalists in accessing specialist provision for children whose behaviour disrupts classes (Galloway and Goodwin 1987), it is important to note that such terms are largely subjective and often do not clearly relate to specific behaviours. In many cases such labels are reflections of a teacher's mounting concern or anxiety about the impact of a child's behaviour upon others. In his review of the genesis of the 'disruptive pupil', Turkington (1986: 103) notes:

> The definitions adopted for surveys and in published reports were invariably so broad as to allow the inclusion of any incident of misbehaviour. The guiding criterion was the interpretation of the incident rather than the incident itself. This problem was frequently commented on and inevitably implied that pupils defined as 'disruptive' by one teacher or one school

would not be defined in this way by other teachers in the same school or other schools.

Although labelling may be directly related to the freeing of additional resources, in seeking to reduce classroom misbehaviour it is rarely helpful to concern oneself overly with psychological classifications or diagnoses. Rather, it is more important to consider what approaches can be introduced to alleviate or resolve the situation. Such considerations involve a close examination of many factors at three different levels. These, and the approaches associated with them, form the basis of this chapter.

Levels of analysis

The 1980s witnessed a proliferation of interest in ways by which disruptive and challenging behaviour might be tackled in schools. Essentially, approaches were adopted which addressed problems at one or more of three levels: that of the child, the classroom and the school (Elliott and Morris 1991).

When asked to consider the reasons for a child's misbehaviour, many teachers and parents will understandably point to aspects of the child's environment, history or psychological make-up (Miller *et al.* 2002). Environmental factors that are often employed to account for misbehaviour include disruption to family life, poor parenting, socio-economic hardship and physical or sexual abuse. Psychological accounts may focus upon such factors as the child's personality, attitudes, temperament and interpersonal style.

In such accounts, the prime focus usually involves 'within-child' analyses where the source of the problem is located within the child. The child enters the school each day, along with his or her problems, and clashes with teachers and other children are an inevitable consequence. As, in such analyses, the origin of the child's problems is perceived to be located outside of the school gates, it is not surprising that schools feel unsure how best to respond. Often the 'answer' is seen as remedying the child's home circumstances, transferring the child to alternative educational provision, or providing some form of psychological therapy.

It is universally accepted, however, that for the majority of children classroom behaviour may vary considerably, depending upon who is teaching at any given time. Although 'within-child' analyses can provide an indication as to why an individual child has a *propensity* to exhibit problem behaviour in school, these are insufficient as a comprehensive explanation for disruptiveness. A focus on the background and interpersonal dynamics of an individual child neglects the importance of the impact of the teacher in determining what *actually transpires*. The highly skilled teacher may often be able to secure a settled, industrious classroom despite the fact that many of the children have the potential to be extremely challenging. In contrast, a less skilled teacher may be confronted with major disruption even by groups of children who can usually be relied upon to conduct themselves admirably. In surveys of students and their parents, teacher behaviours, in particular, those involving unfair treatment of children, are seen as important precursors to poor classroom behaviour (Miller *et al.* 2002).

During the 1980s attention shifted somewhat from the impact of *individual teachers* upon children's behaviour to that of *schools* as social organisations. Unlike studies conducted during the 1960s that appeared to suggest that differences between schools made little or no impact upon student behaviour and attainment, research during the 1970s (Reynolds *et al.* 1976; Rutter *et al.* 1979) began to suggest that the impact of individual schools as social organisations upon children's general level of performance was significant. Teachers also recognised that the difficulties presented by individual children were often exacerbated or ameliorated by a transfer to an alternative school. It is not simply that the classroom skills of the child's teachers may differ from one school to another but, rather, that the overall general ethos or social climate of each school communicates different messages to the child. For many teachers during the late 1980s and 1990s, it was this 'whole school effect' upon children's behaviour that was targeted as the focus for professional development sessions (Elliott and Morris 1991).

Intervention at the within-child level

The major ways of tackling problems at the within-child level involve a variety of forms of counselling or behavioural techniques. These approaches, of course, have long been misguidedly perceived by some teachers as 'a good talking to' and 'school detention'. Misunderstanding of the precise nature of counselling and behavioural approaches and their potential for teachers has arguably reduced their impact and, in extreme cases, resulted in their being dismissed as of little value for school contexts.

At the most simplistic level, counselling attempts to enable the individual to gain a clearer understanding of his or her attitudes, beliefs, attributions, expectations and values, the impact of others upon his/her behaviour, the nature and impact of his/her behaviour upon others and the relationship of these to the child's psychological and social functioning. In the specific context of challenging behaviour in school, it is generally hoped by school staff that the outcome of counselling will be that the child gains greater self-understanding and that this will lead to a change of behaviour.

Behavioural approaches, in contrast, make rather less demands upon the child's ability to reason and ultimately consider what is the preferred pattern of behaviour (see Chapter 2). With regard to disruptiveness in school, the most widely used technique is contingency contracting. This involves establishing a programme that systematically provides rewards and sanctions demonstrably contingent upon behaviour. The desired behaviours are negotiated, specified and explained to the child. Outcomes directly related to these specified behaviours are made explicit and a system of close monitoring and evaluation is established.

Although it is common for both approaches to be employed in combination, it is important to recognise that, within the context of school, it is the latter approach that often sits more easily within the prevailing power structures.

Counselling, and other forms of talking therapy, are generally based upon the premise that the client recognises that he/she has a problem and wishes to work with another in order to find a solution. Where children have problems that do not directly intrude upon the smooth running of school (e.g. anxiety about peer relationships, grief concerning the loss of a loved family member) the practice of counselling is unlikely to lead to role conflict for the teacher concerned. Many young people who engage in disruptive behaviour in school, however, do not actively seek, or wish to enter into, a counselling relationship, nor do they necessarily wish to reflect upon or change their present circumstances, for often their disruptiveness is proving reinforcing to them.

Although a vast array of differing models of counselling exist, they have in common a general principle that it is the client who has ultimate control, freedom and responsibility to choose what he or she feels is the most effective way forward. The counsellor's task is to help the child gain greater understanding of relevant issues and to empower him/her to decide on a course of action. The decision taken should be accepted and valued by the counsellor. This raises the important question of who in the school can and should engage in the counselling process.

During the 1960s, the notion of the school counsellor, already a fully qualified teacher, who could be non-judgemental and non-authoritarian, gained a degree of popularity. Following the model of the school-based guidance counsellor in the USA, it was anticipated by many that each secondary school would employ a counsellor who would help the child with social, educational and vocational issues. Although the child might be referred by school staff, there would be no doubt that the client was the child rather than the school. In such cases, counsellors would not necessarily see a resolution of those difficulties identified by schools as the central goal of their work.

As educational resources declined and conceptions of the role of the teacher changed to incorporate views of teaching the 'whole child', the notion of the teacher as counsellor gained in popularity. Heads of year or house were increasingly expected to engage in counselling children with a variety of personal and social, as well as educational, problems. Gradually this role was taken up by increasing numbers of classteachers, and skills of counselling (e.g. active listening, reflecting, clarifying and summarising) were widely taught by means of inservice training and published materials (e.g. Langham and Parker 1989).

The value of teachers having basic counselling skills in working with colleagues, young people and their parents has now become widely accepted (Elton Report 1989), although an important distinction should be drawn between the operation of such skills in day-to-day school life and the employment by teachers of counselling as the primary strategy in work with a highly challenging individual.

In contrast with the school counsellor, the teacher's perceived task in 'counselling' challenging children is often to ensure that they are persuaded to change their behaviour in a desired fashion. In such circumstances all of the adult's skills of persuasion may be brought to this task, and existing power differentials are likely to be exploited. In such circumstances is counselling appropriate? Consider, for example, the child who is refusing to wear school uniform and is summoned to the head of year to be 'counselled'. Does the description of the ensuing exchange as counselling mean that the child has a real freedom to make a decision? If the child chooses not to act in accordance with the requirements of the school, is the head of year in a position to accept and value the child's decision? To suggest, as is often the case, that a disinterested head of year is merely helping the child to understand the consequences of continued non-acquiescence, that the child is free to make up his or her own mind in the full knowledge of the likely outcomes, is to debase the notion of what true counselling sets out to achieve. In such situations, and however justifiable it may be, the process is not counselling but exhortation, persuasion and/or threat.

> Counselling is about change – personal change – and as such we cannot, and should not, talk in terms of enforcing counselling on others. It is almost impossible to make people change the more fundamental aspects of themselves *unless they want to*. It is also unethical to try to impose such changes on another person. This is allied at worst to brainwashing or intimidation, and at best to social control.
> (Cowie and Pecherek 1994: 55; emphasis in original)

Such a difficulty, albeit to a lesser extent, may also be encountered by other professionals whose responsibility is to provide support to children with behavioural difficulties. The educational psychologist or LEA behaviour support teacher, although freed from the day-to-day pressure that a child may exert on the classteacher or school management, is still likely to feel a degree of pressure to effect the desired change in the client, to encourage the child to respond in ways which the school, local authority and they themselves might find desirable. This is not, of course, to suggest that the interests of the child are overlooked but, rather, that it may become apparent that the child's interests are best served by ensuring that problem behaviour is reduced. In many circumstances, therefore, it is not clear whether a professional is actually engaging in counselling as understood by the counselling literature or is actually guiding the child to behave in a desired fashion. To illustrate this dilemma, consider the example of Colin.

Colin, aged fourteen, was becoming an increasing problem for his teachers. Although not aggressive or directly challenging to teachers, his continual use of argument, name-calling and general banter towards peers was becoming increasingly disruptive and undermining the quality of many lessons. Colin was somewhat overweight and had a marked physical resemblance to a famous comedian. This attracted risible comment from peers to which he would reply in kind.

At his first interview with the educational psychologist, Colin professed unhappiness at his circumstances and a strong desire that those who were provoking him should be silenced. He agreed to meet with the psychologist over a period of weeks in the hope that ways forward might be deduced.

At an early stage in their sessions, the educational psychologist considered Colin to be locked in a spiral of peer antagonism. As a result, the boy appeared to be unthinkingly engaged in a series of self-defeating behaviours that met neither his needs nor those of others. For this reason, it was considered that counselling should focus upon events in school and Colin would be asked to explore what happened and determine whether he wished change to take place. It was anticipated that Colin's generally good-natured disposition and his obvious desire for a comfortable existence, together with a greater understanding of his own role in provoking conflict, would result in a desire and an ability to modify his behaviour.

Over a number of counselling sessions, Colin's behaviour in school was examined and analysed. Events antecedent to conflict were identified and, using flow-charts on large sheets of paper, Colin was shown how his reactions would often maintain difficulties for himself. Over time, Colin appeared to have much greater insight into the dynamics of his classroom setting and the ways by which he interacted with others.

Once a degree of insight was gained, Colin was reminded that he had earlier expressed a desire to change his circumstances. He was asked what would have to change in order that the verbal aggression and ensuing classroom disruption might be reduced. Colin persisted in his argument that it was his peers, not he, who would have to change, even though he clearly understood his impact upon them. (This is a common feature of work with children where highly contradictory perceptions can be held simultaneously, the less desirable of which may often be maintained by a powerful need to attribute blame to a third party.) During the course of further sessions, Colin came to accept that meaningful change would be likely to take place only if he were to change his normal pattern of classroom behaviour. At this point he announced that he enjoyed the classroom banter – it alleviated the tedium of lessons – and that he had made a decision that he did not want his present circumstances to change. This position was maintained during further follow-up sessions.

The educational psychologist was now in a difficult situation. Within the counselling relationship it had been suggested that Colin should come to his own decisions about future action, based upon the insights and understandings obtained during the sessions. The boy had, however, chosen an unwelcome path that placed him in direct conflict with the school. If he did not change it was clear that a likely outcome would be exclusion followed by an enforced transfer to a disruptive unit. In the opinion of the psychologist this was a most undesirable placement given Colin's circumstances. To what extent, therefore, could the psychologist seek to place greater pressure upon Colin to change his behaviour? The use of behavioural techniques, family controls and school sanctions could be integrated into a programme that might be able to enforce compliance yet would this indicate that the pose adopted in the counselling interview was little more than a sham, that freedom of choice for the child existed only in so far as this represented the desired outcomes of others. On the other hand, was it sufficient for the psychologist to inform the school and local authority that he had done his best but, unfortunately, Colin did not wish to change and thus the case would be closed? The pressure upon local authorities to provide services perceived by schools to be 'effective' might further reduce the appeal of the latter alternative.

In the final analysis it was considered that the risks to Colin of permanent exclusion were so great that the employment of a behaviour modification programme geared to reducing his disruptive behaviour was the most appropriate course of action. Such a programme was subsequently established. This involved itemising and agreeing desired behaviours with Colin, his teachers and his parents. After each lesson his teachers provided him with a score which was recorded on a form. His total daily score was then used to establish the extent to which he would receive a variety of rewards such as pocket money and television.

This programme proved highly effective and, despite his initial reluctance, Colin soon became an enthusiastic participant.

One is left to consider, however, whether this satisfactory end justified the action taken – was it right to take control from the child once he had refused to change in the desired fashion? Despite the fact that Colin appeared not to recognise the contradictions above, it is likely that, with hindsight, the psychologist would have specified the limitations upon the boy's freedom to choose.

It is important to note that fairly intrusive behavioural techniques were required to help Colin to change. While it is widely accepted that the *skills* of counselling are of value to teachers in working with child, parents and colleagues, counselling as a *therapeutic process* is only rarely an effective and sufficient technique for teachers confronted by acts of major indiscipline. Indeed, the series of DfE circulars addressing 'Pupils with Problems' (Department for Education 1994) virtually ignore talking therapies as strategies for helping children with behaviour difficulties.

More recently, many schools have embraced the contribution of mentors whose roles may variously embrace the functions of guidance and of counselling. This reflects a broader trend both in schools and wider communities across the world, with Miller (2002) reporting the existence of more than 7,500 youth mentoring programmes. Mentoring grew in popularity at the end of the 1990s with several large initiatives being introduced into Britain. One scheme, 'industrial mentoring' draws upon volunteers from industry who give up part of their time to assist children of all ages in their learning. The reform of careers and youth services at the end of the 1990s resulted in the development of the Connexions service geared to supporting young people aged thirteen to nineteen. Here each child is provided with a Personal Adviser who assists in a wide range of spheres: academic, vocational and recreational. Excellence in Cities is another Government initiative aimed at improving the educational performance of children from the inner cities. This scheme includes, as a major strand, the employment of school-based learning mentors to work with youngsters. In many schools, mentors are particularly engaged with children experiencing academic or behavioural difficulties.

As with other professionals working alongside schools, there can be tensions about the extent to which mentors should act as advocates for the child when this leads them to challenge the practices of teachers and the decision-making of school management (Marshall *et al.* 2001). Uncertainties as to whether the role requires the mentor to ensure student compliance, what Colley (2003) pejoratively terms 'docility', can lead to difficulties in undertaking a counselling function similar to those noted above. Furthermore, evaluations in the USA suggest that mentor relations may work best where the mentor is not overly wedded to a predetermined agenda. Styles and Morrow (1995), for example, found that it was the experience of a trusting and consistently supportive mentor relationship that predicted a positive outcome for young people, rather than a focus upon specific goals. For many mentors, engaging with and sustaining a meaningful relationship with adolescents, some of whom are likely to hold negative perceptions of adults from the caring professions, is a demanding task (Rhodes 2002) For those employed directly by schools, the task is often complicated by perceived pressure to effect improvement in student behaviour.

Behavioural approaches, in contrast to counselling, have as their primary focus observable behaviours and how these may be modified or shaped (see

Chapter 2) with particular stress placed upon the relationship between be-haviours and their consequences. Put simply, it is considered that behaviour followed by a positive experience is more likely to recur. Behaviour that has no 'pay-off' or, alternatively, an adverse consequence should become less likely to recur. This very simple maxim, stemming originally from work with animals, becomes somewhat problematic, however, when applied to complex social situations such as classrooms or playgrounds.

Unlike animals in experimental situations, humans engage in complex social behaviours, and experience positive and negative results in ways that are not easily reducible to simple cause and effect. The sources of perceived outcomes are similarly many, and the ability of those in authority to control these is comparatively limited. For example, for many adolescents, peer approval is a significantly more powerful factor than any reinforcer (tangible or intangible) which may be at the teacher's disposal.

Behavioural techniques tend to be most effective in settings where the ability to control rewards and sanctions in a consistent and uniform fashion is at its greatest. For this reason, such approaches have become particularly popular in secure settings for children with highly complex and challenging behaviour, as these have relatively high and sustained control over the child's environment and, thus, to the sources of reinforcement. An example of such a setting is Boston Secure Treatment (BST), a maximum-security setting in Massachusetts for children who have been convicted of serious offences such as rape and murder (Elliott 1987). BST operates a highly complex points system for every phase of the child's day from getting up in the morning, having breakfast, attending classes, engaging in group work and therapy, engaging in evening recreation, to going to bed at night. Aggregated scores for the week lead to the children being placed at one of four levels. A child's level is the key factor in determining the privileges that can be enjoyed for the rest of the week. These include such rewards as pocket money, use of radio/TV/computers, use of phones, bedtimes, and the delivery of pizza. Because the children are incarcerated for twenty-four hours a day and priv-ileges are so tightly controlled, the behavioural programme is immensely powerful and provides strong controls on the behaviour of a highly volatile and disordered population.

Although similar programmes can be found in residential special schools for children with behavioural difficulties, it is very difficult to apply these in mainstream school settings. Clearly, such a high degree of control over reinforcement is impossible (and, for many people undesirable) in mainstream schools. These settings can usually offer only a very restricted range of rewards and sanctions, and, given the length of the school day, can exert a direct influence for only six hours on five days a week.

To illustrate, consider the case of Mary, aged fourteen, who is proving to be highly disruptive in her classes. You, as one of her teachers, wish to encour-age her to become more responsive to you by relating such desired behaviour to positive outcomes. What rewards (reinforcements) are open to you? The list is likely to be limited and involve few items that will be perceived as particularly attractive by Mary. Now consider likely rewards that result directly from her disruptiveness. These may include peer approval, amusement at the teacher's discomfort, an escape from perceived boredom, an opportunity to take out her anger towards someone else (a parent, sibling, boyfriend?) on a 'safe' target, an opportunity to mask her insecurities about academic work, the opportunity to exert power/control over another. Where Mary is struggling with major unresolved issues (parental separation, an abusive family, social isolation, low self-esteem) the power of such reinforcers is often likely to be greater than those which adults can substitute.

Furthermore, you are in contact with Mary for only a fraction of her time in school. Although she appears to be presenting difficulties in other lessons, her behaviour does seem inconsistent and clearly differs from one teacher to another. To what extent could you rely upon your colleagues to support you by following the behavioural programme even if you could persuade senior management to establish one? How could you be certain that whatever is set up will not be undermined by Mary's parents, relatives or friends?

The establishment of a behavioural programme for a highly challenging child in a school setting will usually involve close collaboration between teachers, senior management, parents and, in many cases, an external consultant such as an educational psychologist or behaviour support teacher. In drawing up a behavioural programme the following issues will need to be clearly specified (see also Chapter 7):

- a clear definition of the behaviours which are giving cause for concern: information will be required concerning their nature, frequency, intensity, the settings in which they occur – in particular, the extent to which they are situation- or person-specific – which usually requires the establishment of a detailed system of measuring and recording to provide a pre-intervention baseline and demonstrate what gains, if any, are made subsequently;
- precipitating factors which appear to trigger the behaviour and the usual consequences for the child of the behaviour;
- the present and potential range of rewards and sanctions that can be applied at home and at school;
- factors which may undermine the operation of the programme and the means by which these may be overcome;
- complementary ways by which the behaviour difficulties can be addressed (e.g. use of counselling, peer support, amendments to timetabling/ curriculum content and delivery);
- the clear commitment to the programme of all those involved in its operation;

- roles and responsibilities for all those involved in operating and monitoring the programme.

Many attempts to operate individual behavioural programmes founder because there is insufficient attention to detail, progress is not monitored closely and those involved do not adhere closely to agreed action in response to the child's behaviour. Where such failings are not in evidence, behavioural programmes can be very successful. One example, that of Carl, is illustrated below.

Carl, aged nine, attended Hilltown primary school. Located in a highly socially disadvantaged urban area, the school was very experienced in dealing with disaffected, volatile and aggressive children and its teachers were generally highly competent and confident in tackling misbehaviour. Carl, however, was proving too taxing and was at severe risk of being permanently excluded.

Carl could be a pleasant and amiable boy yet he was prone to become defiant and aggressive to adults in authority. When asked to engage in classroom tasks he would often refuse outright and seek to amuse himself by taunting other children or playing with equipment/toys. When confronted by his teacher, he would rapidly become verbally aggressive and begin to shout that no one was going to tell him what to do. If his teacher persisted in demanding that he should acquiesce, Carl would hurl materials around the room prior to running out of school. Although Carl had experienced some difficulties during his infant education, the intensity and frequency of his recent classroom outbursts were not in keeping with his earlier behaviour.

Within the peer group, Carl was perceived as a leader who, through his physical prowess and personal qualities, could control the behaviour of the other members of class. He was skilled in his interactions with peers and appeared to enjoy his influential position. When he wished, he appeared able to relate well to adults. Carl's academic ability was not perceived as problematic, although his behaviour was resulting in underachievement.

Carl was the oldest of three children living at home with their divorced mother. Although Carl's mother was highly concerned about her son's behaviour in school, her attempts to reason with him had proven to be ineffective and she was at a loss to know how to proceed. On occasions, she had stopped him playing out with his friends in the evening or had stopped his pocket money but this 'had not taught him a lesson' and his behaviour had continued unabated.

In his interviews with all concerned, the educational psychologist built up a picture of a boy who had a clear grasp of the nature of his behaviour and its effect upon others. Unlike some children with emotional and behavioural difficulties, Carl appeared not to be overwhelmed by inner tensions, not to have confused attributions as to the intentions of others, did not demonstrate an inability to tolerate perceived provocation or experience an incapacity to maintain acceptable control of his emotions. Rather, it seemed that he enjoyed the exercise of power, found his behaviour in class to be rewarding both in offering him prestige and influence and in providing him with opportunities to avoid undesirable tasks. As Carl's influence with peers grew, and as he passed through to the junior section of the school, he appeared to have gained in confidence to a level that he was now more prepared to challenge school in an outright, defiant fashion. A series of short-term exclusions had made no impact upon his behaviour and it appeared that an inevitable outcome of continued misbehaviour would be permanent exclusion. In such circumstances it appeared essential that Carl should come to recognise the authority of his parents and teachers and be encouraged to participate fully in his education.

In discussions with Carl's mother and teachers, it was agreed that a behavioural programme would be established. This would make highly explicit to Carl exactly what was desired behaviour in school and how this would be related to the exercise of privileges at home. Carl's mother proved highly willing to ensure that agreed outcomes were effected and demonstrated her conviction that she was able to ensure that Carl could not subvert these. (Note: this is an essential element in the operation of such programmes and a lack of parental resolve in carrying out agreed action is often a reason for failure.)

It was decided that the key behaviour to tackle was Carl's propensity to temper tantrums in class and his tendency to storm out of the room. It was explained to him that he would receive a coloured sticker each day if he were able to avoid such responses. If he received a sticker he would be awarded points based upon his behaviour; these would be directly related to pocket money. Stickers and points were entered each day on a chart held by his teachers which would be taken home to be scrutinised by his mother each evening.

In the operation of such programmes, it is important that the child is made aware that privileges such as pocket money, sweets and treats are not always an automatic right. Rewards for desired behaviour, therefore, would normally tend to total little more than that which is already being made available; the key issue is that they are now contingent upon the child's actions. Such a stance helps to reduce the possibility that the child is seen as being rewarded for poor behaviour, or that rewards are perceived as bribes.

Carl's mother wished to add a sanction for severe misbehaviour (i.e. when the sticker was not awarded) and after discussion it was decided that in such cases he would be put into his pyjamas and kept in the house after tea. As Carl enjoyed playing out most evenings, it was clear that he would find this undesirable.

Extensive discussion took place between the educational psychologist, Carl, his mother and teachers in order to ensure that the procedures were fully understood. These were also set out in a letter (see Figure 8.1). Figure 8.2 provides an example of the daily record form.

In these cases a common pattern involves the child obtaining scores which are initially high (a honeymoon period) often followed by a sudden deterioration in behaviour. At such a time, it is easy for the adults concerned to become disheartened and to give up. It is important, therefore, to ensure that everyone concerned adheres closely to the agreed procedures and the child recognises that, unlike many other past attempts to tackle his or her behaviour, the present intervention will be maintained in a consistent and sustained fashion. Such a procedure took place with Carl.

Unlike many children, Carl very quickly reneged on his agreement to maintain a more desirable pattern of behaviour in class. Although Day 1 had witnessed major improvement in his usual behaviour, on the second day he returned to his former behaviour of shouting out, picking arguments with others and refusing to undertake any work. As his teacher attempted to address the situation, Carl threw his books across the room and ran out swearing. Carl did not receive his sticker.

Consequently, that evening the educational psychologist visited Carl's home. Carl was asked to discuss the events of the day and consider the outcomes of his behaviour. He seemed surprised that his mother had stuck to the agreement as in the past she had often been inconsistent in seeing through her threats. As the educational psychologist spoke with Carl and his mother and arranged a home visit later that week from an educational social worker, it would have become clear to Carl that this intervention was not going to go away. Carl's behaviour was subsequently transformed and, during the time that the programme operated (ten weeks), there was no recurrence of such extreme behaviour.

Often behaviour scores are placed on a graph. This helps the practitioner to track changes in behaviour over time. Visual representation of progress can also be highly motivating for all those involved as the child's progress can be made visible and thus provides frequent opportunities for praise and congratulations. In Carl's case, the graph proved highly reinforcing.

It should be recognised that such programmes generally set out to reduce extreme behaviours, to make what are perceived to be intolerable situations manageable. In many cases one would expect children's behaviour to regress after completion of the programme. In successful interventions, however, they do not regress to the former level of severity, intensity or frequency. Although, after the programme was terminated,

Dear Mrs X,

Following our discussion at Hilltown School on 26 March 2002, I thought it would be helpful to make a note of what we agreed about Carl's home–school programme.

1   Carl will be responsible for bringing the form home each evening and returning it to school the following day.
2   The sticker will be necessary each day for Carl to receive any treats that same evening. Should he fail to receive the sticker, he will be sent to his room after tea.
3   When he is successful in obtaining the sticker, Carl may be rewarded with the agreed treats. To receive these, however, he must also obtain a total of nine points for that day.
4   When Carl receives at least nine points he will:
   • be allowed to watch television
   • be permitted to play outside with his friends (if such circumstances as the weather etc. are favourable)
   • receive 60 pence pocket money
   • receive 30 pence for his savings account.
   We agreed that we should stress to Carl that this sum reflects the amount he currently receives and by no means should it be perceived as an *additional* incentive or a bribe to be well behaved. I understand that if Carl succeeds in saving enough money, you are prepared to take him on a shopping trip in order that he might buy some football boots.
5   Any further allowances and treats which you provide will depend upon Carl scoring highly on his weekly total. Attempts will be made, wherever possible, however, to limit the availability of money, sweets, treats and the like from other sources (e.g. relatives, friends), as these will reduce the effectiveness of the programme.
7   Carl will not attempt to influence his teachers by entering into negotiation with them. If this does transpire, his teachers have been asked to place a zero on the record form.
8   Carl's teacher, Mrs Wright, will total the points scored each day and return it to him. You have kindly indicated your willingness to sign the form each evening so that she will be aware that you have seen it.
9   If Carl fails to bring the form home, it should be assumed that he has not behaved appropriately that day and, therefore, the agreed rewards will not follow.
10 I have explained the system to Carl and he appears to understand how it will work.
11 Finally, may I stress again the importance of focusing upon good behaviour and using praise as an important added reward.

I hope that you will feel that this letter represents an accurate account of our agreement. Please contact me as soon as possible if you feel that any changes are needed. If not, we shall aim to start the programme from the beginning of the new term.

   We are grateful for your support and obvious commitment to helping Carl make the most of his education.

Figure 8.1 Letter from the educational psychologist to Carl's mother

Figure 8.2 A completed record form employed for Carl

Carl continued to have difficulties in school from time to time, he was no longer perceived to be particularly difficult, nor did his behaviour warrant further referral to external support agencies.

Factors which reduce the likelihood of effective intervention

It is important to recognise that the successful outcome of the above intervention is not a feature of all behavioural programmes. In the experience of the writers the following factors, if present, greatly reduce the likelihood of a successful home–school behavioural programme:

• The child's behaviour is the result of major emotional confusion and/or a manifestation of severe psychological trauma.
• The child does not have a clear understanding of exactly which behaviours are being addressed and how these will relate to subsequent outcomes.
• The child does not consider that he/she is working with all parties to effect a change in behaviour which is perceived to be helpful for him/her. A strong desire to subvert the programme is clear from the outset.
• Parents are unable or unwilling to suggest rewards which can be made available for desirable behaviour.
• Parents are ambivalent about following through the agreed procedures because they lack the authority or mechanisms of control or because they are concerned that the child will think 'that I don't love him/her' any more.
• Parents do not consider that the behaviour is sufficiently problematic to warrant such concerted intervention.
• Parents are preoccupied with other concerns to an extent that they have insufficient energy/motivation to address the needs of their children.
• Teachers do not have a clear understanding about exactly which behaviours are being addressed. Other issues (e.g. homework completion, where this is not part of the programme) are allowed to affect scores.
• Teachers do not ensure that the monitoring of the scheme is tightly managed. The child's performance is not checked and, where appropriate, praised each day. In secondary schools one member of staff does not assume responsibility for keeping an overview of the programme and addressing weaknesses.
• Teachers fail to appreciate that the programme must be underpinned by skilled and sensitive classroom management.
• External agencies, where these have established the programme, do not maintain an active involvement. As a result, child, parents and teachers may consider that interest in the programme has decreased.
• Regular case discussions are not held and attended by all parties concerned with the operation of the programme.

Intervention at the level of teacher–pupil interaction

It is a truism that, however difficult the child in class, his or her behaviour is determined, to a significant extent, by the effectiveness of the teacher. While few would dispute that at the heart of good teaching is the ability to develop and sustain relationships underpinned by caring and respect (Cothran et al. 2003), such statements offer little practical guidance to those teachers who may find themselves in potentially challenging situations. Beyond the

Rogerian qualities of empathy, warmth, genuineness and unconditional positive regard, essential to many relationships, lies a range of interpersonal behaviours and skills that are common to highly skilled teachers.

During the 1980s, approaches that aimed to tackle school-based disruption concentrated largely upon the development of a range of teacher management skills. These concerned, first, the skills involved in delivering an appropriate curriculum in an educationally sound fashion and, second, those aspects of interpersonal effectiveness by which the authority of the teacher was communicated and accepted. It is the ineffective exercise of these latter skills that often leads to classroom misbehaviour.

The seminal work of Kounin (1970) in the United States suggested that those teachers who were considered to be superior in their management of classroom situations differed from their less effective colleagues not in their response to major acts of indiscipline but, rather, in their ability to prevent difficulties from occurring in the first instance. Kounin's work pointed to the importance of teacher vigilance (or 'withitness'), the need to manage effectively the many demands upon the teacher's attention in the classroom (overlapping), and the skills involved in keeping children alert and free from distraction.

There may be several reasons why teachers fail to be as vigilant as is desirable. In very few cases, some may be unaware of its importance. More often, in circumstances where much effort and concentration is being put into the delivery of complex ideas, or great care is being taken to ensure that the message conveyed is appropriate, teachers, like public speakers more generally, may avoid engaging directly with their audience in order that fewer demands are placed upon their cognitive processing. The demands involved when scanning the classroom environment, thinking about what they are seeing and hearing and considering how they should best respond, while also concentrating upon the content and nature of their delivery, can be highly problematic, particularly for less experienced teachers or those under stress. Such multi-tasking activity also makes significant demands upon teachers' energy levels and can be particularly difficult to maintain when illness or weariness intrude. More worryingly, some teachers reduce their levels of vigilance in circumstances where they have lost confidence in their capacity to prevent or deal with classroom misbehaviour. As a result, a form of 'selective myopia' can result in which the teacher seemingly stops noticing what is happening and has a reduced classroom presence. This can create a vacuum leading to increased dominant or disruptive behaviour on the part of influential members of the student group.

Skilled teachers tend to be able to deal with multiple events in a smooth and authoritative fashion. Not only can they ensure that the classroom runs smoothly, rather like a conductor in an orchestra, they also do not allow intrusive events, such as a wasp flying around the classroom, a child falling off a chair, or the unexpected failure of electronic equipment, to undermine the overarching sense of order. In dealing with overlapping events, such teachers are essentially proactive rather than reactive, and endeavour to convey an impression of quiet confidence whatever the adversity.

In Britain, the work of Robertson (1990) built upon American studies. This work emphasised the nature of teacher authority and how this was signalled through a range of highly subtle verbal and non-verbal cues. From the first meeting of teacher and child, such communication serves to increase or decrease the likelihood of a challenge to the teacher's authority. Many teachers, particularly the less experienced, are unaware of the subtle ways by which children may test them out and only become aware of the potential threat to their authority at a later time. Key non-verbal and verbal behaviours, which add to or diminish the teacher's air of authority, are summarised below:

- eye contact (scanning groups of children);
- one-to-one eye contact;
- rate of speech;
- volume and pitch of speech;
- rhythm, fluency and intonation in delivery;
- pitch of voice;
- body posture and kinaesthetics;
- use of territory/space.

Eye contact

Eye contact is an important element in maintaining alertness, holding the listener's concentration and signalling vigilance. Some speakers have a tendency to focus on objects immediately in front of them or to stare blankly out into space. Others address one part of the audience (usually those in the central region) and appear to ignore the others. It is widely accepted that in addressing any group it is important to suggest to each individual that it is he or she to whom the presentation is being addressed. For teachers, the ability to sweep the classroom visually and give the impression to each child that it is to him or her that the message is being addressed denotes a capacity for vigilance, alertness and a grasp of a professional skill that will be perceived even by very young children.

The individual who controls eye contact in an interaction is generally perceived to be the dominant partner. In direct dealings with children eye contact is likely to be used to convey differing forms of challenge to the teacher. Eyes downcast are usually understood to represent submission or deference to authority; a gaze away, often in a slightly upward direction, suggests sufficient compliance to remain in the speaker's presence but an unwillingness to listen to, or heed, what is being said; a fixed and intense stare, often allied to a rigid posture and a reduction of physical distance, may signal an overt and direct challenge to one's authority and be associated with a degree of physical threat.

It is important to note that these behaviours are conditioned significantly by age, gender and cultural factors. Although enraged infants may stare in a hostile, albeit brief, fashion at the objects of their anger, young children seeking challenge are more likely to employ indirect methods such as averting their eyes and refusing to take notice of the adult. Adolescent girls who wish to signal defiance may similarly avert their gaze while feigning an air of indifference or boredom. The more confrontational 'locked-gaze' behaviours, in a school context, are usually the product of male teacher–male adolescent interactions. This latter situation is particularly problematic and may quickly escalate into physical confrontation.

It is important to note, however, that for children from minority cultures, for example, those of Afro-Caribbean heritage, avoiding eye contact when being chastised is a sign of respect. A failure to recognise cultural differences may increase the likelihood of subsequent conflict.

The skilled teacher reads such signals and draws upon a range of other contextual and interpersonal cues to determine how best to respond, whether to attempt to establish authority in an overt fashion, for example, by saying, 'Look at me when I'm talking to you!', or by using other methods of signalling authority, such as skilfully controlling the dialogue, similarly withholding eye gaze, or appearing not to notice the challenge.

Voice

The voice is another key element in preventing and managing behaviour difficulties. Many individuals project the impression of a lack of confidence in themselves as authority figures by speaking too rapidly or breathlessly, allowing the pitch of their voice to rise when anxious, speaking in a flat, monotone way with little rhythm or cadence and by stammering or struggling to find appropriate words to explain themselves. A common failing resides in the false belief that raising one's voice (by shouting, rather than voice projection) necessarily suggests authority. Although cultural differences vary to the extent that shouting at children is deemed acceptable (e.g. American teachers are often horrified by the raised voices they hear in British classrooms), the effective use of this measure by skilled teachers often serves as an unhelpful model for those who are struggling to demonstrate their authority. What many fail to recognise is that a lowered voice carries a greater suggestion of intent, self-control and authority.

Body language

The third key area concerns the awareness and use of body language (Neill 1991). Anxious teachers tend to adopt rigid, tense postures. They may cross their arms or legs across their body defensively and may feel challenged by a young person's overly relaxed, non-responsive posture (e.g. leaning back in a chair with arms behind head). Relaxed postures reflect status differentials and are a means by which teacher authority may be tested. Similarly, teachers who lack confidence may not circle the classroom environment in a sufficiently casual or extensive manner to suggest that the classroom is their 'territory'. Standing rigidly at the front of the classroom for prolonged periods, staring at the class as a unit in an unfocused manner and adopting defensive mannerisms such as crossing one's arms or rubbing one's face are all behaviours which dramatically increase the likelihood of indiscipline.

Control over communication

At the verbal level it is essential to recognise that authority is usually vested in the individual who is in control of the content and flow of the dialogue. Children may test out adults in authority by posing questions (the answers to which they may have little interest in), making requests, ignoring statements or questions, pausing before replying, and generally seeking control over the communication. Less experienced members of staff may be overly responsive to the child – answering all questions, seeking to maintain a relationship by acquiescing to the child's wishes to as great an extent as possible and proceeding to speak without first gaining the child's full attention. To persevere in such behaviours is to signal to the child that one lacks experience and/or sufficient strength to manage the complexities of classroom life.

Brian, a newly qualified teacher with a class of eight-year-olds, was experiencing considerable difficulties in managing classroom behaviour, despite the fact that he was popular with the class and no one child was displaying severely challenging behaviour. The difficulties he was encountering were largely the result of his own behaviour, as the following event exemplifies.

It was the beginning of the afternoon session and Brian was finishing off his introduction to the class who, seated on the carpet, were breaking off into groups to begin their allotted tasks. The final group, who were going to work in the craft area, were eager to get started, spurred by the knowledge that the area contained a small amount of furry material which was greatly prized by all the children.

Brian's first mistake was to omit to impart some important information about the groups' tasks during the briefing. As the children hurried to the craft table he realised his mistake. His second error was to call further instructions across the room while the children rooted through the materials. As he tried to gain the children's attention (most of whom had their backs to him) he spoke louder with his voice carrying a rather

higher pitch. Finally, he was distracted by another child's desire for attention and he left the group to work unassisted for several minutes. Brian's
behaviour signalled to the whole class that he did not have control over
communication and was unsure as to how this could be gained.

Brian immediately and independently recognised the mistake he had
made with respect to the imparting of directions and, as such, was
unlikely to repeat this error. He had not, however, appreciated that the
tone and pitch of his speech was helping to undermine his authority
and was surprised when this was pointed out to him by an observer.
Fortunately, he was willing to accept help and agreed to the use of
audio recordings of him speaking in the classroom. By modelling voice
projection and intonation and analysing the tapes, Brian's adviser helped
him to become more skilled in the use of his voice, particularly when he
found himself in stressful situations.

Advising and supporting teachers with classroom management problems is
problematic for many reasons: often a conceptual framework for understanding behaviour is lacking, opportunities for colleagues to observe and advise
are limited, and resistance to being observed or accepting proffered advice is
strong.

Skilled professional behaviour often operates at a tacit level and many
highly able teachers find it difficult to articulate what it is exactly that they
do that maintains classroom discipline. The common response of many
experienced teachers when asked about their practice, 'It's just experience,
actually!', is of little help to the novice teacher beset by difficulties.

Although general advice about good practice can be helpful, it is often
only detailed observation of practice that can highlight professional short-
comings; unfortunately, constraints upon staffing rarely render such support
possible.

An ability to control one's classroom is a key skill which lies at the heart
of the teacher's professional identity. Thus for many teachers, in particular
those who are relatively experienced, the suggestion that the misbehaviour
in their classroom stems in part from less than ideal management is highly
threatening and a source of shame. In such cases, there may be strong
pressure to attribute responsibility to the child or children rather than to
oneself. For this reason, struggling teachers may be loath to be observed, and
any advice concerning classroom management may be perceived as a threat
to their professional dignity and thus met by defensiveness, resistance and an
inability to accept personal responsibility.

Despite these difficulties, helping the struggling teacher to develop interpersonal and management skills is generally the single most important means
of reducing the prevalence and intensity of disruptive incidents. Such a view
was endorsed by the Elton Report (1989) which stated that:

1   Teachers' group-management skills are probably the single most import-
    ant factor in achieving good standards of classroom behaviour.
2   These skills can be taught and learned.
3   Practical training in this area is inadequate.

A number of training manuals or packages have been produced to aid teachers
in developing skills for preventing challenging behaviour (e.g. Chisholm
et al. 1986; Rogers 2002). While the delineation of these skills can offer the
new or trainee teacher a valuable conceptual framework to consider his or
her developing knowledge, as has been noted above, for the more experienced
teacher, the ability to manage behaviour is a core professional skill which it
is often considered shameful to lack. For this reason, some teachers may
approach professional development sessions in a defensive manner and feel
constrained in their ability to discuss their difficulties, strengths and weaknesses. If such a dialogue does not take place, professional development in
this area becomes little more than a series of mechanistic prescriptions that
are unlikely to become accommodated within the teacher's existing behavioural repertoire.

As acceptance grows that all children should be included in mainstream
schools, irrespective of the difficulties they encounter, teachers are increasingly finding themselves charged with the education of children with
complex emotional and behavioural difficulties. While accepting the general
principle of inclusive education, teachers may be rather reluctant to accept
students adjudged to have emotional and behavioural difficulties into their
classsrooms (Swinson *et al.* 2003). In such circumstances, it is all the more
important that the nature and role of teachers' management skills is emphasised. Even the most skilled teachers may find their performance deteriorating
when they are under stress, and, in the case of the highly challenging child,
they are less likely to utilise positive strategies when they lack confidence in
their ability to effect behavioural improvement (Poulou & Norwich 2002) .

Intervention at the whole-school level

Research in the 1960s and 1970s appeared to suggest that schools, as individual units, made little impact upon student behaviour or attainment. Large-
scale surveys in the United States (Coleman *et al.* 1966; Jencks *et al.* 1972)
and in Britain (Plowden Report 1967) placed far more emphasis upon family
influences. Subsequently, however, the seminal work of Power *et al.* (1967)
led to a succession of studies (e.g. Reynolds *et al.* 1976; Rutter *et al.* 1979;
Mortimore *et al.* 1988) which provided strong support for the suggestion that schools as social institutions had a significant and differing effect
upon the behaviour and attainment of children.

These findings, together with a general emphasis upon whole-school planning and development, have resulted in most schools attempting to develop

whole-school behaviour policies. Such policies emphasise the importance of shared visions, values and understandings, consistency of expectations, response and management, the structured use of rewards and, to a lesser extent, sanctions for children's behaviour.

Other whole-school initiatives draw upon rather more narrow behavioural principles in the belief that these will result in a climate in which teachers act consistently to reinforce desirable behaviour and eliminate disruptive and uncooperative behaviour. An early programme of this kind for primary schools, BATPACK (Wheldall and Merrett 1985) was commended by the Elton Report, although this has been overtaken in popularity by a highly structured, yet relatively straightforward, American programme, Assertive Discipline (Canter and Canter 1992). Although perceived by some as failing to respect children's and parents' rights (Robinson and Maines 1994), the approach is popular with many teachers who welcome a structured programme in which classroom rules are made clear and relate in contingent fashion to specified rewards and sanctions.

The Assertive Discipline programme is the result of Lee Canter's perception that many teachers with classroom management difficulties are either lacking in assertiveness or are hostile in their dealings with children. It emphasises the importance of making classroom rules and procedures clear and explicit and communicating a strong resolve to back up their instructions with actions where necessary. Where children do not observe the rules, the programme offers a series of punishments, the severity of which usually depends upon the number of times the rules are broken. Sanctions usually range from a warning from the classteacher at the first instance to referral to the headteacher for multiple occurrences.

Despite Government endorsement (DfEE 1998), there has been little structured evaluation of the impact of Assertive Discipline upon schools and much of the current controversy has centred upon philosophical issues concerning the ethics of the techniques advocated (Maines and Robinson 1995; Robinson and Maines 1994; Swinson and Melling 1995). One detailed study of fifteen British primary school classrooms (Nicholls and Houghton 1995), however, indicated that, for some classes, the introduction of Assertive Discipline resulted in an increase in on-task behaviour and a concomitant decrease in the frequency of disruptive behaviour.

A difficulty with programmes such as Assertive Discipline is that while teacher management skills are emphasised in the training manuals, these may be subsequently overlooked in the desire to implement punitive structures for those who misbehave. Thus the programme may become little more than a highly structured system of providing in-class sanctions and referrals to senior management. Rather than using interpersonal skills to prevent or deflect problem situations, the teacher may feel tempted to highlight the 'problem' and seek to invoke punitive consequences in order to demonstrate his or her authority. Thus any attempt to introduce whole-school behaviour programmes should ensure that the day-to-day, preventive skills of the class-room teacher, rather than the school's formal disciplinary procedures, are emphasised.

Furthermore, while the adoption of a whole-school approach is invaluable for increasing the positive climate of school, and should, over time, inevit-ably reduce the frequency and intensity of disruption (see, for example, Elliott and Morris 1991), it is unlikely that establishing and operating a whole-school policy on behaviour is sufficient as a solution to problems currently posed by a particularly difficult child. In such circumstances, an examination of interpersonal dealings at school and in the home, exploration of the poten-tial of behavioural approaches, and a detailed analysis of the suitability of the educational tasks that are being presented are likely to be more promising in the short term.

Summary – what sort of intervention strategy is appropriate?

In attempting to prevent or manage a disruptive situation in the classroom it is necessary to consider the impact of individual child factors, the inter-actional pattern and skills of teachers' classroom management and the impact of the school as a social institution. The intervention strategy that is adopted will depend upon individual circumstances, particularly the extent to which the difficulty is specific or general (see Figure 8.3).

It is important to note that Figure 8.3 refers to an underlying *emphasis* rather than to the employment of discrete strategies. A coherent and struc-tured whole-school approach should reduce the likelihood and frequency of severe behavioural difficulties. Where these do exist, however, improving teachers' classroom management skills and ensuring a high quality of curric-ulum delivery are more likely to produce a solution in the short term. Where

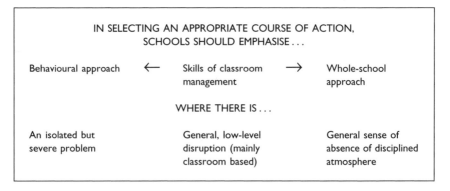

Figure 8.3 Intervention strategies

a school is experiencing difficulty with a particular child, especially where this is not specific to one teacher, a behavioural intervention may be the most productive solution. Ideally, however, intervention should operate at all three levels and, indeed, classroom management and behavioural approaches are often considered as part of a broader whole-school approach (e.g. Galvin *et al.* 1990).

References

Canter, L. and Canter, M. (1992). *Assertive Discipline*. Santa Monica: Lee Canter Associates.

Chisholm, B., Kearney, D., Knight, G., Little, H., Morris, S. and Tweddle, D. (1986). *Preventive Approaches to Disruption*. London: Macmillan.

Coleman, J.S., Campbell, E., Hobson, C., McParland, J., Mood, A., Weinfeld, F. and York, R. (1966). *Equality of Educational Opportunity*. Washington, DC: US Government Printing Office.

Colley, H. (2003). Engagement mentoring for 'disaffected' youth: a new model of mentoring for social inclusion. *British Educational Research Journal*, 29, 521–42.

Cothran, D.J., Kulinna, P.H. and Garrahy, D.A. (2003). 'This is kind of giving a secret away . . .': students' perspectives on effective class management. *Teaching and Teacher Education* 19, 435–44.

Cowie, H. and Pecherek, A. (1994). *Counselling: Approaches and Issues in Education*. London: David Fulton.

Department for Education (DfE) (1994). *Pupils with Problems*. London: DfE.

Department for Education and Employment (DfEE) (1998). *Meeting Special Educational Needs: An Action Programme*. London: DfEE Publications.

Didaskalou, E.S. and Millward, A.J. (2002). Breaking the policy log-jam: comparative perspectives on policy formulation and development for pupils with emotional and behavioural difficulties. *Oxford Review of Education* 28, 109–21.

Elliott, J. (1987). The treatment of serious juvenile delinquents in Massachusetts. *Educational Psychology in Practice* 3(2), 49–52.

Elliott, J. and Morris, J. (1991). Teacher in-service and the promotion of positive behaviour in school. *British Journal of In-Service Education* 17(2), 111–19.

Elton Report (1989). *Discipline in School*. London: HMSO.

Galloway, D. and Goodwin, C. (1987). *The Education of Disturbing Children*. New York: Longman.

Furlong, J. (1985). *The Deviant Pupil: Sociological Perspectives*. Milton Keynes: Open University Press.

Galvin, P., Mercer, S. and Costa, P. (1990). *Building a Better Behaved School*. Harlow: Longman.

Jencks, C., Smith, M., Acland, H., Bane, M.J., Cohen, D., Gintis, H., Heyns, B. and Michelson, S. (1972). *Inequality: A Reassessment of the Effect of Family and Schooling in America*. New York: Basic Books.

Kounin, J.S. (1970). *Discipline and Group Management in Classrooms*. New York: Holt, Rinehart and Winston.

Langham, M. and Parker, V. (1989). *Counselling Skills for Teachers*. Lancaster: Framework Press.

Maines, B. and Robinson, G. (1995). Assertive discipline: no wheels on your wagon – a reply to Swinson and Melling. *Educational Psychology in Practice* 11(3), 9–11.

Marshall, S., Elliott, J.G. and Alborough, C. (2001). *Modelling Connexions? Some Evidence from Personal Adviser Practice*. Newcastle: Newcastle City Council.

Miller, A. (2002). *Mentoring for Students and Young People: A handbook of Effective Practice*. London: Kogan Page.

Miller, A., Ferguson, E. and Moore, E. (2002). Parents' and pupils' causal attributions for difficult classroom behaviour. *British Journal of Educational Psychology* 72, 27–40.

Mortimore, P., Sammons, P., Stoll, L., Lewis, D. and Ecob, R. (1988). *School Matters: The Junior Years*. Wells: Open Books.

Nicholls, D. and Houghton, S. (1995). The effect of Canter's Assertive Discipline Program on teacher and student behaviour. *British Journal of Educational Psychology* 65(2), 197–210.

Neill, S. (1991). *Classroom Nonverbal Interaction*. London: Routledge.

Pearson, G. (1983). *Hooligan: A History of Respectable Fears*. Macmillan.

Plowden Report (1967). *Children and their Primary Schools*. London: HMSO.

Poulou, M. and Norwich, B. (2002). Cognitive, emotional and behavioural responses to students with emotional and behavioural difficulties: a model of decision-making. *British Educational Research Journal* 28, 111–38.

Power, M.J., Alderson, M.R., Phillipson, C.M., Schoenberg, E. and Morris, J.N. (1967). Delinquent schools. *New Society* 10, 542–3.

Reynolds, D., Jones, D. and St Leger, S. (1976). Schools do make a difference. *New Society* 37, 321.

Rhodes, J.E. (2002). *Stand By Me: The Risks and Rewards of Mentoring Today's Youth*. Cambridge, MA: Harvard University Press.

Robertson, J. (1990). *Effective Classroom Control*. London: Hodder and Stoughton.

Robinson, G. and Maines, B. (1994). Jumping on a dated wagon. *Educational Psychology in Practice* 9(4), 195–200.

Rogers, W. (2002). *Classroom Behaviour: A Practical Guide to Effective Teaching, Behaviour Management and Colleague Support*. London: Paul Chapman.

Rutter, M., Maughan, B., Mortimore, P. and Ouston, J. (1979). *Fifteen Thousand Hours*. London: Open Books.

Styles, M.B. and Morrow, K.V. (1995). *Understanding How Youth and Elders form Relationships: A Study of Four Linking Lifetimes Programs*. Philadelphia: Public/Private Ventures.

Swinson, J. and Melling, R. (1995). Assertive Discipline: four wheels on this wagon – a reply to Robinson and Maines. *Educational Psychology in Practice* 11(3), 3–8.

Swinson, J., Woof, C. and Melling, R. (2003). Including emotional and behavioural difficulties pupils in a mainstream comprehensive: a study of the behaviour of pupils and classes. *Educational Psychology in Practice* 19, 65–75.

Turkington, R. (1986). In search of the disruptive pupil: problem behaviour in secondary schools. Unpublished PhD thesis, University of Leeds.

Wheldall, K. and Merrett, F. (1985). *The Behavioural Approach to Teaching Package (BATPACK)*. Birmingham: Positive Products.

Chapter 9

Drug and solvent abuse

The use of drugs to create a sense of well-being has been a feature of many cultures throughout the centuries. Within our own culture the use of alcohol and tobacco has been quite acceptable for many years, although health concerns around the use of tobacco are now greatly reducing its acceptability. For almost as long, the use of illicit drugs has also been an accepted part of life for the literary elite, as Thomas De Quincy's *Confessions of an English Opium Eater* testifies. However, in the past forty years the use of illicit drugs such as heroin, cocaine and cannabis has shown a dramatic increase and has become so endemic that in certain parts of western culture such drug use must be considered the norm. Images of drug use constantly press upon us, and part of that image is of drug abuse being routine among the young. Certainly in the early nineties there was a marked increase in drug use with some reports estimating it being a feature of the lives of 24 per cent of the sixteen-year-olds in the United States (Gilvarry 2000). Of course, under-age drinking is a routine way for many teenagers to demonstrate rebellion and individuality, and it is becoming more common for drug experimentation to be used in similar way – a study in the north-west of England found that half of the children had tried drugs before they were sixteen years of age (Parker *et al.* 1995). Overall, there also continues to be an upward trend of usage in the UK, particularly in cannabis and the 'party drugs' such as ecstasy (Gilvarry *et al.* 1995).

Reasons for drug usage

Adolescence is a time of transition when young people are seeking to establish their own identities. This is partly achieved by experimentation and by challenging adult concepts and expectations. There are, of course, many ways to do this, two of which are under-age drinking and experimenting with drugs. No matter how adolescents try to establish a sense of separate identity, they are very adept at justifying their behaviour, and this can be extremely exasperating for the adults around them. They tend to win in any debate, in part because with adolescence comes the ability to think hypothetically, which is in contrast to the very concrete pattern of thinking which is typical of childhood (Piaget 1952). Because of this, it is important to avoid trying to offer discipline only through debate – such an approach is liable to see the adult losing.

Perhaps even more critically from a drug-usage point of view is the fact that this phase of development is one where the young person feels a need to place great reliance upon friends. Copying the group in dress or behaviour and behaving in ways that win their approval are felt as key elements of being successful as a teenager. If the group of friends views drug experimentation as part of their pastimes, then this can exert a powerful influence upon steering a young person to drug usage.

A great deal of work has been carried out in an effort to try to predict who might become a significant drug user. Consistently, such work shows that although drug users often have personality problems, such as being considered immature, there is no specific personality type that predicts future drug addiction (Ghodse 1995). Family history of drug use may be influential (Hoffmann and Cerbone 2002), and it is therefore important to look at all aspects of the young person's life and functioning in order to understand the origins of the problem, and the factors that are helping to maintain it. Although there can be many reasons for someone to begin taking drugs, a key distinction which needs to be made is between drugs that are being used to cope with the stress of a severe psychiatric illness and their use to be part of a particular youth culture. The former type of user is usually a solitary individual, and often demonstrates many other problems and difficulties. Indeed, recent studies have suggested that perhaps up to one-third of young people who have an addiction problem may have other psychiatric disorders (Hovens et al. 1994) and these often started before the drug abuse began (Christie et al. 1988).

As already mentioned, the origins of abuse are very individual but it has been recognised for some time that such problems can run in families, which has prompted considerable interest in whether addiction problems may actually be inherited. There is evidence that becoming dependent on alcohol may have an inheritable component counting for up to 60 per cent of the influence (Pickens et al. 1991), but it has not been shown that a similar inheritance pattern exists with other forms of addiction. Genetics is not the only way that families influence their children, and indeed a child's desire to copy parents is one of the stronger determinants of future patterns of behaviour. This mechanism is a powerful factor in drug use, for if there is a pattern of parental drug abuse there is a greatly increased likelihood that the child will also develop such a habit (Bewley et al. 1974). For many teenagers, however, one of the strongest influences on their immediate behaviour remains the peer group with which they spend their time. This is reflected in the changes that have occurred in the preferred drug of misuse, which has tended to change with changes in youth culture – the 1960s saw 'flower-power' and LSD as the favoured drug, in the 70s and 80s this changed to heroin and solvents, and in the 90s it has been cannabis and stimulants such as ecstasy.

When is drug use a problem?

For some drugs, such as alcohol and tobacco, usage is so common that it cannot be considered an abnormal activity. In addition, discovering that a teenager has been trying cigarettes or drinking alcohol should not provoke an overreaction. Offering long lectures, or too intense a display of disappointment, runs the risk of seeing the behaviour repeated. Isolated episodes should be treated as such. Recognising that usage is now becoming regular obviously increases adult concern, and encouraging the young person to seek counselling from local youth projects or drug treatment teams is helpful. The ways that parents, teachers and other concerned adults can help are described towards the end of this chapter.

The pattern of usage can be described as addiction when it is causing problems to the young person's health, or alters social or psychological functioning. At this stage advice from the nearest community addiction team can be invaluable, but it is very rare that real help can be given to drug users until they are willing to receive it. Sadly the commonest scenario is that the young person will only seek help as a last resort. In the early 90s persistent addicts usually began the significant drug taking around nineteen years (Gossop et al. 1994b), but the trend is now for usage to start in the early teens (Gilvarry 2000).

When a young person is addicted to drugs the addiction is not only maintained because of the sense of physical craving, but often, more powerfully, by a sense of psychological dependence. In this the addict believes that he or she cannot cope without the drug, and anticipates significant problems if the drug is stopped. It is this anticipation which powerfully contributes to feeling the need to continue. In addition to these elements of dependence, and the problems experienced as a result of the withdrawal of the specific drug, the sense of needing to keep using drugs can also be reinforced if there are significant environmental and social factors. Difficulties within the family, such as seeing marital violence or feeling that parents no longer care about you, can be very potent sources of distress which the young person can only relieve by becoming intoxicated (Braucht et al. 1973). Indeed, sometimes the driving force may be to try to blot out some passage within the adolescent's own past which is just too painful to come to terms with.

Donna was nine years old when her father died in a car crash. In the year before his death there had been concern within the police and social services that he was sexually abusing Donna, but sufficient proof was not found. From the age of twelve years Donna began missing school, and she was frequently in trouble with the police for stealing. No matter what the time of day, or night, she was usually to be found sitting in the local park with a group of older boys, in an intoxicated state. On several occasions she needed to be taken to the local hospital because she had taken a cocktail of pills and alcohol which had rendered her incoherent.

Donna's mother acknowledged that she was not able to control her daughter's behaviour, and four weeks after her fourteenth birthday she was received into the care of the local authority. Initially, she went to live with a local foster family, but she continued to stay out until very late at night, and was usually returned in an intoxicated state either by her friends or the police.

After three months Donna was moved to a children's home which offered closer supervision than the foster family could manage. The first few days were quiet, but Donna gradually became more moody, and would fly into violent rages when thwarted or challenged in any way. She began absconding from the home, and would often be missing for days at a time. When found, she was unkempt and would openly recount stories of criminal activity, drug usage and sexual activity which sometimes included prostitution.

Donna was referred to the local adolescent psychiatry service, and in the sessions there Donna would describe the vivid dreams she had when she tried to sleep. These were always scenes from her early abuse – her bedroom, a sense of being trapped, and feelings of pain and self-disgust. She described how during the day she would sometimes see a flash image of herself in which the front of her nightdress was covered in blood. Donna would avoid looking in a mirror because she said her body disgusted her and explained that the only way she could escape these feelings and images was to 'numb herself' with pills. Donna was, however, adamant that she did not want any psychiatric treatment because she was not a 'nutter'.

After four months in the children's home Donna was arrested for breaking into a chemist's shop. She was remanded to secure accommodation and within two days of arriving began to show the symptoms of withdrawal from sedatives. She successfully completed a withdrawal programme within the secure setting, and after several weeks she began to talk to staff on the unit about her recollections of her abuse.

Donna's story illustrates several of the problems that professionals face when confronted with someone who is routinely abusing drugs. The pattern of self-destruction in this case was being fuelled by recollections of early abuse which were too painful for Donna to deal with. Her method of 'escape' was to be almost permanently intoxicated. Although professional intervention could assist her to deal with these issues, she did not want to cooperate with it, leaving the adults around her feeling powerless to help. Similarly, her drug usage could not be dealt with without her cooperation, and it was only when her general behaviour became totally unruly that formal legal action could be taken. It is sadly true that for most cases of persistent drug usage the situation has to sink to a considerable depth before those concerned for the addict are permitted to offer real help.

An issue that is also of growing significance is the impact of a mother who is using illicit drugs during pregnancy, and its impact upon the infant. There is clear evidence that both perinatal substance abuse and environmental stress in early life produce profound persistent alterations in brain structure and functioning (Thadani 2002). As well as increasing the likelihood of many physical and behavioural disorders (Johnson and Leff 1999), parental drug use also increases the risk of the child abusing drugs when in their teens, although a strong family bond appears to reduce this risk (Hoffmann and Cerbone 2002). Parental abuse of alcohol also increases the risk of the children in the family having drug involvement (Obot *et al.* 2001), as well as increasing their risk of developing mental health and behavioural problems. Recognising that a child's difficulties may be exacerbated by parental substance misuse, and how best to respond (McNamara *et al.* 2000) is becoming an increasingly important task in the childcare field.

Drugs of abuse

Alcohol

The vast majority of senior secondary schoolchildren admit to under-age drinking. Indeed, in a recent survey it was found that over half of fifteen-year-olds in Scotland and Wales had been drunk twice in the previous year (King *et al.* 1996). In some this can be a pattern of quite heavy alcohol consumption, but the problems of dependence tend not to occur until adulthood. As with drug use generally, it is said that the drinking has become problematic when there is a deterioration in day-to-day functioning or in general health. It is important to realise that young people who use many different drugs will frequently also use alcohol, and so a young person who is clearly intoxicated may not only have been drinking.

Effects

Research in recent years has suggested that small amounts of alcohol may be helpful to health by reducing the potential for heart disease (Doll *et al.* 1994). However, chronic abuse of alcohol is clearly not healthy. As with most drugs of abuse, one of the first signs of addiction is that of tolerance. This is where the young person finds that there is a need to drink increasing amounts in order to achieve the same effect of well-being and intoxication. Tolerance occurs because the body, and in particular the liver, becomes more adept at dealing with the alcohol and so minimises its effect more rapidly as time goes on. It is also worth noting that women appear to metabolise alcohol less well than men, and so smaller amounts, at least in the initial stages of chronic abuse, are capable of producing equivalent levels of intoxication (Frezza *et al.* 1990).

Features of withdrawal

The body's increased capacity to cope with alcohol gradually leads to a steady state in which the normal functioning of the body's systems requires a persistent level of alcohol. When this state has been achieved the young person is said to be showing physiological dependence. At this point, if there is a sudden withdrawal of the alcohol, the young person gradually becomes restless, agitated and tremulous. In severe cases the adolescent may become confused, disorientated and have vivid hallucinations. This severe withdrawal picture (known as the delirium tremens) is uncommon in adolescents, but if it should occur, it needs immediate medical treatment.

Initial intervention and responses to acute intoxication

Most adolescents will have episodes when they become significantly intoxicated. The first priority in such situations is to ensure their safety. Because they are liable to vomit, they should not be allowed to lie on their backs, but kept on their sides. With intoxication comes confusion, so a warm soothing tone should be used to keep reassuring them where they are, and that they are safe. Dehydration always follows excess, and is the main cause of the hangover. The drinking of small quantities of water should be encouraged on a frequent basis, and vigilance maintained so that any vomiting does not obstruct the breathing.

If the adolescent is too young to drink, then action needs to be taken. Long lectures or too intense a display of disappointment should be avoided, for this may be counterproductive. It is also important to avoid letting anger colour the intervention. Rather, it should be assumed that such events will happen and the sanction for such behaviour planned in advance. The next day the planned sanction should then be imposed with the minimum of comment. It is the imposition of a sanction that has an impact, not its severity. The cool, brisk intervention is far more effective than long speeches and lengthy punishments. If the episodes begin to form a regular pattern, then a formal behavioural programme (such as described in Chapter 7) may help, recognising, of course, that regular drinking of alcohol is a quite acceptable element of many people's lives.

If the drinking is clearly to excess, and is beginning to cause ill-health or problems with maintaining a daily routine, then the situation has reached the abuse stage. The management of alcohol abuse demonstrates many of the approaches that are used to deal with any drug addiction. First, it is important to recognise that the young person must be willing to cooperate with any treatment regime if it is to stand any chance of success. Admitting adolescents to hospital against their will is possible, but can only be achieved by using the powers of the Mental Health Act (1983). This requires that two doctors agree that the young person:

- is suffering from mental disorder of a nature or degree which warrants the admission; and
- ought to be detained in the interests of his or her own safety or with a view to the protection of another person.

Practitioners are very reluctant to detain people in hospital against their will, and so such a course of action for someone with a drug problem would be very rare, and probably reserved for someone who was acutely intoxicated and out of touch with reality. They would also need to be at risk of harm, or harming others, and even in such circumstances they would be kept in hospital only for as long as they were confused and disorientated.

Detoxification

If the young person is willing to cooperate with the treatment, then referral to the community addiction team is the first step. Usually the team can be approached directly, or the adolescent's general practitioner can make a referral. The first stage of the process is to look for any physical illness that may be increasing the difficulties. Most regimes routinely give courses of vitamins because young people who have been drinking excessively for any period of time usually have had a very poor diet. The second stage is gradually to reduce the amount of alcohol within the young person's system. This detoxification can cause the adolescent to become very ill, and so it is usual to give regular tranquillisers (such as Librium) which help to reduce the worst of the effects that withdrawing the alcohol can cause. Once the effects of stopping the alcohol have been overcome the tranquillisers can be gradually withdrawn and the detoxification programme is complete.

Psychological support

If stopping the drinking is to have any chance of success, it is important that at an early stage the issues which started the drinking, and are maintaining it, are explored and addressed. This can take a variety of forms from brief, focused work which only looks at stopping drinking, to more detailed exploration of life history to understand the origins of the drinking. For most young people detoxification is not necessary, and it is the psychological management which is the central requirement. Community addiction teams obviously have great expertise in this area, but skilled counsellors within doctors' surgeries and schools, as well as psychiatry teams, can offer appropriate support providing they have experience of dealing with such difficulties.

In some young people there are clearly social and psychological problems behind the drinking, and dealing with them can be quite a lengthy process. Many drinkers have developed a belief that they cannot get through a day successfully without drinking, and the use of cognitive techniques can help to address these issues. Many programmes involve the use of groups which allow the members to feel they are not alone in trying to deal with their difficulties, and some organisations such as Alcoholics Anonymous offer a very intensive programme of self-analysis and mutual encouragement.

Over the years there have been various attempts to use behavioural techniques to control drinking habits. The most well established of these is the use of a drugs such as disulfram and acamprosate. With this type of drug in the bloodstream any alcohol creates strong feelings of nausea and physical discomfort, including throbbing headache and palpitations, and the intention is to create a sense of aversion to the thought of any further drinking. The decision to use such an approach is now seen as a last resort, especially in the young, because if the young person is determined to drink despite the treatment, potentially life-threatening complications can occur, such as irregular heartbeat or a dramatic drop in blood pressure.

Sedatives

Effects

As the name implies, this group of drugs tends to reduce brain activity and clinically they are often used to reduce anxiety or induce sleep. They are also capable of reducing muscle activity and so are sometimes used to help with muscle strains and other such injuries. Although barbiturates were the initial drugs of abuse in this group, the benzodiazepines are now mainly used, with temazepam being the drug which has prompted the most concern about illicit use (Ruben and Morrison 1992).

Young people who abuse sedatives often use other types of drugs as well, especially alcohol. Episodes of violent behaviour are sometimes seen in regular abusers, but generally the picture is one of intoxication similar to alcohol.

Features of withdrawal

The drugs within this group cause physical dependence and so, if a regular user is deprived of the drug, there can be a withdrawal syndrome which is similar to the one seen with chronic alcoholism. In mild cases the addict

ALCOHOL

Method of use Drinks.

Effects on user Relaxation and reduced inhibition. Effects begin within ten minutes and can stay in the bloodstream for several hours. Although the user is not aware of it, judgement and manual dexterity are impaired, and so driving while intoxicated is especially dangerous.

In excess Slurred speech and uncoordinated movements. Moods may be exaggerated. Alcohol will increase the effects of any other drugs that are taken.

What to look for Slurred speech and unsteady gait. Very distinctive smell.

Upon withdrawal After acute intoxication – headache and clouded thinking, often with nausea and abdominal pains.
   When dependent upon alcohol – tremors and visual hallucinations. Can become confused and disorientated (delirium tremens).

SEDATIVES

Other names Barbs, and benzodiazepines such as temazepam ('wobbly eggs'), diazepam ('yellows/blues') .

Method of use Ingested, though occasionally injected.

Effects on user Intoxication, with drowsiness, lack of co-ordination and sleepiness.

In excess Sedation and coma.

What they look like Commercial products – usually as tablets or capsules.

What to look for Intoxication, with marked sedation.

Upon withdrawal Depressed or paranoid.

Figure 9.1 Comparison of alcohol and sedatives
Source: Adapted from National Drugs Helpline information

becomes restless and anxious, and has great difficulty sleeping. In more severe cases the young person may go on to have seizures, become delirious, develop a high body temperature (hyperthermia) and a very rapid heartbeat (tachycardia). Such a reaction can be life threatening and so when present immediate medical attention is necessary. While waiting for medical attention, the person should be kept calm, and someone who understands first aid and resuscitation must remain with them.

   Withdrawal from barbiturates usually resolves in about eight to ten days but the longer-acting benzodiazepines cause problems for much longer. Some people still show the effects of withdrawal many months after stopping the drug. The most potent drugs within the group, such as alprazolam (Xanax) and triazolam (Halcion) can produce some of the most severe withdrawal symptoms if they have been the drug of regular abuse.

Detoxification

When it is suspected that someone has a sedative addiction it is important to form a clear picture of how much of the drug they have been taking. A regular heavy user will need the assistance of the community addiction team to detoxify. The first stage in such a process is to transfer from the sedative to a long-acting drug such as diazepam. This is given to minimise the withdrawal effects of the abuse drugs, and ideally a mild intoxication should be created. After stabilisation the dose of diazepam can gradually be reduced, and such a process often needs a lengthy stay within hospital. Sometimes antidepressants which have sedative qualities may be used, especially if the patient has clear disturbances of mood.

Psychological support

Even after a successful detoxification programme young people often continue to experience difficulties with sleep, anxiety, depression, headaches and muscle-aches which is known as the abstinence syndrome. The chronic presence of such symptoms is a very common reason for the person to revert to being a drug user, and so the psychological support described above is an important element in any attempt to stop sedative addiction. Again, if the usage is not severe, then skilled counsellors can help the young person to explore the issues which may have caused the problem, and may develop strategies to reduce the risk of reuse.

Stimulants

Effects

As the name implies, this group of drugs increases certain aspects of thinking and sensation which has led to the use of names such as 'uppers' and 'speed' being used to describe them. Methylamphetamine (crystal, meth, ice) creates a rapid feeling of well-being, vigour and physical power. This is described as the 'rush'. Four to six hours later these feelings of increased well-being give way to a sense of unhappiness, anxiety and depression which is known as 'the crash'. This can sometimes be quite profound and suicidal gestures are not uncommon. The tremendous sense of health decreases each time the drug is used. This increasing tolerance to the drug means that larger and larger doses need to be taken in order to create a similar effect.

Some of the most potent stimulants, for example, smoking methylamphetamine, can produce so intense a change of thinking that the sense of well-being is replaced by a complete disorganisation of thoughts and psychotic symptoms emerge. These psychotic symptoms can usually be distinguished from a severe psychiatric illness because the hallucinations are

---

STIMULANTS

Other names Speed, uppers, whiz, amph, billy, sulphate.

Method of use Sniffed or taken by mouth. Occasionally it is injected.

Effects on user Quickly creates a feeling of energy and confidence, which lasts for about four hours. The typical side-effects are a dry mouth, constipation and an inability to sleep.

In excess Increased pulse rate and blood pressure. There can be marked mood swings, episodes of aggressive behaviour, a sense of panic and even paranoia.

What they look like White, pink or yellow powder, or tablet.

What to look for Energetic, and more intense than usual. Significant mood swings and complaints about side-effects.

Upon withdrawal Depressed, or paranoid.

Figure 9.2 Features of stimulants
Source: Adapted from National Drugs Helpline information

vivid visual ones and occur at a time when the young person is confused and disorientated (Poole and Brabbins 1996).

One of the best-known drugs within this group is cocaine. This comes from the leaves of the coca plant which originally grew in the Andes of South America. It was used by the Incas for some time before becoming a regular treatment in western medicine for such diverse problems as hysteria and asthma. Although Coca-Cola derived its name from the fact that it contained cocaine, this was actually replaced in 1903 by caffeine and, indeed, in the early part of the century cocaine was a little-used drug, only being popular with artists and people of a bohemian lifestyle.

In the 1960s the drug experienced a renewed popularity and rapidly gained the reputation of being 'glamorous', with the commonest methods of use being by injection or inhaling the powdered form. In the 1970s it was found that the potency of taking cocaine could be increased if it was inhaled while being heated with a solvent. This became known as 'freebasing'. A further refinement to the process was developed in the 1980s, when drug suppliers began to heat cocaine and solvents at higher temperatures, which removes the hydrochloride part of the chemical structure. This process also allows impurities to settle to the bottom, leaving brown crystals. It is these crystals which are heated and inhaled, and because of the distinctive crackling sound that they make when they are heated, this form of cocaine has become known as 'crack'. Both refined forms of cocaine give a very intense sense of well-being which lasts only for a brief time and is inevitably followed by a very profound 'crash'. The intensity of both the positive rush and the after-effects make this a highly addictive drug, though there is evidence that smoking the drug is less addictive than injecting it (Gossop *et al.* 1994a).

Cocaine creates a sense of well-being, with the young person often talking excessively and perhaps becoming quite agitated. The crash produces sleeplessness, depression and an increasing craving for more cocaine (Gawin and Ellinwood 1988). The effects can remain evident for several weeks afterwards, with the user showing marked lethargy, apathy and depression.

In the UK about 2 per cent of eleven- to sixteen-year-olds have experimented with cocaine (Wright and Pearl 1990). Regular cocaine usage carries with it significant physical problems. If the drug is taken by means of injection, obviously there are concerns to do with HIV and hepatitis as well as the potential for infections within the blood. The drug itself can cause irregular heartbeats, heart attacks and seizures. Crack, in particular, can damage lungs and cause marked breathing difficulties (Cregler and Mark 1986), and if it is used regularly in pregnancy the baby is always of a low birth weight, and there is an increased likelihood of foetal abnormalities.

Large doses of cocaine can cause people to start having paranoid ideas and sometimes they will have psychotic episodes, with visual and tactile hallucinations, which could last for several days. These are often associated with episodes of violent and antisocial behaviour. These symptoms subside as the drug leaves the system, and if they persist, it may be that the young person has a true psychiatric illness and taking the drug was perhaps their way of trying to cope with it.

Features of withdrawal

The features of withdrawal may begin quite insidiously, with the young person having no idea why he/she is feeling tired, irritable and lethargic, but usually it is characterised by a more dramatic sense of agitation and depression which begins some hours after the last dose. This is followed by an inability to sleep, despite an increasing sense of fatigue, and a gradual reduction in the sense of craving for more cocaine. This initial withdrawal phase ends with the young person feeling totally exhausted, but with an increasing appetite, and sleep patterns which are returning to normal.

After this initial phase there may be several more sequences in which the young person slips into a period of feeling miserable and lethargic, and then returns to feeling more settled and comfortable.

Psychological support

The immediate support of someone in an intoxicated state has been described above. It is always worthwhile to try to determine what the intoxicating agent may be, but always within the context of maintaining a tranquil atmosphere. Treating cocaine addicts rarely requires an alternative drug to

COCAINE AND CRACK

Other names Charlie, coke, snow, freebase, rock, 'C', wash, stone.

Method of use Sniffed, smoked or injected. When smoked crack has an immediate effect which lasts for ten to fifteen minutes.

Effects on user Increases alertness and gives sense of energy. There is a sense of enhanced confidence.

In excess Increased pulse rate and blood pressure. Eyes become light sensitive and pupils dilate. Crack, in particular, also produces agitation, aggressive outbursts and sometimes psychosis or convulsions.

What it looks like White powder, or crystal 'rocks' of crack.

What to look for Energetic, and more intense than usual. To be sniffed the powder needs to be 'cut' so look for razor blade, and tube such as straw. Pipe or syringe if being taken in those ways.

Upon withdrawal Intense craving to repeat experience, and then marked lethargy, with young person becoming depressed, or paranoid.

Figure 9.3 Features of cocaine and crack
Source: Adapted from National Drugs Helpline information

be prescribed, and most treatments depend upon using psychological methods. It appears that cognitive behavioural therapy and contingency management are able to show the best impact upon helping with stimulant misuse and its associated dependence (Rawson *et al.* 2002). As with all drug problems, the source of expert help and advice is the community addiction team. Unfortunately, relapse rates are very common with this drug which is why its use is such a cause for concern.

Opiate drugs

Opiate drugs such as heroin have been prescribed by the medical profession over many years, and at the turn of the century opium dens were features of most large cities. Heroin in the UK is not used as commonly as other drugs of abuse such as alcohol or solvents, but because it can quickly become the dominant focus of the young person's life, addiction is easily established. Many users become criminals to finance the habit. It is reported that in the UK approximately 2 per cent of senior secondary school pupils have tried the drug (Wright and Pearl 1990).

Features of withdrawal

The opiates can be smoked, injected under the skin ('skin popping') or injected into a vein ('main lining'). Tolerance to the drug develops quite quickly,

---

HEROIN

Other names H, horse, scag, smack, snuff, brown, junk, gear, jack.

Method of use Sniffed, smoked ('chasing the dragon') or injected ('main lining').

Effects on user Calming, with a sense of warmth and well-being while intoxicated. Dependence quickly develops.

In excess Increased agitation, aggressive outbursts and sometimes psychosis or convulsions. Loss of consciousness and respiratory failure.

What it looks like White powder or tablets.

What to look for Rather an apathetic mood, and pinpoint pupils. If injecting, then the paraphernalia may be in evidence – needles, syringes, blackened spoons. Needle marks on arms, legs and feet indicate injecting something.

Upon withdrawal Increasing feelings of craving. Sweating and diarrhoea becoming more severe with time, bone pains and pupils dilate.

Figure 9.4 Features of heroin
Source: Adapted from National Drugs Helpline information

and since the young person feels quite unwell as the effect of the drug wears off, addiction to it is rapidly established. If addicts attempt to withdraw they experience severe abstinence symptoms, which begin to appear about eight to twelve hours after the last dose. There is an intense craving to reuse the drug and this is associated with nausea, diarrhoea, a running nose, goosebumps and severe pain within the bones and joints. The young person also begins to sweat profusely, the pupils are very dilated and extreme lethargy is apparent, with repetitive yawning. As well as these physical symptoms, the addict will appear to be markedly anxious, restless and depressed.

Even when these profound problems have been overcome, the young person can, for several months, feel depressed and anxious and have marked difficulty in sleeping.

A habitual user of opiates can experience physical problems from their use. There are problems associated with injecting a drug, but in addition the drug itself can prompt fluid to develop on the lungs or depress the breathing. If the young person takes too large a dose, then a profound reduction in vital signs is seen, with a slowing of respiration and the tell-tale pinpoint pupils.

Psychological support

In an acutely intoxicated situation the general advice of protection and tranquil atmosphere apply. The health risks associated with overdose require extra vigilance for breathing problems, which in extreme cases may need resuscitation measures to be started.

If an addict is seeking help to overcome a drug habit, the addiction team first look to substitute the drug with a synthetic opiate such as methadone, or buprenorphine. If the young person is also abusing other drugs, then these have to be reduced before any effort is made to reduce the dose of synthetic substitute. For some abusers, establishing them on a regular replacement programme is the most that can be achieved. The remainder of the programme is focused on offering psychological insight and support, and the slow and at times faltering process of helping the user rebuild a life.

Hallucinogens

Perhaps the best-known drug within this group is lysergic acid diethylamide (LSD). This drug became very popular in the 1960s and its popularity has continued to rise steadily since then, with 4 per cent of the population reporting having tried it in 1985 compared to 10 per cent in 1992 (Institute for the Study of Drug Dependence 1993). More recently 5–4–4-methyl-amphetamine (MDMA) has become popular among the young. This drug is better known as 'ecstasy'. Also within the group is phencyclidine (PSP), which is also known as 'angel dust', but this has not really become established as a drug of abuse in the UK.

Effects

Hallucinogenic drugs tend not to be drugs of habitual use, but are rather used intermittently to enhance social activities, such as rave dancing. Tolerance rapidly develops and so the young person has to take increasing doses to produce the same effect. These drugs alter perception – visual images will flow together and objects will appear to melt. Thoughts assume an unusual clarity and there is often an apparent distortion of time which can make things appear to move very quickly, or very slowly. When intoxicated with the drug there is usually a feeling of euphoria, but users can feel very panicky, or become paranoid. Switching between such moods can occur abruptly and the distortion of time can make it appear that the bad feelings are lasting for ever. In fact the effects of MDMA and PSP will last for up to eight hours in most cases, although the effects of LSD can last up to twenty-four hours.

When the mood changes are those of panic and fearfulness it is said that the young person is having 'a bad trip'. Such feelings are often associated with breathlessness, and many young people report fearing that they are losing their sanity during such episodes. Although these feelings tend to fade after some hours, they can recur some weeks or months after the drug was last taken. Such re-experiences are known as 'flashbacks' and although usually mild and brief, they can, on occasion, cause a great deal of fear and concern for a loss of sanity in the user.

MDMA – ECSTASY

Other names E, adam, XTC, fantasy, white doves, disco burgers, New Yorkers, Mitsubishis, dolphins, Rolexes.

Method of use Taken orally, effects start after twenty minutes, and can last for several hours.

Effects on user Gives sense of energy, acute thirst.

In excess inability to sleep, depression and paranoia.

What it looks like White, brown, pink or yellow tablets or capsules. Often they may also contain caffeine or household substances.

What to look for Energetic, restless and drinking large amounts of soft drinks.

Upon withdrawal Not considered to be addictive, but can make young person depressed, or paranoid.

Figure 9.5 Features of ecstasy
Source: Adapted from National Drugs Helpline information

LSD

Other names Acid, trips, tabs, blotters, dots.

Method of use By mouth.

Effects on user Hallucinations, especially associated with sounds and colours. Dilated pupils.

In excess Increased pulse rate and blood pressure. Hallucinations can be frightening and can prompt acute anxiety or paranoia.

What it looks like Small tablet or absorbed on to a piece of coloured paper.

What to look for Change in behaviour, with disorientation and recounting of hallucinations.

Upon withdrawal Not known as a problem.

Figure 9.6 Features of LSD
Source: Adapted from National Drugs Helpline information

Psychological support

If PCP is taken in high doses, it is likely to provoke quite marked violent behaviour, often with psychotic symptoms. In such situations the young person is often uncoordinated, blood pressure is quite high and the heart is often erratic in its beat. In such severe toxicity cases the young person needs to be admitted to hospital to minimise the physical effects. For most young people, however, it is a matter of being supportive and offering a calming influence until the effect of the drug subsides. This also involves reassuring them of their safety, and that the effects of the drug will pass.

If the young person is experiencing flashbacks then a similar supportive stance is appropriate. The effects are not a sign that they are going crazy, but in the midst of the experience this might be difficult for them to accept. Referral to a drug counselling service or to their own doctor can put them in touch with people who can re-emphasise this reassurance and this is especially necessary if the flashbacks are becoming a regular occurrence.

Inhalants

Solvents, glues, lighter fuel and the propellants within aerosols have all had a vogue with young people as drugs of abuse. Young people normally experiment with such drugs within groups and continued use is often part of a social routine. The dangers of this type of abuse partially arise from their inflammable nature, and also from the associated risks of choking and suffocation. In the UK the number of deaths appears to be rising, with the 82 deaths in 1983 increasing to 149 in 1990 (Institute for the Study of Drug Dependence 1993).

Effects

Drugs of this group create an immediate sense of light-headedness and this is usually associated with a floating sensation. There is a clouding of thinking and the young person may appear quite drowsy, usually with an associated lightening of mood. Commonly, the organic solvents are put in a plastic bag and inhaled to intensify the effect, and, of course, such a mechanism increases the risk that accidental suffocation will occur. The use of aerosol propellants can also be quite dangerous if the spray is a noxious chemical such as fly spray, and some young people will spray through a cloth to try to strain out these other chemicals.

One of the most dangerous of the group is lighter fuel. This is used by spraying the fuel on to the back of the throat, and because of its irritant nature it tends to prompt swelling of the throat lining, which can cause severe breathing problems.

A young person intoxicated with solvents appears rather drunken, with slurring of speech and a slowing of thought processes. The eyes may be red from the irritant nature of the fumes being inhaled, and some users develop inflamed skin round the nose and mouth, also as a result of this irritation.

Sometimes the young person can have a toxic reaction to a particular inhalant and this causes breathing problems, an increased pulse rate and rapid unconsciousness. This is a potentially fatal situation and requires close medical supervision until the crisis has passed.

INHALANTS

Types Glue, gas, aerosols, lighter fuel, petrol and thinners

Method of use Sniffed or inhaled.

Effects on user Dizziness and intoxication with loss of inhibition. The effects are immediate and last for about thirty minutes.

In excess May experience hallucinations and can kill.

What they look like Commercial products.

What to look for Signs of intoxication. Possibly smell of solvents, soiled plastic bags or discarded empties; excoriated and reddened skin round nose and mouth, sudden onset of acne; running, sniffy nose.

Upon withdrawal Some tolerance, but withdrawal is psychological.

Figure 9.7 Features of inhalants
Source: Adapted from National Drugs Helpline information

Psychological support

Although solvent abusers are usually cheerful and biddable, intoxication can prompt a sense of panic, and during this acute phase the aim should be to offer a calm and non-threatening environment in which the effects can wear off. It is important to monitor breathing and pulse to detect any complications that are arising, but usually the effects will simply pass. The decision as to whether medical assistance is needed is determined by whether physical complications, such as breathing problems, are starting to appear. It is unusual for hospital admission to be needed.

There is little evidence to suggest that young people who regularly use solvents experience withdrawal, and so the major thrust of assistance is trying to understand the origins of the use while looking for signs of underlying psychiatric illness. The approach for families needs to strike a balance between offering support and maintaining a clear rule system which consistently emphasises disapproval of inhalant use. The process of intervention tends to be a slow one. Inhalant use is usually a social activity, and so many young people have no motivation to stop until they outgrow their peer group.

Robert was a fifteen-year-old boy who had begun sniffing glue when he was thirteen. His friends within the neighbourhood had introduced him to its use, and most evenings they would gather in a remote corner of a small wood which was next to the estate where they all lived. Glue had become popular because it was easier to steal than alcohol, and there had been a gradual progression from glue to solvents of various kinds.

Robert and his friends began to miss those lessons at school that they didn't enjoy, preferring to spend the time in the local shopping centre. Robert's group became very adept at stealing from shops, and would plan what they could do to liven up their evenings – on occasion they would bring off-road motorcycles to ride in the wood, or steal a car and drive it at great speed through the estate.

The search for greater excitement led Robert and his friends into more daring thefts, after which the group would gather in their corner of the wood and inhale solvents to enhance their feelings of elation. At fifteen Robert and four of his friends appeared in court on several charges of breaking and entering, and two further court appearances eventually resulted in Robert being given a custodial sentence.

Robert's history illustrates the commonest theme to be found among solvent users. A mixture of peer-group pressure, the search for excitement and accepting delinquent activity as the norm are the elements which tend to maintain solvent use. The lack of motivation to stop means that concerned adults have no real opportunity to intervene. Occasionally the solvent use is a solitary activity to block out psychological or emotional problems, and such users do sometimes recognise that help with these underlying problems is a better solution than solvent usage.

Cannabis

Cannabis is a common drug of experimentation among adolescents and is derived from the cannabis sativa plant. This drug is grown throughout the world and has been used by many cultures over the centuries. In the UK in the early 1990s 3–5 per cent of senior schoolchildren report having tried cannabis (Health Education Authority 1992), but this has increased significantly, and continues to do so (Gilvarry 2000). It occurs in two forms – a mixture of the dried stems, seeds and leaves which is known as marijuana, and the far more potent resin which is derived from the flowering tops of the plants and is known as hashish. Both forms can be taken orally or smoked.

There is a movement which argues that because cannabis in itself is no more dangerous than tobacco and is in such common use it should be legalised. Opponents of this stance point to the fact that most hard-drug users have a history of cannabis use. However, most cannabis users do not go on to become users of hard drugs. In the UK the status of the drug has been changed, putting it in a far less serious category of concern.

The effects of cannabis begin within a few minutes and last for an hour or two. Perception of visual and tactile stimuli are often enhanced, and there is

---

CANNABIS

Other names Pot, dope, grass, puff, ganja, weed, herb, spliff, marijuana, hashish, blow, hemp, draw, smoke, joint, skunk.

Method of use Smoked or occasionally by ingestion with food.

Effects on user Relaxation, sometimes with a heightened awareness of colour and music. Reduced coordination, dilated pupils.

In excess Increased pulse rate and blood pressure. Rarely may be a sense of anxiety which can prompt temporary paranoia.

What it looks like Either a mixture of leaves, stalks and seeds (marijuana), or a solid brown cake (hashish).

What to look for Relaxed, dilated pupils and perhaps rather disinterested demeanour. A strong herbal smell, and sometimes the eyes are reddened.

Upon withdrawal Very rarely a problem.

Figure 9.8 Features of cannabis
Source: Adapted from National Drugs Helpline information

some distortion in the perception of time. At the same time the heart rate may often increase, and fine tremors are not uncommon. The user may feel hungry, and usually the drug increases relaxation, though on occasions it can prompt the young person to become agitated and feel anxious.

In someone who uses the drug quite regularly there can be a pattern of mild withdrawal with irritability and restlessness. In regular use there are concerns about developing psychological dependence. Anyone wishing to withdraw from the drug should be encouraged to pursue the type of approach which is advocated for stopping smoking.

Anabolic steroids

There has in recent years been an increasing concern that anabolic steroids are being used by athletes and body builders to increase their performances. In such cases it is quite common for two or even three different steroids to be used (Perry *et al.* 1990). While this is not strictly a drug of addiction, some young people can come to believe that they must regularly take the drug to maintain a high performance.

In young people regular use of the drug can cause depression, irritability, hostility, aggression and even psychosis. Many of the longer term effects are on the sex organs – erectile problems, shrunken testicles, as well as an increase in the risk of heart and liver problems. If these drugs are used by children, growth problems can develop. There is no recognised withdrawal programme, but many of the psychological principles used in helping other types of drug abuser will apply to these young people too.

General recognition and management of an addict

Certain aspects of teenage rebellion occur so frequently that they should be considered normal. Under-age drinking is an example of this type of behaviour, but although this might be quite typical for this age group, a young person who has developed a dependence on alcohol clearly is not. The regular use of drugs has the potential to have a profound effect upon a young person's future life and functioning and quite naturally parents, and others who come into contact with the young person, become very concerned by such behaviour. However, it is important to realise that many young people move away from drug use without any formal treatment (Biernacki 1986).

Sudden changes of behaviour may be the first indication that a young person is starting to establish a drug habit. The sudden onset of stealing, a marked drop in school performance, changing friendships and alliances, and becoming more irritable and bad tempered can all be features of a young person trying to cope with adolescence, but should also prompt consideration that they may also be abusing drugs.

At this stage it is important to voice suspicions in the correct way. Direct confrontation will only provoke denial and prompt the young person to be more secretive. Suspicion should be followed by a period of looking for supporting signs, especially periods of intoxication. If a drug habit is developing it will be increasingly difficult for a young person to hide the drug's effects.

If the young person presents in an intoxicated state, then protection from harm, and monitoring of breathing and so on, in a calm, reassuring style, is the first priority. Identifying the drug is helpful, because, as indicated above, certain drugs may cause specific health concerns. If the source of the intoxication cannot be identified, then referral to the local casualty department is prudent.

The pattern of response described for alcohol is generally applicable to all drug-usage situations. If the young person agrees to professional help then the local addiction service will decide whether detoxification will be necessary. Although such detoxification is an important step in a successful programme, engaging the young person in appropriate psychological support is the fundamental factor in determining whether drug usage can be stopped. As part of this process it is important to determine whether the young person has any concurrent psychological problems, and, with regard to this, the responses offered by family or classroom may be a significant arena for change. For example, marital conflict may be prompting misery that can only be escaped through drug use. If this family issue is not addressed, then no real progress with the drug use is likely. Similarly, teenagers who are being bullied at school, or are finding the work expectations beyond them, will need to have changes in these areas if motivation for change is to be secured.

Some young people may lack the motivation to stop drug usage, and in such cases the approach needs to be a careful mix of education and gentle encouragement. For some, the most that can be achieved in the short term is harm minimisation – and developments such as needle-exchange programmes and education about which inhalants carry the greatest risk are examples of this approach (Anderson 1990). These young people are often the most frustrating for adults to deal with. They seem deliberately to refuse to accept the advice being offered, and this prompts concerned parents, and teachers, to demand that 'something be done'. Unfortunately, the lack of things that can be done tends to frustrate the adults even more, which can result in the young person losing the adults' support. Recognising that they have to decide about their own life is one of the hardest lessons for any concerned adult to learn. The most assistance that can be offered is to establish clear expectations for behaviour and to stick to them totally. If the drug use is too disruptive for a household or school to tolerate, then intoxication may mean being barred. This is not a punishment for misbehaviour, it is protection for the home or school from further disruption. This 'tough love' approach places a great strain on caring adults but helps to impress upon a user the terms on which they can rejoin their family or community.

Formal treatment programmes

Professional agencies, such as drug-addiction teams, tend to offer treatment which falls into two categories. The first are treatments which focus upon the young person, and may take the form of counselling, behavioural techniques or group meetings. Self-help groups can be beneficial in helping users to recognise that the problems they face are commonly shared, but young people tend to be reluctant to participate in such meetings. The second approach is to focus upon the family, and the network in which the adolescent lives. Whichever type of approach is adopted the aims are broadly similar – to encourage abstinence and enhance those areas of life that are not linked to drug usage. However the multifaceted nature of many young people's drug problems makes it difficult for a single type of intervention to succeed. Because of this, in recent years Multisystemic therapy (Henggeler 1999) has been the focus of considerable research interest. This is a family- and community-focused intervention which tries to address the elements within the individual, school, home, peer group and community that may be contributing to the substance misuse. Its focus is maintaining continual engagement with the programme, and the long-term results are not only very hopeful (Henggeler et al. 2002), but the overall cost of the programme is less than many other options (Schoenwald et al. 1996).

Issues of prevention

The major concerns that exist around drug use has naturally prompted considerable work on programmes of prevention. There is a suggestion that the rate of increase in drug usage is slowing down (Gilvarry 2000), and reviews of school-based prevention programmes show that the most promising prevention approaches target individuals during the beginning of adolescence and teach drug-resistance skills and norm-setting either alone or in combination with general personal and social skills (Botvin 2000). They seem able to significantly reduce adolescent tobacco, alcohol and marijuana use, but their effects may decrease over time, with booster booster interventions being necessary to maintain and in some instances even enhance prevention effects (Griffin *et al.* 2003).

Sources of further help

www.fdap.org.uk
www.aona.co.uk
www.nida.nih.gov
www.adfam.org.uk
www.dare.com
www.eata.org.uk
www.release.org.uk

References

Anderson, H.R. (1990). Increase in deaths from deliberate inhalation of fuel gases, and pressurised aerosols. *British Medical Journal* 301, 41.
Bewley, B., Bland, J. and Harris, R. (1974). Factors associated with the starting of cigarette smoking by primary school children. *British Journal of Preventative and Social Medicine* 28, 37–44.
Biernacki, P. (1986). *Pathways from Heroin Addiction: Recovery without Treatment.* Philadelphia PA; Temple University Press.
Botvin, G.J. (2000). Social and competence enhancement approaches targeting individual-level etiologic factors. *Addictive Behaviors* 25, 887–97.
Braucht, G.N., Brakarsh, D. and Follingstad, D. (1973). Deviant drug use in adolescence: a review of psychosocial correlates. *Psychological Bulletin* 79, 92–106.
Christie, K.A., Burke, J.E. and Regier, D.A. (1988). Epidemiologic evidence for early onset of mental disorders and higher rates of drug abuse in young adults. *American Journal of Psychiatry* 145, 971–5.
Cregler, L.L. and Mark, H. (1986). Medical complications of cocaine abuse. *New England Journal of Medicine* 315, 1495–500.
Doll, R., Peto, R. and Hall, E. (1994). Mortality in relation to consumption of alcohol: 13 years' observations on male British doctors. *British Medical Journal* 309, 911–18.

Frezza, M., di Padova, C. and Pozzato, G. (1990). High blood alcohol levels in women: the role of decreased gastric alcohol dehydrogenase activity and first pass metabolism. *New England Journal of Medicine* 322, 95–9.

Gawin, F. and Ellinwood, E.H. (1988). Cocaine and other stimulants: actions, abuse and treatment. *New England Journal of Medicine* 318, 1173–82.

Ghodse, H. (1995). *Drugs and Addictive Behaviour: A Guide to Treatment.* 2nd edn. London: Blackwell Scientific Publications.

Gilvarry, E. (2000). Substance abuse in young people. *Journal of Child Psychology and Psychiatry* 41, 55–80.

Gilvarry, E., McCarthy, S. and McArdle, P. (1995). Substance use among school children in the North of England. *Drug and Alcohol Dependence* 37, 255–59.

Gossop, M., Griffiths, P. and Powis, B. (1994a). Cocaine: patterns of use, route of administration and severity of dependence. *British Journal of Psychiatry* 164, 660–4.

Gossop, M., Griffiths, P. and Strang, J. (1994b). Sex differences in patterns of drug taking behaviour. *British Journal of Psychiatry* 164, 101–4.

Griffin, K.W., Botvin, G.J., Nichols, T.R. and Doyle, M.M. (2003). Effectiveness of a universal drug abuse prevention approach for youth at high risk for substance use initiation. *Preventive Medicine* 36, 1–7.

Health Education Authority (1992). *Tomorrow's Young People. 9–15 Year Olds Look at Alcohol, Drugs, Exercise and Smoking.* London: Health Education Authority.

Henggeler, S. (1999). Multisystemic therapy. *Child Psychology and Psychiatry Review* 4, 2–10.

Henggeler, S., Clingempeel, W.G., Brondino, M.J. and Pickrel, S.G. (2002). Four-year follow-up of multisystemic therapy with substance-abusing and substance-dependent juvenile offenders. *Journal of the American Academy of Child and Adolescent Psychiatry* 41, 868–74.

Hoffmann, J.P. and Cerbone, F.G. (2002). Parental substance use disorder and the risk of adolescent drug abuse: an event history analysis. *Drug and Alcohol Dependence* 66, 255–64.

Hovens, J.G.F.M., Cantwell, D.P. and Kiriakos, R. (1994). Psychiatric co-morbidity in hospitalised adolescent substance abusers. *Journal of the American Academy of Child and Adolescent Psychiatry* 33, 476–83.

Institute for the Study of Drug Dependence (1993). *National Audit of Drug Misuse in Britain 1992* London: Institute for the Study of Drug Dependence.

Johnson, J.L. and Leff, M. (1999). Children of substance abusers: Overview of research findings. *Pediatrics* 103, 1085–99.

King, A., Wold, B., Tudor-Smith, C. and Harel, Y. (1996). *The Health of Youth: A Cross-National Survey.* European Series no. 69. Geneva: WHO Regional Publications.

McNamara, J., Bullock, A. and Grimes, E. (2000). *Bruised Before Birth: Parenting Children Exposed to Parental Substance Abuse.* London; British Agencies for Adoption and Fostering.

Obot, I.S., Wagner, F.A. and Anthony, J.C. (2001). Early onset and recent drug use among children of parents with alcohol problems: data from a national epidemiologic survey. *Drug and Alcohol Dependence* 65, 1–8.

Parker, H., Measham, F., Aldridge, J. (1995). *Drug Futures. Changing Patterns of Drug Use amongst English Youth.* London: Institute for the Study of Drug Dependence.

Perry, P.J., Andersen, K.H. and Yates, W.R. (1990). Illicit anabolic steroid use in athletes. A case series analysis. *American Journal of Sports Medicine* 18, 422–8.

Piaget, J. (1952). *The Origins of Intelligence in Children.* New York: International University Press.

Pickens, R.W., Svikis, D.S. and McGue, M. (1991). Heterogeneity in the inheritance of alcoholism: a study of male and female twins. *Archives of General Psychiatry* 48, 19–28.

Poole, R. and Brabbins, C. (1996). Drug induced psychosis. *British Journal of Psychiatry* 168, 135–8.

Rawson, R.A., Gonzales, R., Brethen, P. (2002). Treatment of methamphetamine use disorders: an update. *Journal of Substance Abuse Treatment* 23, 145–150.

Ruben, S.M. and Morrison, C.L. (1992). Temazepam misuse in a group of injecting drug users. *British Journal of Addiction* 87, 1387–92.

Schoenwald, S., Ward, D., Henggeler, S., Pickrel, S. and Patel, H. (1996). MST treatment of substance abusing or dependent adolescent offenders: costs of reducing incarceration, inpatient, and residential placement. *Journal of Child and Family Studies* 5, 431–44.

Thadani, P.V. (2002). The intersection of stress, drug abuse and development. *Psychoneuroendocrinology* 27, 221–30.

Wright, J.D. and Pearl, L. (1990). Knowledge and experience of young people regarding drug abuse, 1969–1989. *British Medical Journal* 300, 99–103.

Chapter 10

Depression in children

Over recent years, there has been an intense interest in the concept of depression in childhood. The issue is particularly complex because sadness and tears are common parts of all children's lives and so cannot form any true basis for a diagnosis of a depressive illness. In addition, the term itself has become so much part of common usage that it has begun to lose value as a description of a particular illness process. Even within professional circles the word 'depression' is used synonymously to describe three discrete levels (Kazdin 1990):

Depressed mood: a state of profound unhappiness and sense of dejection (dysphoria) that is more than normal sadness. The person cannot see any real bright spots to his or her life, and there is a loss of emotional involvement with either other people or activities. Often it is associated with negative styles of thinking about the young people themselves (giving rise to feelings of failure and guilt) or about the future (giving a sense of hopelessness). Figure 10.1 shows how such thoughts create a wider shift in mood, which then becomes attributed to all aspects of life. The presence of some such feelings is a normal reaction to a distressing event, but they are in proportion to the importance of the event, and the overall intensity is not great.
Depressive syndrome: a cluster of symptoms including depressed mood, tearfulness, irritability, loss of appetite, sleep disturbance, poor concentration and loss of energy.
Depressive disorder: a psychiatric diagnosis of depression, such as the one given in the *Diagnostic and Statistical Manual* (DSM-IV) of the American Psychiatric Association (1994), is based on typical symptoms but they must be present for a specific time, and clearly impair the person's functioning. Persistence and impairment are what distinguishes the disorder from the syndrome.

However, this is not the end to the confusion of terms. For example, some people prefer to use the term 'affective disorder' to describe the family of emotional illnesses, and recently diagnostic labelling has moved from terms such as depression to 'unipolar disorder'. Not surprisingly, with a subject so

When reflecting upon	Personal achievements	Ability to influence events
The past	Feelings of guilt and shame	Fearful of acting in case repeats 'mistakes'
The present	Believes self to be a failure	Feels helpless
The future	Expects the worst to happen	Feels hopeless

Figure 10.1 The way that negative thoughts can become attributed to all aspects of life

littered with terms and titles it is sometimes difficult to understand what is being referred to. (See the glossary for definitions of some of the other terms used when referring to depression and other emotional illnesses.)

It is important to realise that the classification of depressive illness has remained contentious for many years, and over that time there have been many variations in the classification. The discussion so far has looked at what are usually referred to now as major depressive episodes, and are described in the World Health Organization's classification (1992) as endogenous depression. But what about the person who is easily, or chronically, distressed and unhappy? These types of problem have been called neurotic depressions, and they can be distinguished from the other group because the causes, and to some degree the reactions, are merely exaggerations of what we all might feel in similar circumstances. The DSM-IV classification uses a different term for this group, describing it as dysthymic, and this a diagnosis that is beginning to be applied to children. However, it is important not to lose sight of other emotional reactions in children and adolescents that can at first sight appear similar and are a normal age variant. An excellent example of this is the mood lability which is common in the early teenage years, and presents as rapid changes of mood which are sometimes marked. It is occasionally difficult to distinguish this type of marked mood swing from the illness process where profound depression alternates with a very elated and over-cheerful period (known as bipolar illness), but the distinction is important since the ways to respond to these two types of mood variation are substantially different.

Reaching a diagnosis

To confirm that a depressive syndrome is present, the young person must not only appear miserable and unhappy, but demonstrate a negative style of thinking and present a daily routine which illustrates a loss of interest and concentration. For some clinicians, there must be clear anhedonia – which means that the young person has lost all enjoyment of life and now portrays a picture dominated by gloom and despondency.

Julie, a fourteen-year-old girl, presented with a six-week history of not attending school. When asked about this, she explained that for some months she found it difficult to concentrate at school and was concerned that all of her friends had turned against her, and that the teachers no longer liked her. Her mother said that Julie was previously a happy and cheerful girl, but over recent months she had become quiet and withdrawn, and would quickly become tearful and distressed at any difficulty or problem. She no longer went out with her friends, preferring to spend most of her time in her bedroom watching television. She had stopped eating and, although she constantly felt tired, was finding it difficult to settle to sleep and was waking consistently at 4.00 a.m. Throughout the interview, Julie emitted a sense of sadness and misery and, when asked directly, confirmed that she saw no future for herself and had thought about suicide, although she insisted she would not kill herself since she did not want to cause additional distress to her family.

It is only in recent years that it has been established that the definitions of the depressive syndrome and disorder which are used in adults are also the ones to use when trying to assess children, although it is recognized that in children the symptoms may be different depending upon the child's age (Birmaher *et al.* 1998). Previously, there had been a view that depression did not occur until adult life, or, that if it did present in children, it was in a 'masked' form. This theory suggested that a variety of difficulties within childhood, for example, soiling and wetting, were the manifestations of depression in a childhood (Frommer 1968). This theory drew its support, in part, from the fact that conditions such as bedwetting improved when treated with antidepressants, an interesting reversal of the present view on the relevance of antidepressants in depression, as we shall see later.

With the acceptance that adult-type depression is present in children, there has been an increasing interest in whether the mixture of depression and mania, which is seen in adults, can occur in childhood. There has been a gathering agreement that this type of disorder does occur in young people (Biederman 2003), and that children with the bipolar illness should be differentiated from those with depression only (Weller *et al.* 1995), although the symptoms of depression that both groups show are remarkably similar (Depue and Monroe 1978). What prompts perhaps the most controversy in this area is whether the manic part of bipolar disorder does in fact mimic, and perhaps is often mistaken for, severe ADHD (State *et al.* 2002).

Prevalence

Using the adult criteria it has been estimated that about 2 per cent of children develop a depressive illness before they reach puberty (Kashani *et al.*

1983), with perhaps as many as 30 per cent of those who present with depression before puberty going on to show the bipolar illness in later life (Geller *et al.* 1994). In adults the number of people who will have at least one episode of depression before they die (lifetime prevalence of depression) is said to be 15–18 per cent of the population (Wittchen *et al.* 1994), with about 9 per cent of the adult population having a significant depressive illness in any one year. Of course, when considering prevalence, it is important to bear in mind the distinction between the presence of depressive symptoms and the more profound depressive disorder. For example, a community-based study in Cambridge found 21 per cent of the girls reported having symptoms of depression in the previous year, but when a syndrome definition was used the rate was 6 per cent (Cooper and Goodyer 1993). Overall 5–10 per cent of adolescents will have a major depressive illness during their teenage years (Fleming and Offord 1990), with the majority of these starting at around fifteen years of age (Lewinsohn *et al.* 1994).

As has already been pointed out, having symptoms of depression does not mean that the disorder of depression is actually present. Indeed, up to 25 per cent of the general adolescent population show some symptoms of depression at some point (Roberts *et al.* 1990), and although only a small proportion of these will go on to develop the full disorder, this group is more likely to show the full disorder in the following two years than the general population (Weissman *et al.* 1992).

Impact of the disorder

As already described, depressed young people are persistently miserable, gloomy, and unhappy. They may feel so bad that the effort to express such negative emotions is too much, and they then become inert and withdrawn. There is often an associated slowing of speech and movement which can sometimes be mistaken by the uninformed as disinterest. Not surprisingly, such behaviours cause these young people to have impaired peer and family relationships, and there is usually a deterioration in school performance (Puig-Antich *et al.* 1993). In some cases these features rather than the depressive symptoms themselves may be more evident to the casual observer (Kent *et al.* 1995).

A particular problem can occur in adolescence because this period of development does tend to exaggerate existing psychological traits such as needing to tidy or compulsively checking that lights are switched off. If the young person was already prone to be gloomy, then adolescence itself may make this more marked, but such symptoms still fall short of the features that would allow it to be called a depressive illness.

The nature of the disorder can have a significant impact on trying to find out details of history from the young person. The withdrawal and general slowing-up of thought processes mean that they are unlikely to volunteer information and any answers they do give are likely to be slowly given.

Many questions will be met with 'don't know', but since this is almost a universal adolescent reply, it is not very helpful diagnostically.

Causes of depression

There is a great deal of scientific endeavour focused upon trying to understand what causes depression. Although the vast majority of this work is focused on the illness in adults, some parallel work is being undertaken in children. Perhaps predictably the lines of enquiry have been those followed for adults – genetic, brain chemistry, the role of historical themes and significant life events. None of these has so far been proven to be the total explanation for the onset of depression, and at present it seems to be a mixture of the factors that ultimately lead to prompting the illness. Children, perhaps even more than adults, are sensitive to atmospheres and the expectations of a particular situation and perhaps this is relatively more influential in children as a consequence (Kendler *et al.* 1992). Living in an environment that is limited financially, and has few opportunities for play or stimulation, is therefore quite capable of sapping a child's sense of the positive and rendering the start of each day a gloomy prospect.

When considering genetics it is important to distinguish those patients who have bipolar or severe major depressive illness, because this group has inheritability estimates of around 80 per cent. This contrasts with milder forms of the disorder (which make up the vast majority of cases) where the inheritability estimate is between 10 and 50 per cent (McGuffin and Katz 1989). Overall it does appear, based on the evidence from twin studies, that depressive symptoms in young people are inheritable (Rice *et al.* 2002a), with genetic factors becoming more important from childhood to adolescence (Rice *et al.* 2002b). In fact the evidence for any significant genetic effects in these only moderate depression disorders is weak, and it is probably the influence which the family environment exerts which is the most significant factor in these cases (Radke-Yarrow *et al.* 1992). As a general rule the evidence for children and adolescents is that if the illness starts before puberty or is severe, then it is very likely that there is a genetic influence at work (Strober 1992).

One of the most enduring theories in the causation of depression is the amine hypothesis (Deakin and Crow 1986). This suggests that depression arises because there is a problem with a particular family of chemical transmitters, the monoamines. If these are depleted, then depression is said to result. The evidence for this comes from the fact that if drugs are given which are known to reduce monoamines, then depression occurs, and, conversely, many of the drugs used to ease depression are known to increase these brain chemicals. However, depressed young people do not show the same positive response to these drugs as adults do, although it is not clear what implication this has for this particular hypothesis.

Alongside the interest in chemical causes, there has been a vast amount of work done with adults looking at how environmental issues, stress, life events and other such changes in a particular person's circumstances might effect the onset of depressive illness. The facts that for each successive generation the prevalence of depression is increasing and the age of onset is decreasing (Klerman and Weissman 1989) have tended to reinforce the belief that life issues play a significant part in the causation of depression.

One observation which has fuelled much speculation is the way that the prevalence of the illness changes in men and women over time. The rate of depression in adult women has consistently been found to be about twice that of men, although the difference is gradually reducing over time. In children under the age of twelve years, however, it is boys who tend to present more frequently with depression problems (Angold and Rutter 1992). For this difference to be explicable there must be a phase of life when the sex pattern shifts over; that is, a time when the frequency in girls increases and overtakes that of boys. It does, indeed, seem the case that with the onset of adolescence girls begin to show a greater likelihood of developing a depressive illness (McGonagle et al. 1994), with the shift of prevalence having fully occurred by mid-adolescence (Whitaker et al. 1990). How could such a shift be explained? A pointer may be the ways in which the sexes deal with the stress that adolescence imposes. For boys there tends to be an externalising of emotion – they gather in groups and become very action-based. This is often as innocuous as kicking a football around, but can involve more risk-taking behaviour such as driving stolen cars. For girls the mechanism of coping is more typically one of internalising the emotion – long, intimate and heart-felt discussions with close friends are common pastimes, and perhaps this analysing of emotion establishes this as a mechanism to be used when more marked difficulties arise.

One of the factors which is consistently shown to be influential is the family, where it has emerged that severe parental psychiatric illness increases the risk of a poor outcome in the child's illness (Rutter and Quinton 1984). In addition, other strands of work in this area have clearly demonstrated a link between being exposed to marital discord and divorce and developing depressive symptoms (Hetherington et al. 1985). It is less easy to know how to interpret the fact that children of clinically depressed parents are more likely to suffer from a major depressive illness than their peers (Weissman et al. 1987). This could arise from a genetic inheritance, but equally could be the influence of living with a depressed parent and the family environment that such an illness creates.

Associations with other disorders

The type of situation where more than one disorder appears to be present at the same time is called co-morbidity, and with regards to depression there is a strong co-morbidity with oppositional and conduct disorder (Angold and

Costello 1993). Why there should be a link with conduct problems is not understood, but it is probably significant that the overall outcome for young people with conduct problems does not seem to be influenced by whether they have depression or not (Harrington *et al.* 1991). Since there is also no strong family history of depression in such cases, it seems likely that this depression may be a product of young people reflecting upon their adverse life events, rather than a depressive illness acting in a way that causes conduct problems to arise.

It is also common to find conduct disorder and depression co-existing, and when together the young person usually shows more serious levels of maladjustment, especially relating to school success and substance dependence, than would be expected given the adjustment associated with each disorder alone (Marmorstein and Iacono 2003). However the commonest association with depression has been with anxiety disorder, because as many as 75 per cent of depressed young people will show anxiety features (Merikangas and Angst 1994). In the more marked forms, the anxiety tends to precede the onset of the depressive illness (Brady and Kendall 1992) and may herald a more severe form (Bernstein 1991). However, there is no evidence to suggest that this is a particular type of illness, but rather that having two such difficulties occurring together multiplies the impact upon the sufferer's life.

Intervention

As one might imagine, a young person presenting with a depressive illness often has other difficulties and problems associated with it, and it is important that these are assessed and dealt with appropriately (Goodyer *et al.* 1991). In many cases the correct resolution of wider family difficulties, and addressing issues such as poor peer relationships, can have a major beneficial effect upon the young person's mood. It is therefore important to recognise all the elements which may be contributing to the low mood, and to ensure that each element is given due weight in the intervention plan.

The treatment of depressive illness in adults has been exhaustively researched, and several approaches have been delineated. Although somewhat dependent upon the philosophy of the service offering treatment, and the views of the individual, the use of medication has been the first approach to such problems for a long time. In children, however, the picture is less clear. Opinions differ regarding treatment planning and the duration of treatment that is required to prevent relapse. Development of a treatment relationship with the young person and their family is crucial for a successful outcome (Birmaher *et al.* 1998).

Medication

The evidence that medication is helpful in the treatment of depression in adults has become increasingly robust in recent years, with most authorities stating that it has a clear part to play in any treatment approach (Paykel and Priest 1992). As was mentioned earlier, the view that children used to demonstrate depression in a 'masked' way had in part arisen because certain symptoms in children seemed to improve with antidepressants. It is not surprising, therefore, that when the criteria used in adults to diagnose depression is applied to children and teenagers, the treatments which have emerged as valuable in adults have been tried with young people.

The first successful group of antidepressants were the tricyclic antidepressants. Before being superseded by drugs with fewer side-effects they were the main medication used in depression, proving effective in treating the disorder in about 80 per cent of cases. As with all types of antidepressant these drugs show a distinct response profile. There is usually little response in the first two weeks, but then the physical and motor features which are associated with depression, such as appetite, sleep and being slow in movements, begin to improve. The patients usually do not actually feel any better themselves at this stage, but observers see the improvements. It is usually six to eight weeks before the full impact of the drug is felt upon mood. There are many drugs in this group but the commonest, and the only two approved for use with children, are imipramine and amitriptyline. Although effective in adults, patients are often troubled by the side-effects they cause, particularly the heart problems, such as irregular heartbeats. Most patients experience drowsiness, a constant dry mouth, and constipation, and, for some, problems with blurred vision and urine retention can cause discomfort. They are also dangerous if they are taken in overdose. In children, however, the response to these medicines has been poor and they are not considered an effective treatment with children (Ambrosini et al. 1993).

The discovery of another brain chemical transmitter that influences depression (serotonin) produced a new family of drugs which have quickly become the treatment of choice in adult depression. These are usually known as selective serotonin reuptake inhibitors (SSRIs). The most commonly used drug in this family is fluoxetine (Prozac) which has become very popular with middle-class patients, and is the first antidepressant that it is almost fashionable to admit to be taking. Others in the family include fluvoxamine (Faverin) and paroxetine (Seroxat). Although these drugs are far less toxic than the older tricyclics, they do have side-effects of their own, most notably gastrointestinal problems such as nausea and vomiting, which are dose-related. In the United States fluoxetine and fluvoxamine have been approved for use in children and there is some evidence that they reduce depression in the young (Emslie et al. 2002), albeit far less reliably than in adults, and that some – particularly paroxetine – may increase suicidal ideas in this age group. In view of these findings, medication is currently seen as appropriate where the depression is recurrent, chronic, or has not responded to psychological measures (Emslie et al. 1999).

This raises the interesting conundrum of whether childhood depression is actually the same as that seen in adults, or whether the drugs are simply ineffective in the younger age group. Certainly, it is not that the antidepressants are inert when given to children, for there is a great deal of evidence that they exert effects in children with regard to other disorders, such as bedwetting and attention deficit disorder (see Chapter 4). The research effort goes on a pace to try to answer these questions, and the answer will no doubt open new treatment avenues in this age group.

Psychological approaches

Almost since the beginning of modern psychiatry there have been efforts to help people overcome psychological difficulties by using techniques which work with mental processes directly. These have taken many forms, and work which proves that they are as effective as other types of intervention has only recently been forthcoming (Tillett 1996). These approaches may focus upon:

- changing behaviour directly through behavioural programmes;
- changing the thinking processes which are influencing the mood and behaviour – known as cognitive therapy;
- exploring the young person's inner world by looking at history, belief systems and issues such as loss – the basis of most psychotherapies.

Behavioural approaches are discussed in detail elsewhere (Chapter 2), and although the focus will be different for a depressed child, the principles are very similar. The fundamental aim is to focus on behaviours which are maintaining the problem, and reduce them, or introduce new behaviours which are incompatible with being depressed. So, for example, each task completed can be followed by a small reward, and planning the future rewards is an important first step in establishing such programmes. In addition, it is very helpful to establish routine sessions of physical activity, or regularly play favourite games to intrude upon the gloomy mood and, if well chosen, to give islands of positive feeling which can be gradually expanded and intensified. In practice behavioural programmes are not used in isolation, but as part of a wider psychological approach using cognitive therapy.

In recent years the use of cognitive therapy for people with depression has become recognised as a helpful approach, and some work has also been done with children using this technique (Vostanis and Harrington 1994). As described in Chapter 2, this type of therapy is based on the assumption that behaviour and moods are produced as a result of what the person is thinking, and so changing the thinking can change the behaviour. Since its original focus was dealing with depressive illness, it is perhaps not surprising that its value in treating young people has been explored.

In practice this type of intervention depends upon understanding the processes which are governing a particular person's thinking. Although there are several elements to the thinking process, two of the key ones from a therapeutic point of view are cognitive processes and cognitive products. Cognitive processes are the procedures which the brain uses to perceive and interpret experiences. The cognitive products are the thoughts which result from the interpretation and its interaction with experience, opinions and so on. If the young person has distortions in the cognitive processes then it becomes very easy to develop a distorted view of the world, and the depressing thoughts that stem from this act as strong reinforcement that the original view was a correct one. For example, if a young person believes he or she is useless at schoolwork, every low mark or comment by a teacher helps to confirm for the young person that this is a true summary of the situation. This view has been supported by the finding that such negative cognitions (such as self-criticism) are stable and often precede the emergence of depressive symptoms (Nolen-Hoeksema *et al.* 1992).

These cognitive processes can give rise to problems such as depression in two different ways. The first is that there is a necessary skill or area of understanding which the young person still has to grasp fully. An example of this might be needing to develop a way of controlling temper outbursts, or learning to cope with a cutting remark without taking it to heart. The second type of problem is that the thinking becomes distorted in some way, for instance, seeing a group of people talking always makes the young person believe that they are being discussed in a derogatory way.

This type of therapy has been used to treat depression in adults very successfully, and work with depressed young people shows that they have the sort of difficulties that respond to this type of approach. In particular, these young people do not have the skills to solve interpersonal problems easily (Sacco and Graves 1984), and often show a pattern in which they set themselves too high a standard, only then to criticise and punish themselves when these standards are not achieved (Kaslow *et al.* 1984). Perhaps most significant of all, depressed young people always tend to attribute the good things that happen to them to external, specific factors, and the bad things as due to themselves and characteristics that they can't change (Bodiford *et al.* 1988).

The basic approach in cognitive therapy is always one of collaboration, with therapist and patient working as a team. For depressed young people this is often hard to establish, since they feel worthless and without a future. Engaging them in the therapy process usually means that initially they have to be led, and that enthusiasm for help needs to be nurtured and encouraged rather than being the prerequisite to commencing which it is in other types of therapy.

To be of any help it is necessary to gain an understanding of the thoughts that are fuelling the depressive feelings. Typically, this process has three stages. First, it is important to confirm that the young person understands the concepts of emotion – happiness, sadness and so on. Much of the work requires an accurate reporting of feelings and emotions, and so it is vital that these are fully recognised and labelled correctly. Using the knowledge, the young person begins to self-monitor, recording feelings and moods – when they occur and what they are associated with. This allows the young person and therapist together to identify the behavioural sequences which are associated with the problem. In this way the elements that require changing are clarified. This is the starting point for looking at the thought processes. If thought triggers mood which triggers behaviour, then examining the sequences most associated with gloomy moods should help to bring out the originating thoughts.

Having found the thought, then the cognitive restructuring can begin. The overall aim is to help the young person change the underlying cognitive processes which determine the interpretation that is being placed upon events. This is done in as concrete a way as possible, trying all the time to challenge the child's 'beliefs' with evidence that cannot be misinterpreted. Using such techniques helps the young person gradually to replace belief with knowledge, and with that knowledge comes a lessening of symptoms.

Marie was a fifteen-year-old girl who for the last year had felt increasingly miserable and unhappy. One morning her mother had not been able to rouse her for school, and hospital investigations revealed that she had taken about twenty of the tablets her grandmother was prescribed for her anxiety illness. Although her mother said Marie had been a little more subdued in recent weeks, she was shocked by this event, for the family saw Marie as sensible and very level headed. The parents could not identify any particular stresses in Marie's life which might have prompted the overdose, but accepted that since becoming a teenager she had tended to stay in her room and no longer confided in her mother about her problems or worries.

Marie described a pattern of increasing sadness in which she had lost interest in schoolwork and hobbies. She felt her friends no longer liked her, and the overdose had been prompted because she had finally become convinced that all of the girls in her class despised her. She had reached this conclusion because she had come to realise that whenever the girls were whispering together they were making derogatory remarks about her.

The thought identification approach drew out this negative attribution and Marie was asked to think of an alternative explanation for the huddle. She decided upon 'so the boys can't hear', and every time she saw the huddle she used a particular sequence which commenced with visualising a road stop sign and repeating 'stop' under her breath. She then took a deep breath and repeated the new explanation to herself. Self-scoring showed that over the subsequent week her concern about these huddles of girls reduced. Similar measures were used to tackle the other specific issues which arose through the course of therapy, and Marie showed a full return to schoolwork and hobbies, and a new interest in boyfriends, over the next three months. Marie still did not share with her parents, but when therapy ended she was talking intently with her two best friends and was telling them 'everything'!

It is important to realise that there are many variations of the approach that can be adopted, although most use elements of the process described. A more detailed programme for a cognitive therapy package to be used with children is given by Vostanis and Harrington (1994).

The growing body of research in this field shows that it is a successful intervention with young people (Clarke *et al.* 1999), and is more successful than drugs in preventing relapse (Evans *et al.* 1992).

The last intervention which is regularly used to reduce the symptoms of depression is interpersonal psychotherapy. This is a therapy which uses a relationship between patient and therapist as a basis for change, and the focus is very much upon the individual's inner world. The primary aim of such therapy is to give insight into the events and situations that prompted the difficulties, and more importantly into the unresolved issues which are maintaining them. A more detailed discussion of interpersonal psychotherapy can be found in Chapter 2, but when working with a young person who is depressed the therapy is often focused on exploring painful historical events or losses. The theoretical assumption is that the emotional effort of avoiding dealing with these painful elements is prompting the depression, and so recalling them fully and gaining an understanding of them will allow the person to progress. In such a treatment sequence there is nearly always an initial phase in which symptoms become more marked, and new problems may actually arise. This needs to be prepared for, and concerned adults should be primed to expect such a period. The advice for handling such a phase is to recognise the origin of the behaviour, but to maintain the usual rules and expectations. The continuing predictability of all other aspects of the young person's world is a key element in allowing unimpeded concentration on the painful areas which the therapy is addressing.

Outcome

In trying to form a view of how young people with depression might fare in adult life it is important to distinguish those who only have a moderate form of depression from those with severe depression or bipolar illness. As was described earlier, there is probably a genetic loading in the severe disorder groups which makes the development of longer-term problems more likely.

The research evidence suggests that early detection and intervention is effective in ameliorating the poor psychosocial outcome that often accompanies depressive illness (Birmaher et al. 1998), and although having an episode of depression in childhood does make it more likely that there will be episodes of depression in adult life, if there is only one episode throughout the teens and twenties, then the outlook is good (Rao et al. 1995). There are factors that can offer reassurance that this may be the only episode. High self-esteem, good coping skills, school achievement, outside interests and positive relationships with family and friends all seem to exert a positive influence and militate against further recurrence (Compas 1994; Merikangas and Angst 1994). It is also clear that continuation of treatment is necessary in all patients after the acute phase of the illness, and for some long-term maintenance is required if relapse is to be prevented (Birmaher et al. 1998).

The outlook for the severely ill group may be less positive, for it has been estimated that the risk of a repeat episode of depression is about 60 per cent (Harrington et al. 1990), and that as many as 80 per cent of adults with bipolar illness report that their illness started pre-pubertally (Geller et al. 1994). This issue of repeat occurrence is of importance because of the major impact that recurring depressive illness has upon a person's life. It has been established that an adult with a confirmed major depressive illness experiences, on average, between five and six recurrences during his or her lifetime (Zis and Goodwin 1979). These usually take about nine months to be resolved, although about 20 per cent of patients experience depressions that last almost two years (Post and Ballenger 1984). Such predictions have prompted Keller (1994) to conclude that as a general principle depression should be seen as a long-term disorder where patients are vulnerable to relapse.

No matter which type of illness it is, there can be more subtle long-term problems, for although treatment may reduce the immediate depressive symptoms, this is not always followed by improvement in other areas, such as social functioning (Kovacs and Goldston 1991). If the young person has a second episode of depression in adolescence, then there is a far greater likelihood of disruption to interpersonal relationships and a persistent sense of dissatisfaction with life (Rao et al. 1995). Also, as adults, they are more likely to present with overdoses and other suicidal gestures than is the general population (Kovacs et al. 1993).

As well as the factors within the child, there are wider influences which can affect the likelihood of further depressive episodes. For example, if the mother suffers from mood disorders, then this increases the risk of recurrence (Hammen et al. 1990).

Preventative strategies

With the knowledge that exists about predicting the frequency of future problems in at-risk groups, it is natural to ask what is being done to try to prevent this heavy psychological toll on these young people. Some work in adults has looked at whether the continued prescription of antidepressants is able to prevent relapse, and the results suggest long-term treatment does reduce the likelihood of relapse but does not abolish the likelihood of some symptoms returning (Paykel 1993). There is still little evidence that long-term medication reduces the risk of relapse in young people.

In young people the evidence suggests that cognitive therapy is both a positive treatment and that it may reduce the likelihood of recurrence. This therapeutic approach can be combined with the factors which seem to be protective against further relapse: encouragement in developing outside interests; assistance offered to help foster positive relationships with family and friends; teaching good coping skills; correcting any educational deficits so that the young person can experience school achievement. Such a range of measures will also strengthen self-esteem and so reduce the likelihood of further problems.

As might be expected, it has also been shown that a positive emotional atmosphere at home and a perceived sense of family support for the child are far more important in protecting against mental illness than merely having the appearance of an average family make-up (Garrison *et al.* 1997), and indeed the reverse is the case that family discord increases the risk of depressive illness (Nomura *et al.* 2002), as does living with a parent who has a depressive illness (Beardslee *et al.* 1998). Such findings also point to methods by which at-risk children might be made more resilient to the risks to which they are exposed (Place *et al.* 2002), or reduce the presence of vulnerable cognitive mechanisms (Clarke *et al.* 1995).

Conclusion

Depressive illness is a debilitating and often recurrent problem, which exerts influences far beyond the immediate way that it affects the patient. It often seems to begin in adolescence, and although our understanding of it in this age group is increasing there is still much to learn about how it influences the young person's adult life. The treatment in adults is principally by medication and cognitive therapy. Although work still continues to try to find drug treatments that will work in the young, it is cognitive therapy that is attracting most interest in this age group. Clearly depression in the young is a challenging condition in diagnosis, in treatment, and in prevention. The research effort into the illness is great and the next few years are likely to see major changes in this particular area.

Sources of further help

www.nimh.nih.gov/publicat/depchildmenu.cfm
www.rcpsych.ac.uk/info/mhgu/newmhgu25.htm

www.teen-depression.info
www.depressionalliance.org/
www.rcpsych.ac.uk/campaigns/cminds/leaflets/dep/depression.htm

References

Ambrosini, P.J., Bianchi, M.D., Rabinovich, H. and Elia, J. (1993). Antidepressant treatments in children and adolescents. I. Affective disorders. *Journal of the American Academy of Child and Adolescent Psychiatry* 32, 1–6.

American Psychiatric Association (1994). *Diagnostic and Statistical Manual of Mental Disorders.* 4th edn. Washington DC: American Psychiatric Association Press.

Angold, A. and Costello, E. (1993). Depressive co-morbidity in children and adolescents: empirical, theoretical and methodological issues. *American Journal of Psychiatry* 150, 1779–91.

Angold, A. and Rutter, M. (1992). Effects of age and pubertal status on depression in a large clinical sample. *Developmental Psychopathology* 4, 5–28.

Beardslee, W.R., Versage, E.M. and Gladstone, T.R.G. (1998). Children of affectively ill parents: a review of the past 10 years. *Journal of the American Academy of Child and Adolescent Psychiatry* 37(11), 1134–41.

Bernstein, G.A. (1991). Comorbidity and severity of anxiety and depressive disorders in a clinic population. *Journal of the American Academy of Child and Adolescent Psychiatry* 30, 43–50.

Biederman, J. (2003). Pediatric bipolar disorder coming of age. *Biological Psychiatry* 53, 931–4.

Birmaher, B., Brent, D.A. and Benson, R.S. (1998). Summary of the practice parameters for the assessment and treatment of children and adolescents with depressive disorders. *Journal of the American Academy of Child and Adolescent Psychiatry* 37, 1234–38.

Bodiford, C.A., Eisenstadt, R.H., Johnson, J.H. and Bradlyn, A.S. (1988). Comparison of learned helpless cognitions and behaviour in children with high and low scores on the Children's Depression Inventory. *Journal of Clinical Child Psychology* 17, 152–8.

Brady, E.U. and Kendall, P.C. (1992). Comorbidity of anxiety and depression in children and adolescents. *Psychological Bulletin* 111, 244–55.

Clarke, G.N., Hawkins, W., Murphy, M., Sheeber, L.B. and Lewinsohn, P.M. (1995). Targeted prevention of unipolar depressive disorder in an at-risk sample of high school adolescents. *Journal of the American Academy of Child and Adolescent Psychiatry* 34, 312–21.

Clarke, G.N., Rohde, P., Lewinsohn, P.M., Hops, H. and Seeley, J.R. (1999). Cognitive-behavioral treatment of adolescent depression: efficacy of acute group treatment and booster sessions. *Journal of the American Academy of Child Adolescent Psychiatry* 38, 272–9.

Compas, B.E. (1994). Promoting successful coping during adolescence. In M. Rutter (ed.) *Psychosocial Disturbance in Young People: Challenges for Prevention.* Cambridge: Cambridge University Press.

Cooper, P. and Goodyer, I. (1993). A community study of depression in adolescent girls. I. Estimates of symptom and syndrome prevalence. *British Journal of Psychiatry* 163, 369–74.

Deakin, J.F.W. and Crow, T.J. (1986). Monoamines, rewards and punishments – the anatomy and physiology of the affective disorders. In J.F.W. Deakin (ed.) *The Biology of Depression*. London: Royal College of Psychiatrists.

Depue, R. and Monroe, S. (1978). The unipolar–bipolar distinction in the depressive disorders. *Psychological Bulletin* 85, 1001–29.

Emslie, G.J., Walkup, J.T., Pliszka, S.R. and Ernst, M. (1999). Nontricyclic antidepressants; current trends in children and adolescents. *Journal of the American Academy of Child Adolescent Psychiatry* 38, 517–28.

Emslie, G.J., Heiligenstein, J.H., Wagner, K.D., Hoog, S.L., Ernest, D.E., Brown, E., Nilsson, M. and Jacobson, J.G. (2002). Fluoxetine for acute treatment of depression in children and adolescents: a placebo-controlled, randomized clinical trial. *Journal of the American Academy of Child and Adolescent Psychiatry* 41, 1205–15.

Evans, M., Hollon, S. and De Rubeis, R. (1992). Differential relapse following cognitive therapy and pharmacology for depression. *Archives of General Psychiatry* 49, 802–8.

Fleming, J. and Offord, D. (1990). Epidemiology of childhood depressive disorders: a critical review. *Journal of the American Academy of Child and Adolescent Psychiatry* 29, 571–80.

Frommer, E. (1968). Depressive illness in children. *British Journal of Psychiatry* Spec. Pub. 2, 117–36.

Garrison, C.Z., Waller, J.L., Cuffe, S.P. and McKeown, R.E. (1997). Incidence of major depressive disorder and dysthymia in young adolescents. *Journal of the American Academy of Child and Adolescent Psychiatry* 36, 458–65.

Geller, B., Fox, B.S. and Clark, K.A. (1994). Rate and predictors of prepubertal bipolarity during follow-up of 6 to 12 year-old depressed children. *Journal of the American Academy of Child and Adolescent Psychiatry* 33, 461–8.

Goodyer, I.M., Germany, E., Gowrusankur, J. and Altham, P. (1991). Social influences on the course of anxious and depressive disorders in school age children. *British Journal of Psychiatry* 158, 676–84.

Hammen, C., Burge, D., Burney, E. and Adrian, C. (1990). Longitudinal study of diagnoses in children of women with unipolar and bipolar affective illness. *Archives of General Psychiatry* 47, 1112–17.

Harrington, R.C., Fudge, H., Rutter, M., Pickles, A. and Hill, J. (1990). Adult outcomes of childhood and adolescent depression. I. Psychiatric status. *Archives of General Psychiatry* 47, 465–73.

Harrington, R.C., Fudge, H., Rutter, M., Pickles, A. and Hill, J. (1991). Adult outcomes of childhood and adolescent depression. III. Risk for antisocial. *Journal of the American Academy of Child and Adolescent Psychiatry* 30, 434–9.

Hetherington, E.M., Cox, M. and Cox, R. (1985). Long term effects of divorce and remarriage on the adjustment of children. *Journal of the American Academy of Child and Adolescent Psychiatry* 24, 518–30.

Kashani, J., McGee, R.O., Clarkson, S.E. and Anderson, J.C. (1983). The nature and prevalence of major and minor depression in a sample of nine-year-old children. *Archives of General Psychiatry* 40, 1217–27.

Kaslow, N.J., Rehm, L. and Siegel, A.W. (1984). Social-cognitive and cognitive correlates of depression in children. *Journal of Abnormal Child Psychology* 12, 605–20.

Kazdin, A. (1990). Childhood depression. *Journal of Child Psychology and Psychiatry* 31, 121–60.

Keller, M.B. (1994). Depression: a long term illness. *British Journal of Psychiatry* 165 (suppl. 26), 9–15.

Kendler, K., Neale, M., Kessler, R., Heath, A. and Eaves, L. (1992). A population-based twin study of major depression in women: the impact of varying definitions of illness. *Archives of General Psychiatry* 49, 257–66.

Kent, L., Vostanis, P. and Feehan, C. (1995). Teacher reported characteristics of children with depression. *Educational and Child Psychology* 12, 62–70.

Klerman, G.L. and Weissman, M.M. (1989). Increasing rates of depression. *Journal of the American Medical Association* 261, 2229–35.

Kovacs, M. and Goldston, D. (1991). Cognitive and social cognitive development of depressed children and adolescents. *Journal of the American Academy of Child and Adolescent Psychiatry* 30, 388–92.

Kovacs, M., Goldston, D. and Gatonis, C. (1993). Suicidal behaviors and childhood onset depressive disorders: a longitudinal investigation. *Journal of the American Academy of Child and Adolescent Psychiatry* 32, 8–20.

Lewinsohn, P., Clark, G., Seeley, J. and Rohde, P. (1994). Major depression in community adolescents: age of onset, episode duration, and time to recurrence. *Journal of the American Academy of Child and Adolescent Psychiatry* 33, 809–18.

McGonagle, K., Zhao, S. and Nelson, C. (1994). Lifetime and 12 month prevalence of DSM-III-R psychiatric disorders in the United States: results from the national co-morbidity survey. *Archives of General Psychiatry* 51, 8–19.

McGuffin, P. and Katz, R. (1989). The genetics of depression and manic depressive disorder. *British Journal of Psychiatry* 155, 294–304.

Marmorstein, N.R. and Iacono, W.G. (2003). Major depression and conduct disorder in a twin sample: gender, functioning, and risk for future psychopathology. *Journal of the American Academy of Child Adolescent Psychiatry* 42, 225–33.

Merikangas, K.R. and Angst, J. (1994). The challenge of depressive disorders in adolescence. In M. Rutter (ed.) *Psychosocial Disturbances in Young People: Challenges for Prevention.* Cambridge: Cambridge University Press.

Nolen-Hoeksema, S., Girgus, J. and Seligman, M. (1992). Predictors and consequences of childhood depressive symptoms. *Journal of Abnormal Psychology* 101, 405–22.

Nomura, Y., Wickramaratne, P.J., Warner, V., Mufson, L. and Weissman, M.M. (2002). Family discord, parental depression, and psychopathology in offspring: ten-year follow-up. *Journal of the American Academy of Child and Adolescent Psychiatry* 41, 402–9.

Paykel, E.S. (1993). The place of antidepressants in long-term treatment. In S.A. Montgomery and J.H. Corn (eds) *Psychopharmacology of Depression.* Oxford: Oxford University Press.

Paykel, E.S. and Priest, R.G. (1992). Recognition and management of depression in general practice: consensus statement. *British Medical Journal* 305 1198–202.

Place, M., Reynolds, J., Cousins, A. and O'Neill, S. (2002). Developing a resilience package for vulnerable children. *Child and Adolescent Mental Health* 7, 162–67.

Post, R. and Ballenger, J. (1984). *Neurobiology of Mood Disorders.* Baltimore: Williams and Wilkins.

Puig-Antich, J., Kaufman, J., Ryan, N. and Williamson, D. (1993). The psychosocial functioning and family environment of depressed patients. *Journal of the American Academy of Child and Adolescent Psychiatry* 32, 244–53.

Radke-Yarrow, M., Nottelman, E., Martinez, P. and Fox, M.B. (1992). Young children of affectively ill parents: A longitudinal study of psychosocial development. *Journal of the American Academy of Child and Adolescent Psychiatry* 31, 68–77.

Rao, U., Ryan, N.D., Birmaher, B. and Dahl, R.E. (1995). Unipolar depression in adolescents: clinical outcome in adulthood. *Journal of the American Academy of Child and Adolescent Psychiatry* 34, 566–78.

Rice, F., Harold, G. and Thapar, A. (2002a). The genetic aetiology of childhood depression: a review. *Journal of Child Psychology and Psychiatry* 43, 65–79.

Rice, F., Harold, G. and Thapar, A. (2002b). Assessing the effects of age, sex and shared environment on the genetic aetiology of depression in childhood and adolescence. *Journal of Child Psychology and Psychiatry* 43, 1039–51.

Roberts, R.E., Andrews, J.A., Lewinsohn, P.M. and Hops, H. (1990). Assessment of depression in adolescents using the Center for Epidemiological Studies Depression Scale. *Journal of Consulting and Clinical Psychology* 2, 122–8.

Rutter, M. and Quinton, D. (1984). Parental psychiatric disorder: effects on children. *Psychological Medicine* 14, 853–80.

Sacco, W.P. and Graves, D.J. (1984). Childhood depression, interpersonal problem-solving and self ratings of performance. *Journal of Clinical Child Psychology* 13, 10–15.

State, R.C., Altshuler, L.L. and Frye, M.A. (2002). Mania and attention deficit hyperactivity disorder in a prepubertal child: diagnostic and treatment challenges. *American Journal of Psychiatry* 159, 918–25.

Strober, M. (1992). Relevance of early age-of-onset in genetic studies of bipolar affective disorder. *Journal of the American Academy of Child and Adolescent Psychiatry* 31, 606–10.

Tillett, R. (1996). Psychotherapy assessment and treatment selection. *British Journal of Psychiatry* 168, 10–15.

Vostanis, P. and Harrington, R. (1994). Cognitive-behavioural treatment of depressive disorder in child psychiatric patients: rationale and description of treatment package. *European Journal of Child and Adolescent Psychiatry* 3, 111–23.

Weissman, M.M., Fendrich, M., Warner, V. and Wickramaratne, P. (1992). Incidence of psychiatric disorder in offspring at high and low risk for depression. *Journal of the American Academy of Child and Adolescent Psychiatry* 31, 640–8.

Weissman, M., Gammon, G., John, K. and Merikangas, K. (1987). Children of depressed parents. *Archives of General Psychiatry* 44, 847–53.

Weller, E.B., Weller, R.A. and Fristad, M.A. (1995). Bipolar disorder in children: misdiagnosis, underdiagnosis, and future directions. *Journal of the American Academy of Child and Adolescent Psychiatry* 34, 709–14.

Whitaker, A., Johnson, J., Shaffer, D. and Rapoport, J. (1990). Uncommon troubles in young people: prevalence estimates of selected psychiatric disorders in a non-referred adolescent population. *Archives of General Psychiatry* 47, 487–96.

Wittchen, H.-U., Knauper, B. and Kessler, R.C. (1994). Lifetime risk of depression. *British Journal of Psychiatry* 165, (suppl. 26), 16–22.

World Health Organization (1992). *The ICD-10 Classification of Mental and Behavioural Disorders. Clinical Descriptions and Diagnostic Guidelines.* Geneva: World Health Organization.

Zis, A.P. and Goodwin, F.K. (1979). Major affective disorder as a recurrent illness: a critical review. *Archives of General Psychiatry* 36, 835–9.

Chapter 11

Dyslexia

Introduction

In every country one can find a significant number of children whose performance in reading, writing and spelling is deemed problematic. Although the origins of such difficulties can be easily explained for some children – for example, because of hearing/visual impairment, autism, brain damage – there are many others, often in mainstream schools, for whom the cause is less evident. Many of this latter group are considered to have a specific disorder, developmental dyslexia, which although far from understood, is believed to have an underlying neurological cause and be particularly related to language.

The focus of this chapter concerns not only what is meant by the term dyslexia but, perhaps more importantly, the extent to which this term adds to our ability to understand and remedy the problems of children who have difficulty in learning to read.

In a British Psychological Society (BPS) Working Party Report (1999) dyslexia is given a 'working definition': 'Dyslexia is evident when accurate and fluent word reading and/or spelling develops very incompletely or with great difficulty. This focuses on literacy learning at the "word" level and implies that the problem is severe and persistent despite appropriate learning opportunities. It provides the basis for a staged process of assessment through teaching' (1999: 64).

Following the conclusions from a similar exercise in the Netherlands (Gersons-Wolfensberger and Ruijssenaars 1997), the Working Party chose to use a definition that was essentially descriptive and lacked explanatory elements. The fact that the definition could incorporate different causal explanations was seen as a virtue.

A rather more detailed definition is provided by the Orton Dyslexia Society. Here dyslexia is seen as:

> one of several distinct learning disabilities. It is a specific language-based disorder of constitutional origin characterized by difficulties in

single word decoding, usually reflecting insufficient phonological processing abilities. These difficulties in single word decoding are often unexpected in relation to age and other cognitive and academic abilities; they
are not the result of generalized developmental disability or sensory
impairment. Dyslexia is manifested by variable difficulty with different
forms of language, often including, in addition to problems reading, a
conspicuous problem with acquiring proficiency in writing and spelling.

(Lyon 1995: 9)

Such a definition of dyslexia reflects the influence of a growing, and increasingly sophisticated, research base which appears to point strongly towards
language processing as the basis for the problems observed. Despite this,
dyslexia remains a highly controversial condition, with some denying its
very existence and others arguing that the diagnosis, however valid, is of
little value to practitioners.

An increasing number of educationalists, objecting to dyslexia's quasi-
medical tone, prefer to speak of 'specific learning difficulties'. Unlike the
use of the term 'dyslexia', which tends to involve a diagnosis by means of
symptoms and signs (British Psychological Society 1999), 'specific learning
difficulties' is essentially an exclusionary construct that refers to a situation
where the child's level of functioning in reading and writing and associated
areas is significantly weaker than one would expect on the basis of his or
her general academic or cognitive performance. Rather than being wholly
synonymous terms, then, dyslexia may be considered to be one common type
of specific learning difficulty.

There have been many accounts in the popular press of children who have
struggled through their education under great stress, who, it was subsequently discovered, were shown to be dyslexic. This finding, it is sometimes
alleged, proved to be a turning point in their lives as they could now benefit
from remedial teaching geared for dyslexics and begin to make the gains
which one would anticipate given their intellectual abilities. For other individuals, however, a failure to diagnose the condition, it is frequently alleged,
resulted in a ruined education and limited options in adult life. For some,
litigation is now a justifiable consequence. The following quotation, taken from
a newspaper article, is representative of many:

A 22 year old woman was condemned to 'temporary menial tasks' because her former schools did not realise she was dyslexic, the High Court
heard yesterday. Pamela Phelps claims that she is of average intelligence
but because her learning difficulty was not discovered until two months
before she left school, she never learned to read and write properly . . . It
was not the disorder that prevented her from being able to read. She had
originally been 'lumped in' with children of low intelligence when she
needed special tuition.

Tests were carried out on her at infant, junior and comprehensive schools. At the age of 10 she was found to be four years behind in reading and writing skills but the reason was never identified.

(*Guardian*, 27 July 1997: 5)

The above account suggests that if a diagnosis of dyslexia had been arrived at earlier, appropriate treatment would have resolved her difficulties. In July 2000, Ms Phelps' case was upheld and she was awarded substantial damages (see *The Times* Law Report of 28 July 2000 for details). However, her primary school had not failed to recognise that she had reading difficulties – this was the reason for her referral to an educational psychologist. When transferring to secondary school she had a reading age equivalent of seven years and three months. Any secondary school in such a situation should ensure that help is given to remedy such difficulties as, without specialist teaching, problems of this severity are highly unlikely to be overcome (Brooks 2002). However, the high visibility of the case was not simply because a child with reading difficulties failed to be given sufficient help but, rather, because dyslexia was not formally diagnosed. Such a diagnosis, it was argued, would have pointed to appropriate intervention, a multi-sensory, structured approach to the teaching of reading. However, any child with such severe reading difficulties is likely to benefit from such a programme. A key question that follows, therefore, is whether differential diagnosis is important for indicating the most appropriate form of intervention.

In order to ascertain the educational value of a diagnosis of dyslexia three important issues relating to conceptualisation, intervention and the provision of resources need to be considered:

1 Is dyslexia a meaningful condition for differentiating between children with reading difficulties? Can one locate children with literacy difficulties into clear dyslexic/non-dyslexic groupings?
2 To what extent does the dyslexic label guide the educator in devising appropriate forms of intervention?
3 To what extent should the dyslexic label result in the child receiving additional school/LEA resources and/or special examination arrangements which would not otherwise be made available?

Is dyslexia a meaningful condition for differentiating between children with reading difficulties? Can one locate children with literacy difficulties into clear dyslexic/non-dyslexic groupings?

While there is no such thing as a typical dyslexic, there are a number of underlying signs and symptoms which are often associated with the condition. These may include:

- speech and language difficulties (particularly as a young child);
- poor short-term verbal memory;
- difficulties in ordering and sequencing;
- clumsiness;
- lack of consistent hand preference;
- frequent use of letter reversals (b for d, p for q);
- poor verbal fluency.

Such difficulties, however, are also frequently found in people without reading difficulties and in poor readers who are not considered to be dyslexic. Furthermore, it is a point of some debate whether such symptoms are causes or consequences of reading failure. Thus, as is so often the case with the types of problem discussed in this book, the existence of certain signs and symptoms does not necessarily assist the practitioner in making a diagnosis.

There are many reasons why a child may experience difficulties in learning to read. Heaton and Winterton (1996) suggest that key factors are:

- low intelligence;
- inadequate schooling in the form of poor teaching or inappropriate content;
- socio-economic disadvantage;
- physical disability (e.g. hearing or visual difficulties);
- 'visible' neurological impairment which goes beyond reading and writing;
- emotional and behavioural factors which might affect attention, concentration and responsiveness to teacher direction, thus jeopardising the child's ability to learn;
- dyslexia.

One of the major difficulties of such analyses is that dyslexia may simply be defined and identified by the absence of the first six factors (Lyon 1995). Difficulties abound here particularly with respect to the relationship of intelligence to dyslexia (see below) and the significance of socio-economic factors. Dyslexia has been criticised as a 'middle-class syndrome', for, as Rutter (1978) points out, consideration of social factors may rule out the possibility of a diagnosis of dyslexia in those from disadvantaged backgrounds. In recent times, therefore, defining dyslexia on the basis of exclusionary factors has become less acceptable (Coltheart and Jackson 1998).

For dyslexia to be meaningfully differentiated from other forms of reading difficulty, one would require differences in underlying cause, presenting symptoms, prognosis and/or responsivity to differing forms of intervention (Pumfrey 1996). For each of these, however, evidence is currently inconclusive. This is largely because of theoretical disagreement about the more general development of language and the particular patterns of difficulty which are encompassed by the terms dyslexia and specific learning difficulties (Pumfrey and Reason 1991).

Given the lack of current consensus about what constitutes dyslexia, it is hardly surprising that estimates of its prevalence vary substantially. One estimate (Crisfield 1996) suggests that as much as 10 per cent of the population may have 'mild' developmental dyslexia and 4 per cent 'severe' dyslexia. In contrast, the Dyslexia Institute estimates that between 4 and 5 per cent of children, totalling 375,000 pupils in UK schools, are currently affected by dyslexia. While research suggests that the incidence is similar for both boys and girls, Dyslexia Institute data (see website) suggests that additional teaching is three times more likely to be provided to boys.

Dyslexia is perceived as a problem in developed countries around the world (Grigorenko 2001) although rates of reading difficulty are particularly high in English-speaking countries primarily, it is believed, because of the highly irregular nature of the English language.

What causes dyslexia?

Factors underpinning dyslexia can be considered at a variety of levels: the biological, the cognitive and the behavioural (British Psychological Society 1999).

Biological factors

No single cause of dyslexia has been discovered and it is highly likely that the various difficulties with which this term is associated have differing causes. Much work has focused on biomedical accounts which emphasise brain structure and genetic influences. Although in most individuals, the left hemisphere of the brain is usually larger than the right, it has been argued that this may be less evident in dyslexics. This, together with other neurological findings, has led to the suggestion that dyslexia results from ineffective operation of the two sides of the brain. In relation to the dominant emphasis upon impairment of phonological representation (Snowling 2000), it is argued that this can be traced to the left hemisphere. However, while abnormalities in the brains of dyslexic individuals have been frequently found, any link between structural and functional differences is still unclear, and comparative studies of brain structures of those with and without reading difficulties have not provided consistent findings (Grigorenko 2001). Practitioners, therefore, should be circumspect about any claims for intervention based upon brain studies particularly as our currently limited knowledge has, rather unfortunately, sometimes resulted in oversimplistic analyses and claims.

The common finding that dyslexia runs in families has resulted in a familiar genes versus environment debate. While it is quite possible that the quality of a child's literacy experiences will be significantly affected by living with one or more parents who have encountered difficulties in learning to read, the existence of a genetic component in reading performance generally (Wadsworth et al. 2002), and dyslexia in particular, is increasingly strong (Schulte-Korne 2001). In the Colorado Family Reading Study, for example, it was found that boys born to a dyslexic parent ran a 35–40 per cent risk of developing dyslexia themselves (tending to the higher figure if the dyslexic parent was male), whereas girls ran a 17–18 per cent risk irrespective of the parent's gender. Where neither parent was dyslexic, the risks for boys and girls was 5–10 per cent and 1–2 per cent respectively (De Fries 1991).

It is unlikely that a specific gene defect will be identified; rather, greater understanding of the interaction of several genes may ultimately prove informative (Schulte-Korne 2001) although this is unlikely to assist the teacher confronted by a child experiencing difficulty in learning (Plomin and Walker 2003). While genes may not cause reading difficulties directly, they serve to increase the likelihood that an individual will be affected (Plomin and Rutter 1998). Thus it would appear that genetic susceptibility for some individuals will be minimised or maximised by subsequent life experiences.

Visual-processing factors

The role of visual-processing deficiencies has often been seen as a key element of dyslexia, although its perceived relative importance to language-processing deficits has tended to fluctuate (Rayner 1993). The development of our understanding of the role of visual factors has not been assisted by journalists' overenthusiasm for much-heralded 'miracle cures' which have often promised more than could be delivered and have not been subsequently validated by well-designed research evaluations.

Key areas of debate in this field concern the effectiveness of eye movements, the difficulties that may result from an inability to coordinate binocular vision and the inhibiting effect of oversensitivity to light.

THE IMPORTANCE OF EYE MOVEMENTS

It has been noted by clinicians that many dyslexics scan from right to left rather than in the direction of normal Western print order. Pavlidis (1981) argued that, in reading, dyslexics tend to be less skilled in scanning texts, experience difficulties in fixating upon text and are less likely to make jumps (saccades) from one chunk of print to the next in the most efficient fashion. Such ideas, however, are now less influential and it is increasingly considered that, rather than a cause of dyslexia, the role of eye movements may be a reflection of an underlying language-processing difficulty (Miles and Miles 1990).

DIFFICULTIES IN COORDINATING BINOCULAR VISION

It has been argued (Stein and Fowler 1982; Stein 1993) that many dyslexic children fail to establish dominance in one eye when reading print, thus giving the reader the perception that the words are moving around the page. For such individuals, Stein recommends monocular occlusion, a process which involves children wearing glasses with one lens frosted over or covered by tape. These are then worn for reading and close work for a period of approximately six months. Although Stein reports that reading performance improves greatly when binocular difficulties are stabilised, it is important to note that others are critical of the data interpretation (Bishop 1989) or have not found replication studies to be supportive of the theory (Wilsher 1990). It is no longer widely thought that addressing ocular-dominance difficulties represents a significant method of treatment.

SENSITIVITY TO LIGHT (SCOTOPIC SENSITIVITY SYNDROME)

Periodically there is a burst of newspaper speculation about a wonder cure for dyslexics which involves the use of tinted lenses to reduce glare from bright lighting or white page backgrounds and limit the strain upon eyes resulting from sustained focusing. Irlen (1983), who is largely credited with developing this technique, claimed that between 50 and 75 per cent of children with dyslexic profiles may suffer from such sensitivity.

In response to the widespread publicity which resulted from Irlen's work, Wilkins (2003) designed the Intuitive Colorimeter, a piece of apparatus which can throw light of various shades and strength on to texts, that is now employed by some optometrists. Assessment, with the aid of this machine, it is argued, permits the prescription of coloured lenses individually tailored to the client's specific requirements.

The validity of such procedures continues to be a topic of debate. While practitioners may be able to identify individual children whose reading appeared to have improved following the prescription of coloured lenses, many researchers remain sceptical about the evidence for the approach (Shute 1991). Certainly, it is unlikely that the method will address the problems of children with complex decoding difficulties and Wilkins (2003), a leading advocate of the use of coloured overlays, argues that while these often lead to gains in reading speed, children diagnosed as dyslexic do not appear to benefit more than any other children, with or without reading difficulties.

Research into the field of visual processing suggests that it is highly unlikely that such factors can be considered to be significant causes of dyslexia. Indeed, a recent state of the art review of developmental dyslexia (Grigorenko 2001), makes no reference to these. Although visual problems and their various treatments are still associated with dyslexia in the popular press, researchers (e.g. Wilkins 2003) are increasingly understanding dyslexia and scotopic sensitivity as problems with different symptoms and origins.

Phonological processing

The most influential theories about dyslexia (e.g. Goswami 2000, 2002; Snowling 2000) now focus upon deficits in phonological awareness (i.e. the ability to recognise different sounds in spoken language) and knowledge about the relationship between written and spoken parts of speech, often referred to as grapheme–phoneme correspondence. Phonemes are the smallest units of sound which enable one to distinguish one word from another. They can consist of either individual or combinations of letters. Graphemes are the written forms of phonemes.

The emphasis upon phonological awareness was stimulated by research findings (Bradley and Bryant 1983; Lundberg 1994) indicating that young pre-readers who showed difficulties in perceiving rhyme and alliteration and segmenting words into their constituent sounds were more likely to demonstrate dyslexic profiles later in life. It is argued that the beginning reader needs to be able to perceive phonemes in syllables and words and then be able to manipulate these in order to be able to make a connection between speech and writing and to employ an alphabetic system to read and spell (Adams 1990). Other researchers (e.g. Fletcher *et al.* 1994) point out that while a major indicator of phonological weakness is an inability to segment spoken words phonemically, other related difficulties include imprecision in naming objects at speed (Katz and Shankweiler 1985) and limited short-term verbal memory (Brady 1991).

Interest in the role of phonological factors in reading has also been spurred by intervention studies such as that of Lundberg, Frost and Petersen (1988) which showed that pre-school children who receive phonological awareness training through listening and rhyming games make greater gains in reading and spelling than comparable control groups (for detailed discussion of the long-term outcomes of this study, see Lundberg, 1994). However, not all intervention studies have resulted in gains, and undertaking phonological training in the complex world of the classroom may be problematic. In a longitudinal study involving the tuition of five-year-olds in phonological skills by classroom volunteers, no significant gains were found three years later in reading accuracy, comprehension or spelling (Elliott *et al.* 2000).

In order to assess phonological strengths and weaknesses, several measures have been designed. The Phonological Abilities Test (Muter *et al.* 1997) is designed primarily for children aged from five to seven years. Measures consist of four phonological awareness subtests (rhyme detection, rhyme production, phoneme deletion and word completion) together with measures of speech rate (repeating words as quickly as possible) and letter knowledge. The test is deemed to be a valuable instrument for identifying children at risk of reading failure because of their slow phonological development.

A broadly similar measure, the Phonological Assessment Battery (PhAB) (Frederickson *et al.* 1997) is claimed by its authors to have: 'considerable potential both for identifying poor readers with phonological difficulties and children with specific learning difficulties (dyslexia)'. The PhAB contains subtests which assess Naming Speed, Fluency (e.g. name as many animals as you can), Rhyme Awareness, Alliteration (where each word has the same initial sound) and Spoonerisms (which involve the ability to switch initial sounds from one word to another). A number of studies are currently being conducted to ascertain the utility of this measure, some criticisms having been made about the value of the subtests (Whittaker 1996). It has also been argued that it may be only those phonological skills which are used directly in reading which when taught explicitly will lead to gains in reading (Solity 1996).

Phonological deficit theory is now widely considered to be the dominant cognitive theory for the underlying cause of dyslexia (Ramus *et al.* 2003). It is important to recognise, however, that while deficiencies in phonological awareness appear to be the most significant factors in studies of children with reading difficulties:

- we are a long way from being clear about which aspects of phonological processing are the most important for reading acquisition;
- it is unclear which groups of children, if any, should receive training in phonological skills (e.g. all preschool children, pre-readers who appear to be encountering phonological difficulties, or older children who have been identified as failed readers);
- the nature and content of appropriate phonological training programmes are yet to be determined. Furthermore, we do not know whether such training can be taught in isolation or, alternatively, whether it should be explicitly linked with the teaching of reading (Hatcher *et al.* 1994).

There is far more agreement about the statement that reading difficulties should not be considered as unitary. The nature of reading problems, their symptoms and their causes, are likely to vary substantially from one child to the next. Thus it would be unwise to employ phonological, or even language, difficulties as a global explanation (Nicolson and Fawcett 1995).

Despite the difficulties involved in agreeing upon an understanding of dyslexia, there is no shortage of assessment tools, many of which are marketed directly to teachers (who, it is suggested, will then refer suitable cases to an educational psychologist). A short review of some current measures can be found in the British Psychological Society Working Party Report (1999: 104–19).

The role of intelligence in the diagnosis of dyslexia

A cartoon published some years ago in a popular children's comic showed a young man fishing by a riverbank. His exaggerated facial features were drawn in a fashion suggestive that his intellectual ability was limited. A gamekeeper, pointing to a 'No Fishing' sign was pictured shouting to him, 'Can't you read?' Because of the widely held association between illiteracy and intellectual impairment, the reader was invited to find this scenario humorous.

At the heart of the dyslexia debate lies the thorny issue of intelligence. In work with those with reading difficulties, the frequent parental comment, 'I know he can't read but he's not daft!' typically reflects the concern and frustration often felt by those who perceive the stigmatising impact of their child's difficulties in learning to read. In our society illiteracy is often perceived as shameful and, as demonstrated in the children's cartoon, indicative of limited intellectual functioning. The humiliation involved can be a painful experience that is carried into, and sustained throughout, adulthood (McNulty 2003). It is no wonder, then, that parents are often happy for their child to receive a quasi-medical diagnosis of dyslexia. In the minds of many, such a diagnosis helps to separate intellectual from literacy weakness and offers a picture of the dyslexic as someone who, while perfectly 'normal', has a particular difficulty which hinders their development in a highly specific area of functioning. In addition, as is the case in medicine, it is hoped that a diagnosis will help to indicate an effective method of intervention.

For many, then, the dyslexic is typically frustrated and thwarted by being unable to read and write at a level commensurate with his or her intellectual functioning. Thus it is unsurprising that perhaps the a widely used criterion employed in diagnosis is whether there is a discrepancy between IQ and measured reading ability (Presland 1991). The most common method of ascertaining this is by predicting an individual's expected reading score on the basis of his or her IQ score. Where the difference between predicted and actual scores is great, the practitioner may suspect that a specific difficulty is present (McNab 1994).

Although the employment of IQ tests, such as the British Ability Scales (Elliott *et al.* 1983) or the Wechsler Intelligence Scales for Children (Wechsler 1992), is frequently included in assessment for dyslexia, there is a lack of consensus as to whether the practitioner should focus upon total IQ score or either the verbal or non-verbal subscales in isolation. Some commentators stress that an important diagnostic component is the particular performance of the individual on a specific group of subtests (which usually includes both verbal and non-verbal measures) considered to be particularly indicative of dyslexia. In the most widely employed IQ measure, the Wechsler Scales, key subtests are considered to be Arithmetic, Digit Span (a measure of short-term memory which requires the child to repeat increasingly lengthy strings of numbers spoken aloud by the examiner), Coding (where the child must match and draw symbols and shapes under time restriction) and Information (a test of general knowledge). Although such measures have been widely employed (Dudley-Marling 1981), it is now accepted that they have little diagnostic utility for individual children (British Psychological Society 1999).

Increasingly, findings from research studies are resulting in recognition that dyslexia (or specific learning difficulties) is largely independent of intellectual functioning (e.g. Fletcher *et al.* 1994; Stanovich and Stanovich 1997). While poor readers with lower IQ scores may, by virtue of their more limited reasoning skills, be less able to use meaning, inference and syntactical knowledge to help them to make sense of text, they tend to experience no greater problems than their 'dyslexic' peers when they try to read individual words – the crucial area for dyslexia (Stanovich 1991). Such findings, then, seriously call into question the suggestion that dyslexics can be differentiated on the basis of discrepancies between intellectual functioning and reading ability.

Despite recognition by such organisations as the Dyslexia Institute (2002) that dyslexia can occur at any level of intellectual ability, the IQ-reading ability discrepancy continues to be widely employed as an index of dyslexia by researchers and practitioners. In the USA, this serves as an important criterion that offers those with such a discrepancy greater opportunities to access special programmes. The thinking here is that those with low IQs are less likely to benefit from such assistance. Thus, the application of the IQ-achievement discrepancy model serves to exclude some children from specialised intervention (Catts *et al.* 2003).

In the UK, educational psychologists appear equally likely to search for discrepancies. In one survey (Pumfrey and Reason 1991), 80 per cent of a sample of educational psychologists indicated that discrepancies of one kind or another were sought when an assessment of an individual with suspected specific learning difficulties was being undertaken.

In one study, typical of those in this area, Ellis *et al.* (1996) sought to explore whether children identified as dyslexic differed from other groupings. One approach is to examine whether there are underlying differences between dyslexics and younger children whose reading skills are at a similar level.

> If dyslexics perform worse on a given task than children of the same age and IQ who are reading normally (chronological age controls) but similarly to younger normal readers (reading age controls), then it is possible that the dyslexic performance simply reflects the level they have attained in the development of reading. That is, their differences from chronological age controls could be a consequence of their failure to learn to read normally rather than reflecting some underlying cause of dyslexia. If, in contrast, the dyslexics perform worse than both the chronological age controls and the reading age controls on a given task, then that task might indeed be tapping some process whose deficient functioning lies close to the origin of dyslexia itself.
>
> (Ellis *et al.* 1996: 32)

In order to explore whether children identified as dyslexic did differ from other groupings, Ellis *et al.* (1996) identified and compared four groups of readers, all of whose reading age equivalents were in a similar range, 7.03–8.06 years. The groupings were as follows:

1 children categorised as dyslexic (mean age 10:03, mean IQ 118);
2 younger, normal readers (mean age 7:11, mean IQ 107);
3 ordinary poor readers (mean age 10:04, mean IQ 80);
4 precocious readers (mean age 6:02, mean IQ 126).

All the children were given a battery of tests including measures of phonological awareness, reading (letter matching, word recognition, non-word reading and reading passages of text), and visual processing, including visual matching and memory.

The findings indicated that the profiles of the dyslexic children were highly similar to those of the other groups. The authors concluded that: 'dyslexics are more like other children reading at the same level than they are unlike' (Ellis *et al.* 1996: 53). At present, there is little evidence that IQ can identify subgroups that assist in the planning of specific interventions (Catts *et al.* 2003).

An interesting study conducted by Klassen (2001) compared the progress of sixty-seven students with severe reading difficulties, all of whom were receiving special educational provision in mainstream secondary schools. The average gain in reading word performance over the course of a year was approximately six months. The students' IQ had no relationship to the amount of progress recorded, a finding that led to the conclusion that special assistance should be provided to all readers, without reference to IQ score.

As noted above, one reason why dyslexia is a sought-after diagnosis is that there is a very real danger that reading difficulty will be equated with limited academic ability. When this is the case, some children may encounter low teacher, peer and, possibly, parental expectations of their performance and intellectual challenge may be minimised. Because of the widespread perception that the dyslexic is often highly intelligent, it is often hoped that being assigned such a label will raise teacher expectations. In turn, it is hoped that this would result in the provision of a stimulating, demanding education which will stretch rather than demotivate the child. An example of the power of such labels is provided in the case study of Aidan, below.

Aidan, aged thirteen, was the younger of two brothers, both of whom had a long-standing history of reading difficulty. He attended a local comprehensive school, which, while enjoying a sound record of public examination success, employed a rigid system of streaming, based upon end-of-term examinations.

Assessment of Aidan's reading demonstrated a significant mismatch between his reading accuracy and reading comprehension (as measured by a standardised reading test). Aidan's reading accuracy was consistent with that of an average nine-year-old while his comprehension was superior by approximately two and a half years. Aidan's performance on a standardised spelling test was at an age equivalence of eight years and four months.

Intellectual assessment, using the Wechsler Intelligence Scales for Children (Revised), indicated that Aidan was functioning within the top 5 per cent of the population. He performed well on spatial tasks (such as recreating patterns using wooden blocks and ordering pictures to tell a story) and excelled on a number of verbal measures involving general knowledge, comprehension and reasoning. His only significant weakness involved a short-term memory task where he was required to repeat a string of numbers spoken aloud.

It was clear that Aidan could compensate for his poor decoding skills by employing his high intellect to assist him to make sense of text. In a manner similar to that when one is attempting to master a foreign language, he would use his understanding of the grammatical structures of language, and inferential skills, to guess words difficult to recognise and thus draw meaning from the text.

Reliance upon internal examinations for streaming decisions had resulted in Aidan being placed in the lowest stream. In discussion with him, it became clear that this was proving highly problematic. Aidan complained that his classmates often teased him for displaying enthusiasm in class and for the fact that his orientation to school life and peer relationships often seemed to mark him out as different. A further frustration stemmed from what was, for him, an unstimulating and unchallenging curriculum. Although Aidan experienced difficulty in achieving high grades in his examinations, this was largely a reflection of his underdeveloped literacy skills rather than an inability to understand the ideas and concepts which were presented to him. His teachers confirmed the fact that he was quick to grasp ideas and had a sound analytic ability yet, surprisingly, the possibility of inappropriate placement had not appeared to register with them.

In a series of meetings with school staff, the educational psychologist highlighted Aidan's superior intellectual ability, his frustration with the content of many of his lessons and his unhappiness in being placed within a class of somewhat disaffected, unmotivated youngsters. After prolonged debate, the teachers accepted the recommendation that Aidan should be placed in a higher stream. Furthermore, it was agreed that his written performance in end of term examinations should not be seen as adequately representing his learning. Aidan's teachers were asked to ensure that his schoolwork was intellectually challenging and not impeded by his difficulties in reading. This, of course, made significant demands upon his teachers who, in large part, were enthusiastic and diligent in tailoring aspects of their lesson delivery to meet his needs.

As notetaking was an important element of schoolwork, Aidan was subsequently encouraged to record notes using audiotapes. This necessitated the employment of a highly structured filing system in order to ensure ready access to these materials. Aidan's capacity for organisation, coupled with a high level of motivation and support from volunteer sixth formers, ensured that this proved highly effective. Direct intervention aimed at helping him to develop reading and spelling skills continued outside of classroom hours. Some months later his teachers reported that Aidan was far more cheerful and, despite ongoing difficulties with reading and spelling, was making excellent progress in his learning.

The key issue here is not that intelligence proved to be an important factor in diagnosing dyslexia. Nor can it be considered that by demonstrating his above-average intelligence, the appropriate 'treatment' was indicated. What intellectual assessment did help to highlight was that Aidan's ability to grasp and work with difficult ideas and concepts was being obscured by an inappropriate system of assessment placing too great a reliance upon written scripts. Confirmation of Aidan's abilities by the educational psychologist resulted in a changed classroom environment and higher teacher expectations, which, while not a 'cure' for his literacy difficulties, at least ensured that intellectual challenge was maintained.

The above case study serves as a good illustration of the benefits to an individual of a diagnosis of dyslexia. Not only did Aidan receive a more appropriate education, recognition of his intellectual abilities may have helped him to cope with the threats to his self-esteem caused by his placement and treatment by his peers. There is much evidence (e.g. Edwards 1994) that the dyslexic child may be treated harshly, feel humiliated, be discriminated against or undervalued, experience a range of highly negative emotions, and, as a result, develop a diminished sense of self. However, we should question whether such experiences are any less demeaning or harmful for those poor readers who are not labelled dyslexic. Indeed, does the case for sensitivity and special treatment for the dyslexic leave other poor readers to feel even more stigmatised as a result? It is possible that what may benefit some will prove costly to others. This is not to say that the unfortunate experiences of some dyslexics should be discounted, rather that schools need to provide sensitive and supportive environments for all children who encounter learning difficulties.

To what extent does the dyslexic label guide the educator in devising appropriate forms of intervention?

As has been noted, it has often proven difficult to differentiate between dyslexic and other poor readers. If causes and symptoms cannot be clearly identified for such a subgroup, does a diagnosis of dyslexia assist in formulating a clear intervention strategy?

It is generally considered that dyslexic children require teaching approaches which focus upon the ability to decode words using a knowledge of letter sounds, singly and in combination. Perhaps the associated teaching technique most associated with dyslexic children is multisensory learning. This highly structured approach involves the child learning the names, sounds and shapes of letters by accessing a number of sensory channels – hearing, touch, vision and movement. Such work is conducted individually or in small groups either in school or, typically, in a specialist centre for dyslexic children. A variety of multisensory programmes exist, some of the most common being based upon the Fernald Approach (Fernald 1943) and the Orton-Gillingham Method (Orton 1967). An outline description of these and other common approaches is provided by Pumfrey (1991: ch. 6).

Increasing realisation of the importance of phonological awareness has resulted in this receiving much greater emphasis in schools, particularly in work with the very young and those experiencing reading difficulties. Lessons typically involve the use of relatively straightforward, recognisable games designed to develop the child's ability to perceive and discriminate sounds in speech. It would appear that young children at risk of reading failure can be helped by programmes that combine phonological awareness training with teaching of letter–sound correspondence (Schneider *et al.* 2000).

Much debate has focused upon whether the teaching of reading should focus upon the explicit instruction of decoding skills involving knowledge of letters and letter combinations or through 'whole-language' approaches in which phonic knowledge is acquired explicitly, or implicitly, through everyday reading and writing activities. It is important here to recognise that the naturalistic, whole-language (sometimes misleadingly called the 'real books') approach to instruction, undertaken in isolation, may be less suited to those children who experience complex reading difficulties: 'Wherever children who cannot discover the alphabetic principle independently are denied explicit instruction on the regularities and conventions of the letter strings, reading disability may well be the eventual consequence' (Adams and Bruck 1993: 131). Similarly, it would appear inappropriate to focus exclusively upon the processing of letter strings. Activities may soon become sterile, artificial and unattractive to children. The work of practitioners and researchers from the psycholinguistic, or 'whole-language', tradition has highlighted the importance of literacy as a means of communication, emphasised the importance of storytelling and stressed that interventions should reflect the fact that learning to read, like all learning, takes place in a social context. Clearly, teaching which draws upon approaches from these very diverse theoretical traditions would seem necessary for all children (Reason 1990). More recently, mainstream practice in England has moved closer towards more structured teaching approaches. In particular, the introduction of the National Literacy

Strategy has led to greater emphasis upon the teaching of reading at the word level involving a cumulative sequence of phonics targets that, to a significant extent, mirrors traditional dyslexia programmes (Piotrowski and Reason 2000).

Many practitioners and researchers cite the importance of early diagnosis and intervention (Miles and Miles 1984). It is argued that, if tackled early, with specialised and structured teaching, many children can be helped to progress to functioning within normal levels. The value of early, specialised intervention, however, is appropriate for all children with reading difficulties. The much-vaunted Reading Recovery Programme (Clay 1985), for example, has demonstrated the effectiveness of daily, individual intervention with a wide spectrum of poor readers (Hurry 1996). It is, perhaps, somewhat disingenuous to state that, if dyslexia is not recognised and remediated swiftly, the problem will become greater – for such a statement is equally true for all children encountering reading difficulties.

As yet, there is insufficient evidence that there exists any particular teaching approach which is more appropriate for dyslexic children than for other poor readers (Presland 1991; Stanovich 1991; Vellutino *et al.* 2000). It appears likely that both groups benefit from a range of approaches which incorporate those traditionally associated with dyslexia – 'phonic, structured, sequential, cumulative and thorough' (Presland 1991: 218) – together with those which emphasise authentic tasks involving notions of contextualisation, communication, shared reading, relaxation, storytelling and parental support. This does not, of course, mean that one should no longer seek to provide an approach that is individually tailored to the needs of specific children, rather that one should not devise an intervention programme on the basis of a dyslexic/non-dyslexic categorisation.

There are many excellent texts which provide practical guidance to teachers working with dyslexic children. In line with the arguments above, however, these would also appear to be valuable for any child experiencing reading difficulty.

To what extent should the dyslexic label result in the child receiving additional school/LEA resources and/or special examination arrangements which would not otherwise be made available?

Although the British Psychological Society's Report (1999) dispensed with the notion that dyslexia was the preserve of the more intellectually able child, this perception continues to persist among the teaching and educational psychology professions and with the lay public (Regan and Woods 2000; Paradice 2001).

At present, discrepancy models make little significant impact upon choice of intervention approaches; in reality, they are often used to aid decision-making about which children should receive additional support and other resources. Underlying this thinking is the issue of potential (Elliott 2000), that is, a belief that children's underlying weaknesses inhibit the realisation of that which they could achieve. Most commonly, we are presented with an image of an able child whose condition does not permit maximisation of his or her potential. Such children, it is often argued, would benefit more readily from the provision of additional resources (e.g. a word processor, part-time one-to-one adult support) than, say, a child whose poor reading stems from more global difficulties. At present, therefore, a child with reading difficulties and an IQ of 80 is less likely to receive additional support than one with a similar reading profile but an IQ of 120. Such a situation hardly reflects growing research evidence that IQ has almost no value in predicting reading development in poor readers (Francis *et al.* 1996).

The case study of Aidan has indicated that it can be very valuable to recognise that reading difficulties may mask true levels of intellectual functioning. As a result of such a finding, teachers may address the content and mode of their educational delivery in order to ensure that the child is more appropriately challenged. Recognition of the need to assist the child in such a fashion, however, does not mean that his or her needs for additional resources are greater than those of less able poor readers. Indeed, it is arguable that ongoing adult support, guidance and regulation may be more necessary in the case of those with more global difficulties.

Special arrangements for public examinations

Another area of controversy surrounds special arrangements for public examinations taken by children with specific learning difficulties. Each year, the Joint Council for the GCSE outlines procedures for identifying those children who may require special examination arrangements. The vast majority of candidates having special arrangements are deemed to be dyslexic (Dolman 2003).

The 2003–4 criteria for specific learning difficulties are presented in Figure 11.1. It is expected that those seeking special arrangements will set out full details about the nature and history of the child's difficulties (including a report by an educational psychologist or specialist teacher prepared within two years prior to the examination), how these disadvantage the candidate and an account of the arrangements which have been made by the school to assist the child.

The special arrangements permitted for GCSE examinations for children with learning difficulties (such as dyslexia) include:

- an additional time allowance (up to 25 per cent);
- the reading aloud (or taping) of questions to candidates (where there is evidence of a significant discrepancy between reading ability and reasoning ability);

LEARNING DIFFICULTIES (INCLUDING NEUROLOGICAL DYSFUNCTION)

Candidates are likely to have experienced difficulties in at least one of the areas given below.

Reading Accuracy This would include candidates who are unlikely to be able to read the examination material with sufficient accuracy to avoid making mistakes which will affect the understanding of what they read.

Reading Speed This will be a particular problem where the speed of reading is so slow that the candidate loses the sense of what he or she reads.

Spelling This will include candidates with spelling difficulties that significantly slow their work rate and result in the use of alternative words that are easier to spell or candidates who are unlikely to achieve any score in the marking of spelling.

Handwriting Speed Candidates whose handwriting speed is so slow that it presents a particular problem should be trained to communicate the information required by questions as briefly as possible wherever this is appropriate. Where such a strategy is not sufficient, special arrangements may need to be sought.

Handwriting Legibility This may relate to writing under time pressure and in such cases the previous section will apply. There are, however, candidates whose scripts are illegible despite their being allowed to write more slowly.

Other Difficulties As well as the preceding areas of difficulty, some candidates have other specific problems, e.g. attention and concentration, clumsiness and disorganisation of such severity as to prevent a candidate from demonstrating attainment. Such difficulties as these and others are often found to be associated with neurological dysfunction.

Figure 11.1 Learning disabilities criteria which may result in special examination arrangements for 2004
Source: Joint Council for General Qualifications

- access to a word processor where this is the candidate's usual method of communication (note: the use of spell checks is forbidden);
- the provision of a transcript of any section of the candidate's script which is difficult to decipher;
- the use of an amanuensis;
- coloured overlays are permitted for those with visual difficulties.

Although reading difficulties will be found in candidates throughout all of the GCSE grade range, special arrangements under the category of 'learning disabilities' are intended solely for those with the cognitive capacity to participate meaningfully in the content of the examination at the level entered. In order to benefit from those examination concessions noted above, it is usually expected that there should be a significant discrepancy between the candidate's cognitive (intelligence test) assessments and literacy skills. The use of a discrepancy criterion, of course, excludes large numbers of children for whom such arrangements might prove beneficial and, in practice, only a very small proportion of children with reading difficulties will receive such assistance. Concerns have been expressed, however, about exactly what levels of performance are appropriate and whether inequities exist (Woods 2003). Sawyer *et al.* (1991), for example, found that psychologists' requests for additional time were based on candidates' reading accuracy age equivalencies ranging from seven to fourteen years regardless of the fact that the performance of many was of a standard which enabled them to read typical examination passages with little difficulty.

Such allowances, however, do not necessarily offer significant advantage to candidates. The use of additional time, for example, may prove counterproductive. In several cases it has been shown that rather than assisting the candidate to proof-read and edit their work (not always an attractive task for such individuals), the additional period has been inappropriately used to continue to write. This additional work may often prove to be inaccurate or betray a lack of understanding of the material which otherwise might have not been apparent (Hedderly 1996).

The use of an amanuensis tends to be more appropriate to students with physical disability rather than special reading difficulties. The benefits are questionable as students may find the use of a scribe more difficult than anticipated (Collins 2003).

The reading aloud of questions is more likely to prove beneficial, as an inability to grasp exactly what is being asked is greatly disadvantageous to any candidate. Of course, such provision is likely to benefit all children with reading difficulties, not merely those who are eligible on the basis of their higher reasoning ability. It is arguable that any differences in ability or understanding of content would still be demonstrated by the quality of the children's responses. In practice, however, to provide readers to all children who would profit from such a service would require time, personnel and organisation which would stretch the capacity of schools and examination boards. Thus, as with additional educational resourcing, those who are deemed to have most 'true ability' are provided with assistance less readily available to other poor readers.

Outcomes

Contrary to media accounts, a diagnosis of dyslexia and specialised intervention rarely results in immediate and rapid gains. As yet, there is little evidence for any particular treatment beyond the realm of educational practice. Recently, however, the claims of researchers, who have studied the impact of an exercise-based intervention entitled 'dyslexia, dyspraxia attention-deficit treatment' (DDAT) (Reynolds *et al.* 2003), have received much attention. Their study suggested that an exercise programme emphasising a variety of forms of sensory stimulation resulted in gains in reading performance. However, severe methodological flaws in the study (Snowling and Hulme 2003; Stein 2003) have since led many to discount the findings.

Although improvements in reading performance are to be anticipated, given an appropriate educational diet, it is likely that difficulties, particularly those relating to phonological awareness, will persist into adulthood (Snowling *et al*. 1997). In addition, many will take with them the burden of associated emotional insecurity and low self-esteem (McNulty 2003). Given this picture, it is hardly surprising that there is some (albeit limited) evidence that dyslexics tend to stop their education at an earlier age and have less success in employment (Spreen 1987). We are, however, familiar with accounts of many famous people such as Churchill and Leonardo da Vinci who, despite reading and spelling difficulties, achieved greatness. From such individuals, perhaps, we should recognise the fact that reading difficulties are not necessarily barriers to success. In addition to tackling reading difficulties directly, therefore, parents, teachers and others should ensure that assistance focuses upon the use of technological aids, the development of organisational strategies and, perhaps most importantly, the enhancement of the child's perceived competence and sense of self-esteem.

Conclusions

Rutter (1998) has criticised the dyslexia literature on the grounds that attempts have been made to define the term before it has been made clear what exactly is being investigated. It now seems likely that dyslexia will be defined as a specific language-based condition with an underlying neurological basis. As a result, advances in educational and medical research may eventually lead to meaningful discrimination between dyslexics and other poor readers. What is less clear is whether this will result in differential forms of intervention and treatment for dyslexics and non-dyslexics. As yet, a diagnosis of dyslexia, while often welcomed as a means of gaining resources or reducing the stigma attached to reading difficulty, offers little guidance to those whose task it is to provide appropriate learning experiences.

The literature is replete with a huge variety of intervention techniques, some which directly address specific visual- or language-based problems, some which are based upon techniques used for pre- and early readers, some which draw upon existing or new technologies to tackle or circumvent literacy difficulties, and others which merely reflect good practice in the teaching of reading (e.g. paired or shared reading). It seems likely that, despite the contradictions and inconsistencies of professional opinion (Bus 1989), decisions about the nature of intervention should continue to reflect children's individual needs rather than simple categorisation into one of two camps. Similarly, at the current time, there would appear to be insufficient moral or empirical grounds for allocating additional resources to those who are labelled dyslexic while leaving other poor readers – those, perhaps, deemed to have limited potential – to struggle unaided.

An alternative approach is to dispense with differentiation on the basis of discrepancies between reading ability and other skills. Instead, reading impairment could simply be defined on the basis of age-related reading skills, and the form of intervention would be determined by the individual's particular profile (Coltheart and Jackson 1998). This would, of course, weaken the argument for focussing resources upon a particular subset of poor readers, the dyslexics. However, given that about 20 per cent of children in English-speaking countries experience reading problems (Grigorenko 2001), the financial implications of such a conceptualisation would be highly unattractive to policy makers and budget holders. It would seem, therefore, that resource considerations will ensure that poor readers will continue to be split into dyslexic/non-dyslexic groupings with differing access to resources and special consideration.

Sources of further help

Local education authority support services

If there are concerns about a child's reading development, the local education authority's educational psychology or learning support services are often a valuable source of help in assessing the child's needs and in advising upon appropriate sources of support and assistance.

Voluntary bodies

The British Dyslexia Association (BDA), 98 London Road, Reading, Berkshire RG1 5AU. http://www.bda-dyslexia.org.uk
The Dyslexia Institute, 133 Gresham Road, Staines, Middlesex TW18 2AJ. http://www.dyslexia-inst.org.uk

Public examinations

For further information about special arrangements for public examinations for children with special educational needs, contact: Joint Forum for GCSE and GCE, Devas Street, Manchester M15 6EX. http://www.jcgq.org. uk/Publications_and_Common_Docs/Regs_&_Guidance.pdf

Research reports

A research report on the effectiveness of different strategies for teaching reading is available on http://www.dfes.gov.uk/research. A detailed review of

the nature and treatment of scotopic sensitivity is available on http//
www.essex.ac.uk/psychology/overlays

References

Adams, M.J. (1990). *Beginning to Read: Thinking and Learning about Print*. Cambridge,
    MA: MIT Press.
Adams, M.J. and Bruck, M. (1993). Word recognition: the interface of educational
    policies and scientific research. *Reading and Writing: An Interdisciplinary Journal* 5,
    113–39.
Bishop, D.V. (1989). Unstable vergence control and dyslexia – a critique. *British
    Journal of Ophthalmology* 73, 223–45.
Bradley, L. and Bryant, P.E. (1983). Categorising sounds and learning to read:
    a causal connection. *Nature* 301, 419–21.
Brady, S.A. (1991). The role of working memory in reading disability. In S.A.
    Brady and D.P. Shankweiler (eds) *Phonological Processes in Literacy: A Tribute to
    Isabelle Y. Liberman*. Hillsdale, NJ: Erlbaum.
British Psychological Society (1999). *Dyslexia, Literacy and Psychological Assessment.:
    Report by a Working Party of the Division of Educational and Child Psychology of the
    British Psychological Society*. Leicester: British Psychological Society.
Brooks, G. (2002). What works for children with literacy difficulties? The effectiveness
    of intervention schemes. *Department for Education and Skills Research Report 380*.
    London: DfES.
Bus, A.G. (1989). How are recommendations concerning reading and spelling disab-
    ilities arrived at and why do experts disagree? *Psychology in the Schools* 26, 54–61.
Catts, H.W., Hogan, T.P. and Fey, M.E. (2003). Subgrouping poor readers on the
    basis of individual differences in reading-related abilities. *Journal of Learning
    Disabilities* 36, 151–64.
Clay, M. (1985). *The Early Detection of Reading Difficulties*. Auckland: Heinemann.
Collins, E. (2003). It's really hard, this dictation business; observations on the use of
    an amanuensis in examinations. *Support for Learning* 18, 66–70.
Coltheart, M. and Jackson, N.E. (1998). Defining dyslexia. *Child Psychology and
    Psychiatry Review* 3(1), 12–16.
Crisfield, J. (ed.) (1996). *The Dyslexia Handbook 1996*. Reading: British Dyslexia
    Association.
De Fries, J.C. (1991). Genetics and dyslexia: an overview. In M.J. Snowling and M.
    Thomson (eds) *Dyslexia: Integrating Theory and Practice*. London: Whurr Publishers.
Dolman, E. (2003). Equality of opportunities in the examinations of the General
    Certificate of Secondary Education: a response to Woods. *The Psychology of Education
    Review* 27(2), 19–21.
Dudley-Marling, C. (1981). WISC and WISC(R) profiles of learning disabled children:
    a review. *Learning Disabilities Quarterly* 4, 307–19.
Dyslexia Institute (2002). Frequently asked questions on dyslexia by teachers, SENCos
    and parents. http://www.dyslexia-inst.org.uk/faqs.htm.
Edwards, J. (1994). *The Scars of Dyslexia*. London: Cassell.
Elliott, C.D., Murray, D.J. and Pearson, L. (1983). *British Ability Scales*. Windsor:
    NFER-Nelson.

Elliott, J.G. (2000). Dynamic assessment in educational contexts: purpose and promise. In C. Lidz and J.G. Elliott (eds) *Dynamic Assessment: Prevailing Models and Applications*. New York: JAI Press.

Elliott, J.G., Arthurs, J. and Williams, R. (2000). Volunteer support in the primary classroom: the long-term impact of one initiative upon reading performance. *British Educational Research Journal* 26, 227–44.

Ellis, A.W., McDougall, S.J. and Monk, A.F. (1996). Are dyslexics different? I. A comparison between dyslexics, reading age controls, poor readers and precocious readers. *Dyslexia* 2, 31–58.

Fernald, G. (1943). *Remedial Techniques in the Basic School Subjects*. New York: McGraw-Hill.

Fletcher, J.M., Shaywitz, S.E., Shankweiler, D., Katz, L., Liberman, I., Stuebing, K., Francis, D.J., Fowler, A. and Shaywitz, B.A. (1994). Cognitive profiles of reading disability: comparisons of discrepancy and low achievement definitions. *Journal of Educational Psychology* 86, 6–23.

Francis, D.J., Shaywitz, S.E., Stuebing, K., Shaywitz, B.A. and Fletcher, J.M. (1996). Developmental lag versus deficit models of reading disability: a longitudinal individual growth curves analysis. *Journal of Educational Psychology* 88, 3–17.

Frederickson, N., Frith, U. and Reason, R. (1997). *Phonological Assessment Battery*. Windsor: NFER-Nelson.

Gersons-Wolfensberger, D.C.M. and Ruijssenaars, W.A. (1997). Definition and treatment of dyslexia: a report by the Committee on Dyslexia of the Health Council of the Netherlands. *Journal of Learning Disabilities* 30, 209–13.

Goswami, U. (2000). Phonological representations, reading development and dyslexia: towards a cross-linguistic theoretical framework. *Dyslexia* 6, 133–51.

Goswami, U. (2002). Phonology, reading development, and dyslexia: a cross-linguistic perspective. *Annals of Dyslexia* 52, 141–63.

Grigorenko, E.L. (2001). Developmental dyslexia: an update on genes, brains, and environments. *Journal of Child Psychology and Psychiatry* 42, 91–125.

Hatcher, P., Hulme, C. and Ellis, A.W. (1994). Ameliorating early reading failure by integrating the teaching of reading and phonological skills: the phonological linkage hypothesis. *Child Development* 65(1), 41–57.

Heaton, P. and Winterton, P. (1996). *Dealing with Dyslexia*. 2nd edn. London: Whurr Publishers.

Hedderly, R. (1996). Assessing pupils with specific learning difficulties for examination special arrangements at GCSE, 'A' level and degree level. *Educational Psychology in Practice* 12(1), 36–44.

Hurry, J. (1996). What is so special about Reading Recovery? *The Curriculum Journal* 7(1), 93–108.

Irlen, H. (1983). Successful treatment of learning disabilities. Paper presented at the 91st Annual Convention of the American Psychological Association, Anaheim, CA.

Katz, R.B. and Shankweiler, D.P. (1985). Receptive naming and the detection of word retrieval deficits in the beginning reader. *Cortex* 21, 617–25.

Klassen, R. (2001). 'After the Statement': reading progress made by secondary students with specific literacy difficulty provision. *Educational Psychology in Practice* 17, 121–33.

Lundberg, I. (1994). Reading difficulties can be predicted and prevented: a Scandinavian perspective on phonological awareness and reading. In C. Hulme and M. Snowling (eds) *Reading Development and Dyslexia*. London: Whurr Publishers.

Lundberg, I., Frost, J. and Petersen, O.P. (1988). Effects of an extensive programme for stimulating phonological awareness in pre-school children. *Reading Research Quarterly* 33, 263–84.

Lyon, G.R. (1995). Towards a definition of dyslexia. *Annals of Dyslexia* 45, 3–27.

McNab, I. (1994). Specific learning difficulties: how severe is severe? *BAS Information Booklet*. Windsor: NFER-Nelson.

McNulty, M.A. (2003). Dyslexia and the life course. *Journal of Learning Disabilities* 36, 363–81.

Miles, T.R. and Miles, E. (1984). *Teaching Needs of Seven Year Old Dyslexic Pupils*. London: Department for Education and Science.

Miles, T.R. and Miles, E. (1990). *Dyslexia: A Hundred Years on*. Milton Keynes: Open University Press.

Muter, V., Hulme, C. and Snowling, M.J. (1997). *The Phonological Abilities Test*. London: The Psychological Corporation.

Nicolson, R.I. and Fawcett, A.J. (1995). Dyslexia is more than a phonological disability. *Dyslexia* 1, 19–36.

Orton, J.L. (1967). The Orton–Gillingham Approach. In J. Mooney (ed.) *The Disabled Reader*. Baltimore, MD: Johns Hopkins University Press.

Paradice, R. (2001). An investigation into the social construction of dyslexia. *Educational Psychology in Practice* 17, 213–25.

Pavlidis, G. (1981). Do eye movements hold the key to dyslexia? *Neuropsychologia* 19, 57–64.

Piotrowski, J. and Reason, R. (2000). The National Literacy Strategy and dyslexia: a comparison of teaching methods and materials. *Support for Learning* 15, 51–7.

Plomin, R. and Walker, S.O. (2003). Genetics and educational psychology. *British Journal of Educational Psychology* 73, 3–14.

Plomin, R. and Rutter, M. (1998). Child development, molecular genetics, and what to do with genes once they are found. *Child Development* 69, 1223–42.

Presland, J. (1991). Explaining away dyslexia. *Educational Psychology in Practice* 6(4), 215–21.

Pumfrey, P. (1991). *Improving Children's Reading in the Junior School: Challenges and Responses*. London: Cassell.

Pumfrey, P. (1996). *Specific Developmental Dyslexia: Basics to Back?* Leicester: British Psychological Society.

Pumfrey, P. and Reason, R. (1991). *Specific Learning Difficulties (Dyslexia): Challenges and Responses*. London: Routledge.

Ramus, F., Pidgeon, E. and Frith, U. (2003). The relationship between motor control and phonology in dyslexic children. *Journal of Child Psychology and Psychiatry* 44, 712–22.

Rayner, K. (1993). Visual processes in reading: directions for research and theory. In D.M. Willows, R. Kruk and E. Corcos (eds) *Visual Processes in Reading and Reading Disabilities*. Hillsdale, NJ: Lawrence Erlbaum Associates.

Reason, R. (1990). Reconciling different approaches to intervention. In P. Pumfrey and C. Elliott (eds), *Children's Difficulties in Reading, Spelling and Writing*. London: Falmer.

Regan, T. and Woods, K. (2000). Teachers' understandings of dyslexia.: implications for educational psychology practice. *Educational Psychology in Practice* 16, 333–47.

Reynolds, D., Nicolson, R.I. and Hambly, H. (2003). Evaluation of an exercise-based treatment for children with reading difficulties. *Dyslexia: An International Journal of Research and Practice* 9, 48–71.

Rutter, M. (1978). Prevalence and types of dyslexia. In A.L. Benton and D. Pearl (eds) *Dyslexia: An Appraisal of Current Knowledge.* New York: Oxford University Press.

Rutter, M. (1998). Dyslexia: approaches to validation. *Child Psychology and Psychiatry Review* 3(1), 24–5.

Sawyer, C., Ferguson, L., Hayward, M. and Cunningham, L. (1991). On reading and the GCSE. *The Psychologist* 4(5), 221–2.

Schneider, W., Roth, E. and Ennemoser, M. (2000). Training phonological skills and letter knowledge in children at risk for dyslexia: a comparison of three kindergarten intervention programs. *Journal of Educational Psychology* 92, 284–95.

Schulte-Korne, G. (2001). Genetics of reading and spelling disorder. *Journal of Child Psychology and Psychiatry* 42, 985–97.

Shute, R. (1991). Treating dyslexia with tinted lenses: a review of the evidence. *Research in Education* 46, 39–48.

Snowling, M.J. (2000). Dyslexia. 2nd edn. Oxford: Blackwell.

Snowling, M.J. and Hulme, C. (2003). A critique of claims from Reynolds, Nicolson and Hambly (2003) that DDAT is an effective treatment for children with reading difficulties – 'lies, damned lies and (inappropriate) statistics?' *Dyslexia: An International Journal of Research and Practice* 9, 127–133.

Snowling, M.J., Nation, K., Moxham, P., Gallagher, A. and Frith, U. (1997). Phonological processing deficits in dyslexic students: a preliminary account. *Journal of Research in Reading* 20, 31–34.

Solity, J. (1996). Phonological awareness: learning disabilities revisited? *Educational and Child Psychology* 13(3), 103–13.

Spreen, O. (1987). *Learning Disabled Children Growing Up: A Follow-Up into Adulthood.* Lisse, Netherlands: Swets and Zeitlinger.

Stanovich, K.E. (1991). Discrepancy definitions of reading disability: has intelligence led us astray? *Reading Research Quarterly* 26, 7–29.

Stanovich, K.E. and Stanovich, P.J. (1997). Further thoughts on aptitude/achievement discrepancy. *Educational Psychology in Practice* 13(1), 3–8.

Stein, J.F. (1993). Visuospatial perception in disabled readers. In D.M. Willows, R. Kruk and E. Corcos (eds) *Visual Processes in Reading and Reading Disabilities.* Hillsdale, NJ: Lawrence Erlbaum Associates.

Stein, J.F. (2003). Evaluation of an exercise-based treatment for children with reading difficulties. *Dyslexia: An International Journal of Research and Practice* 9, 122–6.

Stein, J.F. and Fowler, S. (1982). Ocular motor dyslexia. *Dyslexia Review* 5, 25–8.

Vellutino, F.R., Scanlon, D.M. and Lyon, G.R. (2000). Differentiating between difficult-to-remediate and readily remediated poor readers: more evidence against the IQ achievement discrepancy definition of reading disability. *Journal of Learning Disabilities* 33, 223–8.

Wadsworth, S.J., Corley, R.P., Hewitt, J.K., Plomin, R. and DeFries, J.C. (2002). Parent–offspring resemblance for reading performance at 7, 12 and 16 years of age in the Colorado Adoption Project. *Journal of Child Psychology and Psychiatry* 43, 769–74.

Wechsler, D. (1992). *Wechsler Intelligence Scale for Children – Third Edition, UK* London: Psychological Corporation.

Whittaker, M. (1996). Phonological assessment of specific learning difficulties: a critique of the Phonological Assessment Battery. *Educational Psychology in Practice* 12(2), 67–73.

Wilkins, A. (2003). *Reading through Colour*. London: Wiley.

Wilsher, C.R. (1990). Treatments for dyslexia: proven or unproven? In G. Hales, M. Hales, T. Miles and A. Summerfield (eds) *Meeting Points in Dyslexia: Proceedings of the First International Conference of the British Dyslexia Association*. Reading: British Dyslexia Association.

Woods, K. (2003). Equality of opportunities in the examinations of the General Certificate of Secondary Education. *The Psychology of Education Review* 27(2), 3–16.

Chapter 12

Developmental coordination disorder (dyspraxia)

The clumsy individual is a long-standing and traditional figure of fun although this often masks the distressing and incapacitating nature of such problems. While clinical accounts of motor difficulties have featured in the scientific literature throughout the twentieth century, it is only relatively recently that detailed consideration has been given to the particular needs of this population. Growing interest in this field has led to a proliferation of terms to describe this condition that has not always resulted in conceptual clarity. Terms employed include: developmental dyspraxia, minimal brain dysfunction, perceptuo-motor dysfunction, sensory integrative dysfunction, apraxia, physical awkwardness, developmental coordination disorder and the clumsy child syndrome. Most common in the UK is the term dyspraxia. Derived from Greek, *dys* is a prefix meaning 'bad'. 'Praxis' relates to 'the learned ability to plan and carry out sequences of controlled movements in order to achieve an objective' (Ripley *et al.* 1999: 1). This emphasis upon planning highlights a strong cognitive element that impacts upon motor skills and coordinated movements.

Despite the hold the term dyspraxia has among the lay public and, in the UK, by health and education professionals (Peters *et al.* 2001), developmental coordination disorder (DCD) has been chosen by most international specialists as the preferred term (Polatajko *et al.* 1995a). According to the American Psychiatry Association's, Diagnostic and Statistical Manual (DSM-IV) (APA 1994), four criteria are listed for DCD:

1   there is a significant impairment in the development of motor coordination;
2   the condition interferes with the academic progress of the child or with day-to-day activities;
3   the condition is not due to a general medical condition such as cerebral palsy or muscular dystrophy;
4   the condition is not primarily due to mental retardation.

While the term DCD is now used in the majority of scientific publications, it remains, 'a fuzzy term without a precise definition' that describes 'a broad band of mild motor problems that researchers and practitioners are still struggling to refine' (Cermak *et al.* 2002: 22). DCD, it is argued (e.g. Kaplan *et al.* 1998), is unlikely to be a discrete condition, and almost certainly describes a heterogeneous grouping of difficulties. Attempts to derive discrete subtypes, however, have resulted in only minimal success (Dewey 2002).

DCD's conceptual relationship with dyspraxia is similarly uncertain. Kimball (2002: 210) considers it 'debatable' whether the two terms are synonymous, and some consider that dyspraxia may describe a subgroup of children who have more severe motor planning problems. Others, however, suggest that the two conditions are different in essence rather than merely degree. Kirby and Drew (2003) differentiate between dyspraxia and DCD by contending that the former places greater emphasis upon planning. For these authors, DCD relates more closely to coordination and execution. Whereas the dyspraxic 'does not know what to do and how to move . . . the child with DCD has difficulties with coordination and execution' (2003: 6). Dewey and Kaplan (1994) take a different view and distinguish between three main groups of children with DCD: those with problems of balance, coordination and carrying out everyday motor activities, those who experience difficulty in planning and subsequently undertaking a series of motor actions (the group who are seen by many as being dyspraxic), and those who have problems in both of the above. Yet again, others differentiate between planning/sequencing and motor execution in relation to dyspraxia. In cases of ideomotor dyspraxia, the individual is seen as experiencing difficulty in performing even simple motor tasks when requested. This is less of a difficulty in the case of ideational dyspraxia where it is undertaking a sequence of multistep motor tasks rather than executing simple movements that is seen as particularly problematic. While it is helpful to differentiate between cognition and action components of motor difficulties, it should be noted that current conceptualisations and labels do not consistently reflect this distinction (Missiuna and Polatajko 1995).

Prevalence

It is difficult to obtain a consensus about prevalence rates as different degrees of severity and forms of difficulty are often employed. DSM-IV and the World Health Organization's classification system (ICD-10) (1992), both provide estimates that approximately 6 per cent of children between the ages of five and eleven exhibit DCD. Wright and Sugden (1996) leading researchers in the field suggest rates of 4.5–5 per cent. As dyspraxia is often seen as involving a smaller proportion of those with more complex motor and cognitive difficulties, the Dyspraxia Foundation's estimate that 2 per cent of the general population are affected is understandable. Males are twice as likely to be affected, although the ratio of boys to girls in clinical samples (e.g. Miller *et al.* 2001) tends to be higher; this most likely reflecting the greater salience of boys with such problems. The condition becomes less pre-valent in adulthood although difficulties often persist (Cantell *et al.* 1994).

Symptoms

If one itemised the various symptoms of DCD and dyspraxia described in the literature, the resulting list would be very long. A high proportion of, but not all, children with DCD reach motor milestones (e.g. crawling, walking, speaking) at a later than average age. Others tend to show difficulties only with respect to the acquisition of more complex motor skills.

In addition to general difficulties of gross and fine motor coordination, common symptoms include: poor organisational skills, poor sense of direction, poor short-term memory, sensitivity to touch (including intolerance of having nails cut or hair and teeth brushed), and difficulty in establishing hand dominance. In addition, such children often exhibit emotional and behavioural difficulties such as obsessive or phobic behaviour, poor social maturity and skills, and a tendency to impatience.

The nature and impact of symptoms vary according to the child's age although in many cases a meaningful difficulty is often not identified until the child starts school. However, from early infancy, the child with DCD is more likely to exhibit attentional, feeding and sleeping difficulties. As noted above, independent crawling and walking may be delayed. During the primary school years, managing the difficulties that result from their poor gross and fine motor actions, and coping with the threat to their sense of self that results from this, are often key tasks. In adolescence, problems stemming from poor peer relations and, as academic and self-regulatory demands increase, a disorganised and unsystematic approach to learning often become increasingly salient.

In addition to a tendency to emotional immaturity, there appear to be a variety of secondary socio-emotional and behavioural problems that may result from the individual's difficulty in coping with the shame and embarrassment that the less physically adept so often experience in childhood. In the early years of life, play has a strong motoric nature and, as the child moves through the school years, poor performance in sports and other physical pursuits becomes a hindrance to achieving social status leading to a greater likelihood of exclusion from the peer group (Smyth 1992). As described in the case study below, children with DCD can easily become isolated onlookers (Smyth and Anderson 2000). While emotional and behavioural problems may not emerge until adolescence (Hellgren *et al.* 1994) their social foundations can begin from a relatively early age. Short and Crawford (1984) noted that self-esteem difficulties for children with motor impairments increase considerably between the ages of five and seven. Schoemaker and Kalverboer (1994) found that six-year-olds with movement problems considered themselves to be less socially competent, and tended to be more anxious and introverted than their peers. Similarly, Losse *et al.* (1991) noted that the teenagers in their sample reported difficulties in making friendships.

> Among this group are children who find it difficult to concentrate at school and become the class nuisance, children who are unhappy in school because they are bullied or socially isolated, children who cope with their clumsiness by becoming the class clown and children who withdraw completely from participation and remain unnoticed until it is too late to help them.
>
> (Henderson and Sugden 1992: 6)

Given the above, it is hardly surprising that many such children have difficulties with academic subjects at school, despite their generally average IQ profile. In particular, studies have repeatedly demonstrated difficulties with written language, spelling and arithmetic (Fletcher-Flinn *et al.* 1997; Dewey and Kaplan 1994; Kadesjo and Gillberg 1999).

Danny's parents recognised early in his infancy that his motor skills were failing to develop in line with those of his peers. Rather than achieving the usual walking milestones, he tended to sit and watch others and liked to be carried. As he matured, he often bumped into inanimate objects, had a poor sense of balance, and encountered difficulty with dressing and tying laces. When seated, he would lock his legs behind the legs of his chair as if to anchor himself into a stable position from which he would not slide. Riding a bike or roller skating were activities that were beyond his capabilities. Food was regularly spilled when eating and a plastic table cloth that could be easily wiped clean proved indispensible. Although he received physiotherapy, his parents believe that this achieved little. At school, Danny proved to be an excellent reader and a quick learner although his handwriting was poor. For several years, he was provided with remedial handwriting exercises by occupational therapists and teachers but these only served to make him feel increasingly frustrated and self-conscious. As a young child, he tended to avoid the rough and tumble of the playground preferring sedentary activities such as playing on the computer or reading. He enjoys film and drama, often creating complex imaginary plots in his head, but avoids singing and dancing. As a fourteen year old, Danny's parents still feel that they must organise his daily life as he appears to have little sense of time, and continues to react to events, rather than planning ahead. He appears uninterested in his personal appearance and his mother feels obliged to assist in his daily grooming.

Danny's parents have always been far more concerned about his social than his physical difficulties. Watching him enter the schoolyard as an eight-year-old, his mother noted that he circled the periphery, hoping to be invited over to join his peers. When he commenced secondary school, Danny's earlier experience of relative social isolation as a young child was replaced by the challenges of a more hostile environment and he soon became a victim of bullying. Transfer to another school with stronger teacher regulation has proven beneficial and he has been far happier in this more structured environment. Harassment has now ceased and his mother often invites his schoolmates over to the house. Sadly, reciprocal invitations to their homes are relatively rare.

Co-morbidity

Children with motor difficulties often display features of other conditions such as Asperger's syndrome, dyslexia and attention deficit disorders. In a study of children with ADHD, Kadesjo and Gillberg (2001) found that 47 per cent had DCD. Kaplan *et al.* (1998) found that 69 per cent of their ADHD and 63 per cent of their dyslexic samples had DCD. In an examination of DCD clinic samples in Canada, Miller *et al.* (2001) found that where co-morbidities were evident, 41 per cent had reports of attention deficit disorder, 38 per cent demonstrated a learning disability, 3 per cent showed developmental delay, and 18 per cent had other co-morbidities. Portwood (1999) reported that approximately half of the clinical cases with which she was working experienced difficulty with language production.

Gaining a clear picture of clinical samples is often compounded by a tendency only to examine for DCD/dyspraxia in cases of severe difficulty (Ramus *et al.* 2003). Language problems are also often difficult to classify and the dyspraxic child may be seen by some to have semantic pragmatic disorder, a term used to describe difficulty in grasping the meaning of language used in its social context. Thus differential diagnosis may, in part, be determined by whether this is undertaken by a psychologist, psychiatrist, physiotherapist, speech and language therapist or paediatrician (Kirby 1999).

Causes

While the causes of DCD/dyspraxia are unknown, it is generally considered that these involve multiple factors that result in immature or atypical brain development (Kaplan *et al.* 1998). However, given that identifiable neurological disorders are exclusionary criteria for a diagnosis of DCD, this is a rather grey area (Dewey and Wilson 2001). Certainly research in this field is considerably less advanced than that in other areas such as dyslexia. Thus, while texts such as those of Portwood (1999), Macintyre (2001) and Kirby and Drew (2003) provide simple descriptions of how the brain functions and offer suggestions as to the origins of such conditions, this is still little more than speculative. As with most developmental disorders, there appears to be some family link with regard to motor difficulties that may be indicative of a genetic component.

At the cognitive level, a range of processing deficits has been examined. Problems have been found in visual perception (Lord and Hulme 1987), kinaesthetic perception (concerning awareness of limb position and movement – Laszlo *et al.* 1988b), the transfer of information from one sensory modality – e.g. vision, vestibular (inner-ear) functioning, proprioception, touch) – to another (Newnham and McKenzie 1993), and the ability to select the most appropriate motor responses (van Dellen and Geuze 1988) and programme these in an effective fashion (Smyth 1991). A recent line of research (Mandich *et al.* 2002, 2003) has found that children with DCD have particular difficulty with inhibitory function; they tend to encounter difficulty ignoring irrelevant information and suppressing the production of unwanted responses. Such responses may concern either motor or cognitive (e.g. attention) functions.

In a wide-ranging review of motor control in children with DCD, Williams (2002: 137) states that, despite the rather limited amount of research available, the following underlying difficulties are often observed:

- significantly slower reaction – movement and times;
- universal difficulty with timing (e.g. rhythmic) control;
- frequent difficulty with force control (i.e. exerting an appropriate amount of pressure);
- over-reliance upon visual information as a means to regulate posture/balance;
- greater vulnerability to situations where balance is disturbed (perturbation);
- an inability to adapt quickly to changes in movement demands;
- inefficient coordination of muscle-group activation to regulate balance;
- poor intersensory integration, especially concerning visual and proprioceptive information.

Assessment of motor skills

While a degree of conceptual and diagnostic confusion continues to prevail, researchers and clinicians are agreed that early recognition and assessment of children's motor difficulties are essential (Polatajko *et al.* 1995a). Not only can various forms of physical therapy be introduced but, equally important, all those who live and work with the child can be sensitised to the broader difficulties concerned, helped to modify the child's environment, and recognise the need to minimise potential threats to the child's social and emotional well-being.

While a variety of tools are employed, there is still no 'gold standard' of assessment instruments for DCD (Sugden and Chambers 2003: 15). One of the most widely employed standardised measures for children is the Movement

Assessment Battery for Children (M-ABC) (Henderson and Sugden 1992). Originally published two decades earlier as the Test of Motor Impairment (TOMI), this measure is concerned with both gross and fine motor skills and assesses manual dexterity, ball skills and balance. It is designed for use with children aged between four and twelve years. As in the case of other popular measures, the M-ABC has been criticised for lacking a sound theoretical base (Cantell and Kooistra 2002). Other widely employed measures are the Bruininks-Oseretsky Test of Motor Proficiency (BPTMP) (Bruininks 1978) and the Developmental Test of Visual-Motor Integration (VMI) (Beery 1997). While the VMI is a popular measure with occupational therapists, Missiuna and Pollock (1995) have recommended that it should be supplemented by assessment of the child's grasp, and of the time taken to complete to complete the test. It is important to note, however, that correlation between measures is not always high and the two most popular tests, the M-ABC and the BOTMP do not consistently identify the same children as having motor impairments (Dewey and Wilson 2001). To overcome this, it is recommended that test results should be combined with observations of specialist clinicians (Crawford *et al.* 2001).

As measures that require individualised assessment of performance on standardised tasks are highly time-consuming and thus expensive for screening purposes, a variety of checklists have become available for this purpose. Some are designed to be completed by parents – the Developmental Coordination Disorder Questionnaire (DCDQ) (Wilson *et al.* 2000). Others, such as that forming part of the M-ABC, are geared for teacher completion. The M-ABC Checklist requires teachers to rate the motor performance of children, aged between four and twelve years, on forty-eight items of daily life in school. The Checklist is divided into four sections that consider progressively more complex situations. Thus, the first section includes items where both the child is stationary and the environment stable; the fourth, and final, section includes those where the child is moving and the environment is changing.

Schoemaker *et al.* (2003) testify to the Checklist's psychometric properties although they found evidence that the measure, covering a broader range of motor skills, did not always confirm diagnoses derived from the M-ABC Test. Although it was anticipated that the Checklist would identify more children with motor problems (Henderson and Sugden 1992), there is some evidence to suggest that, for some age groups, it may identify a significant number of false positives thus resulting in time-consuming and unnecessary diagnostic follow-up investigations (Schoemaker *et al.* 2003). It also appears that the Checklist may fail to highlight the movement problems of some children that are revealed by the Test (Junaid *et al.* 2000).

Irrespective as to whether psychiatric classification systems or standardised measures of motor skill are employed, there is no clear, widely agreed quantifiable means of determining DCD or dyspraxia. Thus, while for DCD, DSM-IV makes reference to significant impairment of motor skills, there is no consensus as to what this means in practice. The situation is similar for ICD-10. In a similar vein, Lewis (2003) notes that studies using the M-ABC have utilised a range of cut-off points for identifying children with DCD ranging from the fifth to the twentieth centile.

Intervention

Intervention programmes may involve one or both of two broad forms (Sugden and Chambers 2003). A focus can be placed upon addressing underlying processes of motor performance such as those concerning perception, memory, vision and kinaesthetics (sometimes known as 'bottom-up' approaches) or, alternatively, emphasis can be placed upon helping them to tackle task-specific problems ('top-down' approaches).

Bottom-up approaches tend to be clustered into sensory integration training, process-orientated treatment or perceptual motor training (Mandich *et al.* 2001). Sensory integration, originally designed for children with learning disabilities, is based upon a belief that providing sensory stimulation will lead to an improvement in brain and motor functioning. Therapy involves full body movements that provide various forms of sensory stimulation – for example, vestibular, proprioception (awareness of one's own body) and tactile. Much of the thinking in this area stems from the work of Ayres who defined sensory integration as

> a neurological process that organizes sensation from one's own body and from the environment, and makes it possible to use the body effectively within the environment. The spatial and temporal aspects of inputs from different sensory modalities are interpreted, associated and unified.
>
> (Ayres 1989: 11)

Process-orientated treatment centres upon developing children's sense of movement (kinaesthesia) as this is seen as essential to the acquisition and performance of skilled motor performance (Laszlo and Bairstow 1985).

Perceptual-motor training is predicated on the assumption of a causal relationship between motor skills and underlying perceptual processes. The approach involves the child in performing a range of fine and gross motor activities in order to enhance skills required for optimal functioning.

The evidence in support of bottom-up approaches is generally equivocal and, where gains on test measures have been shown, there is an underlying question as to their generalisability to other situations and contexts (Mandich *et al.* 2001). Davidson and Williams (2000), for example, carried out a ten-week individualised programme of therapy that was followed by a year's activities recommended to the children's parents and teachers. The programme emphasised sensory integration of vestibular functioning, body awareness and touch, and perceptual-motor training of fine and gross motor activities.

Although there was small improvement in some areas of functioning at twelve-month follow-up, the authors concluded that the clinical benefit of the intervention could not be demonstrated. Another research group (Laszlo and Bairstow 1985; Laszlo et al. 1988a) has produced evidence supporting the efficacy of their kinaesthetic approach; however, their experimental design has been criticised and other studies have failed to show similar gains (e.g. Polatajko et al. 1995b; Sims et al. 1996a, 1996b).

In a review of processing deficits in DCD, Wilson and McKenzie (1998) noted that while impaired processing of visual information appeared to be a significant factor of children with DCD, no studies had examined whether training to improve visuospatial processing would result in improved motor coordination problems. However, a recent review of the role of visual perception in DCD (Rösblad 2002) concludes that there is little evidence to suggest that this a major factor.

While it is clear that children with DCD experience a range of perceptual difficulties, any causal relationship between these and functional motor performance remains unclear (Mandich et al. 2001)

Top-down approaches appear to offer greater potential. The emphasis of such interventions is upon addressing directly specific difficulties encountered in the child's daily life. Thus specific tasks that the child would normally encounter are identified and guidance is given on how these can be undertaken. Where necessary, the task is broken down into discrete steps that can be taught in isolation before being subsequently linked together. A second, cognitive, component of such approaches involves teaching the child various problem-solving strategies that are related to the performance of particular motor tasks.

Although it is generally argued that intervention can prove helpful, there is a dearth of well-controlled studies that can help indicate what forms of treatment are most effective with the various types of difficulties encountered. Chu (1998) argued that research of this kind was virtually non-existent although, more recently, researchers have begun to undertake evaluations. As is the case in many clinical fields, the absence of a control group is a common feature. This is unsurprising given the concerns of many about the ethics of having groups of needy children who receive no intervention (Howard 1998).

Much of the earlier treatment evaluation work focused upon bottom-up approaches, although it would appear that the emphasis is shifting; two recent meta-analyses of research studies having pointed to the greater efficacy of top-down approaches (Pless and Carlsson 2000; Chen et al. in press). In their recent review of six top-down approaches, Chen and colleagues found that these resulted in significant gains in motor skill acquisition and rather weaker indications of transfer of motor skills. However, it was acknowledged that these results have to be treated with caution (described by the authors as 'suggestive' rather than 'confirmatory') as the studies involved relatively small samples and none utilised control groups. Furthermore, all the studies ignored social and communication skills, which, as has been demonstrated in the case study of Danny above, often prove to be the more incapacitating difficulties.

One of the top-down programmes currently receiving significant attention in the literature is the Cognitive Orientation to daily Occupational Performance (CO-OP) (Polatajko *et al.* 2001a, 2001b). Reflecting a general shift towards the utilisation of cognitive approaches for those with special needs (Figg and Elliott 2003), the CO-OP is an individualised programme involving twelve one-hour training sessions. The programme has three major objectives: skill acquisition, cognitive strategy development and generalisation and transfer. Initially, children are asked to select three skills that are important to them in daily life. During the intervention phases they are continually asked to analyse their performance and, where difficulties emerge, identify and try out possible means of overcoming these. The cognitive strategy employed, with theoretical and clinical roots in the work of Vygotsky, Feuerstein and Meichenbaum, is similar to many existing approaches in special education (Ashman and Conway 1997). These emphasise a cyclical process involving selecting goals, planning the means to undertake the task, carrying this out, and evaluating its effectiveness.

A repeated difficulty in intervention programmes concerns the problem of generalisation and transfer. While children with various forms of special need can often be taught knowledge or skills in a specific context, too often this new learning cannot be demonstrated at other times and in other settings. To help overcome this, CO-OP continually emphasises the application of strategies to everyday situations on the part of both the children and their parents (see Polatajko *et al.* 2001a, for further details).

Polatajko *et al.* (2001b) have suggested four particular reasons for the apparent efficacy of their approach:

1   Children select their own tasks which might result in enhanced motivation and greater understanding of goals.
2   The approach utilises verbal self-guidance that can subsequently develop into an internal means of self-regulation.
3   Emphasis is placed upon gaining rapport between therapist and child that facilitates a discovery-based approach to problems and solutions.
4   Children are asked to evaluate their performance. Recognition of their gains may result in a heightened sense of self-efficacy and confidence to tackle other motor difficulties.

In their review of several top-down approaches, Chen *et al.* (in press) found that CO-OP demonstrated the largest gains in skill acquisition. While there was some evidence that it resulted in skill transfer, this was weaker than for skill acquisition. Chen *et al.* suggest that this relatively weaker effect may be explained by the criteria employed, standardised measures, as these shared few characteristics with the children's self-selected tasks and may have appeared less meaningful to them.

Many of the interventions described in the literature are conducted by highly skilled psysiotherapists and occupational therapists. Clearly, with prevalence rates so high, it is important that others, in daily contact with the child, are enabled to assist in programmes. Noting a dearth of controlled studies examining the efficacy of such approaches, Sugden and Chambers (2003) carried out a detailed evaluation of a top-down (task-orientated) programme (Henderson and Sugden 1992) in which teachers and parents were asked to provide individualised sessions lasting approximately twenty minutes for three to four sessions a week. The approach involved children performing functional tasks in (preferably) everyday settings and emphasised a problem-solving approach involving the planning, execution and evaluation of action. The teachers and parents involved in the intervention were charged with selecting appropriate skills (e.g. the manipulation of objects) and locating these in relevant settings. A high proportion of the children made, and sustained, gains as measured by the M-ABC and teacher and parent reports. Of course, fixed-term intervention studies undertaken by prestigious university researchers are more likely to result in parental and teacher engagement than everyday clinical recommendation. Such programmes do require commitment and time and teachers often encounter difficulties in providing individualised programmes. While some of the activities in the Sugden and Chambers study – for example, correctly gripping writing equipment or cutlery – were ongoing and thus dealt with routinely, both the teacher and parent groups reported that it had often been hard to find time in the daily routine to fit in the extra activities involved. To assist them, some teachers had drawn upon the services of teaching assistants, and several parents had enlisted the help of other family members. A further difficulty, noted by the authors, was that some children appeared to have gained little benefit despite regular intervention. Whether these individuals would have benefited more greatly from specialist intervention was unclear. Clearly, as with most developmental conditions, it is unlikely that children with DCD can be deemed to represent an homogeneous population that will respond similarly to one form of intervention. While teachers and parents may make an important contribution to intervention, it is important to make a distinction between roles. 'To pass responsibility for remediation to the school is to fail to distinguish between therapeutic intervention and educational practice' (Stephenson et al. 1991: 111).

In addition to supporting therapists in delivering therapy, parents and teachers need to focus upon whether there is a need to modify the child's environment. Many of the secondary difficulties that arise are less likely to occur if accommodations are made. Thus teachers are advised to substitute handouts or other note forms for conventional means of student written recording (Johnstone and Garcia 1994). Here, electronic aids may prove valuable, for example, children should be taught to use a keyboard early rather than labour with handwriting as this often continues to be slow and effortful (Missiuna and Pollock 1995). Very helpful practical guides on meeting the needs of this population are provided by Kirby 1999; Portwood 1999, 2000; Macintyre 2000, 2001; May-Benson *et al.* 2002; and Kirby and Drew 2003. A text for parents and teachers, widely perceived as helpful (Missiuna 2003) can be obtained electronically.

Prognosis

At one time it was considered that clumsiness reflected developmental delay that would become resolved spontaneously by adolescence (Gubbay 1978) although this is now recognised to be incorrect. Studies, however, are equivocal and have provided contradictory findings (Cantell and Kooistra 2002). This most likely reflects real differences in prognosis for individual children. In addition, prognosis is affected by the complex interrelationship of overlapping conditions such as attention deficit disorder (Sugden and Wright 1998). What is clear is that, although a number of children outgrow their motor difficulties, for many, problems continue in adulthood and can affect occupational choices (Rasmussen and Gillberg 2000). Two studies, each involving ten-year follow-up investigations of children deemed clumsy at ages five and six (Losse *et al.* 1991; Cantell *et al.* 1994) found continuing evidence of motor difficulties in mid-adolescence. The latter study also noted that, in comparison with controls, they also had lower levels of achievement and aspiration.

Sources of further help

www.dyspraxiafoundation.org.uk
www.fhs.mcmaster.ca/canchild/. This site provides a valuable series of information guides for parents, teachers, youth workers, language therapists and other health professionals.

References

American Psychiatric Association (APA) (1994). *Diagnostic and Statistical Manual of Mental Disorders*. 4th edn. Washington, DC: American Psychiatric Association Press.
Ashman, A.F. and Conway, R.N.F. (1997). *An Introduction to Cognitive Education: Theory and Applications*. London: Routledge.
Ayres, A.J. (1989). *Sensory Integration and Praxis Tests*. Los Angeles, CA: Western Psychological Services.
Beery, K.E. (1997). *Developmental Test of Visual–Motor Integration*. 4th edn, revised. Los Angeles: Western Psychological Services.
Bruininks, R.H. (1978). *Bruininks-Oseretsky Test of Motor Proficiency Examiners' Manual*. Circle Pines, MI: American Guidance Service.

256 Developmental coordination disorder

Cantell, M.H. and Kooistra, L. (2002). Long-term outcomes of developmental coordination disorder. In S.A. Cermak and D. Larkin (eds) *Developmental Cordination Disorder*. Albany, NY: Delmar.

Cantell, M.H., Smyth, M.M. and Ahonen, T.P. (1994). Clumsiness in adolescence: educational, motor, and social outcomes of motor delay detected at 5 years. *Adapted Physical Activity Quarterly* 11, 115–29.

Cermak, S.A., Gubbay, S.S. and Larkin, D. (2002). What is developmental coordination disorder? In S.A. Cermak and D. Larkin, (eds) *Developmental Cordination Disorder*. Albany, NY: Delmar.

Chen, H.S., Tickle-Degnen, L. and Cermak, S. (in press). The treatment effectiveness of top-down approaches for children with developmental coordination disorder: a meta-analysis. *American Journal of Occupational Therapy*

Chu, S. (1998). Developmental dyspraxia 2: evaluation and treatment. *British Journal of Therapy and Rehabilitation* 5(4), 176–180.

Crawford, S., Wilson, B. and Dewey, D. (2001). Identifying developmental coordination disorder: consistency between tests. *Physical and Occupational Therapy in Pediatrics* 20(2/3), 29–50.

Davidson, T. and Williams, B. (2000). Occupational therapy for children with Developmental Coordination Disorder: a study of the effectiveness of a combined sensory integration and perceptual-motor intervention. *British Journal of Occupational Therapy* 63(10), 495–9.

Dewey, D. (2002). Subtypes of developmental coordination disorder. In S.A. Cermak and D. Larkin, (eds) *Developmental Cordination Disorder*. Albany, NY: Delmar.

Dewey, D. and Kaplan, B.J. (1994). Subtyping of developmental motor deficits. *Developmental Neuropsychology* 7, 197–206.

Dewey, D. and Wilson, B.N. (2001). Developmental coordination disorder: what is it? In C. Missiuna (ed.) *Children with Developmental Coordination Disorder: Strategies for Success*. New York: Haworth Press.

Figg, J. and Elliott, J.G. (eds) (2003). *Cognitive Education. Educational and Child Psychology* 20(2), themed edition.

Fletcher-Flinn, C., Elmes, H. and Strugnell, D. (1997). Visual-perceptual and phonological factors in the acquisition of literacy among children with congenital developmental coordination disorder. *Developmental Medicine and Child Neurology* 39, 158–66.

Gubbay, S. (1978). The management of developmental apraxia. *Developmental Medicine and Child Neurology* 20, 643–6.

Hellgren, L., Gillberg, C., Bagenholm, A. and Gillberg, I.C. (1994). Children with deficits in attention, motor control and perception (DAMP) almost grown up: general health at 16 years. *Developmental Medicine and Child Neurology* 35, 881–92.

Henderson, S.E. and Sugden, D.A. (1992). *The Movement Assessment Battery for Children*. San Antonio, TX: The Psychological Corporation.

Howard, L. (1998). Dyspraxia: an update of current practice. *British Journal of Therapy and Rehabilitation* 5(3), 118–19.

Johnstone, B. and Garcia, L. (1994). Neuropsychological evaluation and academic implications for developmental coordination disorder: a case study. *Developmental Neuropsychology* 10, 369–75.

Junaid, K., Harris, S.R., Fulmer, A. and Carswell, A. (2000). Teachers' use of the MABC Checklist to identify children with motor dificulties. *Pediatric Physical Therapy* 12, 158–63.

Kadesjo, B. and Gillberg, C. (1999). Developmental coordination disorder in Swedish 7-year-old children. *Journal of the American Academy of Child and Adolescent Psychiatry* 38, 820–28.

Kadesjo, B. and Gillberg, C. (2001). The comorbidity of ADHD in the general population of Swedish school-age children. *Journal of Child Psychology and Psychiatry* 42, 487–92.

Kaplan, B.J., Wilson, B.N., Dewey, D. and Crawford, S.G. (1998). DCD may not be a discrete disorder. *Human Movement Science* 17, 471–90.

Kimball, J.G. (2002). Developmental coordination disorder from a sensory integration perspective. In S.A. Cermak and D. Larkin (eds) *Developmental Coordination Disorder*. Albany, NY: Delmar.

Kirby, A. (1999). *Dyspraxia: The Hidden Handicap*. London: Souvenir Press.

Kirby, A. and Drew, S. (2003). *Guide to Dyspraxia, and Developmental Coordination Disorders*. London: David Fulton Publishers.

Laszlo, J.I. and Bairstow, P.J. (1985). *Perceptual-Motor Behaviour: Developmental Assessment and Therapy*. London: Holt, Rinehart and Winston.

Laszlo, J.I., Bairstow, P.J. and Bartrip, J. (1988a). A new approach to treatment of perceptuo-motor dysfunction: previously called clumsiness. *Support for Learning* 3, 35–40.

Laszlo, J.I., Bairstow, P.J., Bartrip, J. and Rolfe, U.T. (1988b). Clumsiness or perceptuo-motor dysfunction? In A.M. Colley and J.R. Beech (eds) *Cognition and Action in Skilled Behaviour* (pp. 293–309). Amsterdam: Elsevier Science Publishers.

Lewis, V. (2003). *Development and Disability*. 2nd edn. Oxford: Blackwell.

Lord, R. and Hulme, C. (1987). Perceptual judgements of normal and clumsy children. *Developmental Medicine and Child Neurology* 29, 250–7.

Losse, A., Henderson, S.E., Elliman, D., Hall, D., Knight, E. and Jongmans, M. (1991). Clumsiness in children – do they grow out of it? A 10-year follow-up study. *Developmental Medicine and Child Neurology* 33, 55–68.

Macintyre, C. (2001). *Dyspraxia 5–11: A Practical Guide*. London: David Fulton Publishers.

Mandich, A.D., Buckolz, E. and Polatajko, H.J. (2002). On the ability of children with developmental coordination disorder (DCD) to inhibit response initiation: the Simon effect. *Brain and Cognition* 50, 150–62.

Mandich, A.D., Buckolz, E. and Polatajko, H.J. (2003). Children with developmental coordination disorder (DCD) and their ability to disengage ongoing attentional focus: more on inhibitory function. *Brain and Cognition* 51, 346–56.

Mandich, A.D., Polatajko, H.J., Macnab, J.J. and Miller, L.T. (2001). Treatment of children with Developmental Coordination Disorders. What is the evidence? *Physical and Occupational Therapy in Pediatrics* 20(2/3), 51–68.

May-Benson, T., Ingolia, P. and Koomar, J. (2002). Accommodations to functional settings for children with developmental coordination disorder. In S.A. Cermak and D. Larkin, (eds) *Developmental Cordination Disorder*. Albany, NY: Delmar.

Miller, L.T., Missiuna, C., Macnab, J.J., Malloy-Miller, T. and Polatajko, H.J. (2001). Clinical description of children with developmental coordination disorder. *Canadian Journal of Occupational Therapy* 68(1), 5–15.

Missiuna, C. (2003). *Children with developmental coordination disorder: at home and in the classroom*. 5th edn. McMaster University, Hamilton, ON: CanChild Centre for Childhood Disability Research. Also available at www.fhs.mcmaster. ca/canchild/.

Missiuna, C. and Polatajko, H.J. (1995). Developmental dyspraxia by any other name: are they all just clumsy children? *American Journal of Occupational Therapy* 49, 619–28.

Missiuna, C. and Pollock, N. (1995). Beyond the norms: need for multiple sources of data in the assessment of children. *Physical and Occupational Therapy in Pediatrics* 15, 57–71.

Newnham, C. and McKenzie, B.E. (1993). Cross-modal transfer of sequential visual and haptic shape information by clumsy children. *Perception* 22, 1061–73.

Peters, J.M., Barnett, A.L. and Henderson, S.E. (2001). Clumsiness, dyspraxia and developmental coordination disorder: how do health and educational professionals in the U.K. define the terms? *Child: Care, Health and Development* 27, 399–412.

Pless, M. and Carlsson, M. (2000). Effects of motor skill intervention on developmental coordination disorder: a meta-analysis. *Adapted Physical Activity Quarterly* 17(4), 381–401.

Polatajko, H.J., Fox, A.M. and Missiuna, C. (1995a). An international consensus on children with developmental coordination disorder. *Canadian Journal of Occupational Therapy* 62, 3–6.

Polatajko, H.J., Macnab, J.J., Anstett, B., Malloymiller, T., Murphy, K. and Noh, S. (1995b). A clinical trial of the process-oriented treatment approach for children with Developmental Coordination Disorder. *Developmental Medicine and Child Neurology* 37, 310–19.

Polatajko, H.J., Mandich, A.D., Miller, L.T. and Macnab, J.J. (2001a). Cognitive orientation to daily occupational performance (CO-OP): Part II – the evidence. *Physical and Occupational Therapy in Paediatrics* 20(2/3), 83–106.

Polatajko, H.J., Mandich, A.D., Missiuna, C., Miller, L.T., Macnab, J.J., Malloy-Miller, T. and Kinsella, E.A. (2001b). Cognitive orientation to daily occupational performance (CO-OP): Part III – the protocol in brief. *Physical and Occupational Therapy in Paediatrics* 20(2/3), 107–23.

Portwood, M.M. (1999). *Developmental Dyspraxia – Identification and Intervention*. London: David Fulton Publishers.

Portwood, M.M. (2000). *Understanding Developmental Dyspraxia: A Textbook for Students and Professionals*. London: David Fulton Publishers.

Ramus, F., Pidgeon, E. and Frith, U. (2003). Motor control and phonology in dyslexic children. *Journal of Child Psychology and Psychiatry* 44, 712–22.

Rasmussen, P. and Gillberg, C. (2000). Natural outcome of ADHD with DCD at age 22 years: a controlled, longitudinal, community-based study. *Journal of the American Academy of Child and Adolescent Psychiatry* 39, 1424–31.

Ripley, K., Daines, R. and Barrett, J. (1999). *Dyspraxia: A Guide for Teachers and Parents*. London: David Fulton Publishers.

Rösblad, B. (2002). Visual perception in children with developmental coordination disorder. In S.A. Cermak and D. Larkin (eds) *Developmental Cordination Disorder*. Albany, NY: Delmar.

Schoemaker, M.M. and Kalverboer, A.F. (1994). Social and affective problems of children who are clumsy: how early do they begin? *Adapted Physical Activity Quarterly* 11, 130–40.

Schoemaker, M.M., Smits-Engelsman, B.C.M. and Jongmans, M.J. (2003). Psychometric properties of the Movement Assessment Battery for Children Checklist as a screening instrument for children with a developmental co-ordination disorder. *British Journal of Educational Psychology* 73, 425–41.

Short, H. and Crawford, J. (1984). Last to be chosen: the awkward child. *Pivot* 2, 32–36.

Sims, K., Henderson, S.E., Hulme, C. and Morton, J. (1996a). The remediation of clumsiness: an evaluation of Laszlo's kinaesthetic approach (part one). *Developmental Medicine and Child Neurology* 38, 976–87.

Sims, K., Henderson, S.E., Morton, J. and Hulme, C. (1996b). The remediation of clumsiness: is kinaesthesis the answer? (part two). *Developmental Medicine and Child Neurology* 38, 988–97.

Smyth, T.R. (1991). Abnormal clumsiness in children: a programming defect? *Child: Care, Health and Development* 17, 283–94.

Smyth, T.R. (1992). Impaired motor skill (clumsiness) in otherwise normal children: a review. *Child: Care, Health and Development* 18, 283–300.

Smyth, T.R. and Anderson, H.I. (2000). Coping with clumsiness in the school playground: social and physical play in children with and coordination impairments. *British Journal of Developmental Psychology* 18, 389–413.

Stephenson, E., McKay, C. and Chesson, R. (1991). The identification and treatment of motor/learning difficulties: parents' perceptions and the role of the therapist. *Child: Care, Health and Development* 17, 91–113.

Sugden, D.A. and Chambers, M.E. (2003). Intervention in children with Developmental Coordination Disorder: the role of parents and teachers. *British Journal of Educational Psychology* 73, 545–561.

van Dellen, T. and Geuze, K.H. (1988). Motor response programming in clumsy children. *Journal of Child Psychology and Psychiatry* 29, 489–500.

Williams, H.G. (2002). Motor control in children with developmental coordination disorder. In S.A. Cermak and D. Larkin (eds) *Developmental Cordination Disorder*. Albany, NY: Delmar.

Wilson, B.N., Kaplan, B.J., Crawford, S.G., Campbell, A. and Dewey, D. (2000). Reliability and validity of a parent questionnaire on childhood motor skills. *American Journal of Occupational Therapy* 54, 484–93.

Wilson, P.H. and McKenzie, B.E. (1998). Information processing deficits associated with developmental co-ordination disorder: a meta-analysis of research findings. *Journal of Child Psychology and Psychiatry* 39, 829–40.

World Health Organization (1992). *International Statistical Classification of Diseases and Related Health Problems*. 10th edn, vol. 1 ICD-10. Geneva: World Health Organization.

Wright, H.C. and Sugden, D.A. (1996). A two-step procedure for the identification of children with developmental coordination disorder in Singapore. *Developmental Medecine and Child Neurology* 38, 1099–1105.

Glossary

Affect is defined by the *Oxford English Dictionary* as a feeling or emotion, and so an affective disorder is an illness which results in disturbances to feelings and emotions. This can take two forms: the flattened and inert feelings of depression; or mania.

Agoraphobia is an abnormal fear of open and/or public spaces.

Anhedonia means that the young person has lost all enjoyment in life and now portrays a picture of gloom and despondency.

Antigens are substances which the human body sees as harmful and produces antibodies to neutralise their effect.

Beta blockers are drugs which block certain nerve receptors in the nervous system. This blocking prevents these nerves from working.

Bipolar illness is diagnosed in anyone who has had a manic episode which alternates with depressive disorder. It is not necessary for one illness to follow the other, though they sometimes do; the fact that both illnesses have occurred is sufficient to describe the problem as bipolar.

Conduct disorder is a specific diagnostic category which is used to describe the pattern of behaviour where there is repetitive and persistent misbehaviour (such as fighting, bullying, destroying property, and stealing) which is far more than would be expected for a child of that age.

Flashbacks are the re-experiencing of feelings, images or even physical sensations which are associated with a traumatic event of some kind, and cause distress when they are re-experienced.

Hallucinations are false perceptions and may involve any of the senses. The most well known is a hallucination involving hearing in which people believe they are hearing voices which are talking to them. This is often a feature of schizophrenic illness.

Hepatitis is an inflammation of the liver caused by infection, or the build-up of toxic substances. If persistent it can lead to permanent failure of parts, or all, of the liver.

Hyperactivity is a label denoting that a child shows significant overactivity and an increased tempo of physical activity. The term is sometimes applied (wrongly) to describe all types of attention problem, though in fact this forms one element of one type of attention deficit disorder.

Intermittent reinforcement describes a schedule where reinforcement does not always follow the target behaviour. Intermittent reinforcement is more likely than continuous reinforcement to result in persistent behaviour which is resistant to extinction.

Kinaesthesia concerns the brain's awareness of the position and movement of the body and limbs.

Kleinian therapy is a style of individual therapy that is often seen as particularly appropriate for children. It is based on a view that the beginnings of the superego can be identified within the first two years of life, and that any analysis should focus upon the infantile stages of development when anxiety and aggressive impulses are thought to have their origin. The other major element is the assumption that the most important drives that a person experiences are the aggressive ones.

Mania is an illness where the patient superficially appears very happy and energetic, with a greatly elated mood. Patients usually have very grandiose plans and ideas, but leap from subject to subject in a rapid fashion. The mood is quite unstable with aggression and violent outbursts often flaring up. This is classified as a psychotic illness.

MAOIs, the monoamine oxidase inhibitors, form a class of drug most commonly used to treat depressive illness. They interfere with the destruction of the monoamines in the brain. These drugs do have to be used with great care because they react with many other drugs, such as cough mixtures, and certain foods, such as cheese and yeast extract products.

Neurosis is a mild form of psychiatric illness involving symptoms of anxiety and stress. Unlike the psychoses, there is no loss of external reality.

Oligoantigenic is a term which is used to describe something that is least likely to provoke an adverse reaction from the body's self-defence mechanisms because it contains no antigens.

Phobia is an intense, abnormal fear of a relatively harmless object or situation.

Phonological awareness concerns the ability to recognise different sounds in spoken language.

Proprioception concerns an individual's sensation, stemming from muscles and joints, as to their body position and movement.

Psychosis is a severe mental illness, the hallmark of which is a loss of contact with external reality. It can be caused by medical problems such as infections or toxicity due to drugs but mostly is caused by major psychiatric illness. Usually these patients have hallucinations and delusions, the nature of which helps to distinguish the type of disorder. Problems to do with thinking and thought processes are usually seen in schizophrenia, whereas themes that are dominated by feelings and moods are seen in the affective disorders.

Secondary sexual characteristics   are those sex-specific features of development which appear at puberty. These include the development of pubic hair, the deepening of the voice, and in boys, the beginning of beard growth.

Short-term memory   refers to that aspect of memory where a small number of chunks of information are held for a limited period of time (e.g. 'holding on' to a telephone number while searching for a pencil).

Unipolar illness   is when the person only seems to suffer from a depressive element, and there is no suggestion that manic symptoms may surface later.

Vestibular   refers to the sensory process, stemming from within the inner ear, that concerns balance and awareness of gravity and movement.

Visuospatial processing   relates to one's use of vision in perceiving the spatial relationship between objects. This includes awareness of relative size, position, direction, depth and movement.

Index